T0203301

Metaheuristics for Intelligent Electrical Networks

Metaheuristics Set

coordinated by
Nicolas Monmarché and Patrick Siarry

Volume 10

Metaheuristics for Intelligent Electrical Networks

Frédéric Héliodore
Amir Nakib
Boussaad Ismail
Salma Ouchraa
Laurent Schmitt

WILEY

First published 2017 in Great Britain and the United States by ISTE Ltd and John Wiley & Sons, Inc.

ISTE Ltd
27-37 St George's Road
London SW19 4EU
UK

www.iste.co.uk

John Wiley & Sons, Inc.
111 River Street
Hoboken, NJ 07030
USA

www.wiley.com

Library of Congress Control Number: 2017946567

British Library Cataloguing-in-Publication Data
A CIP record for this book is available from the British Library
ISBN 978-1-84821-809-3

Contents

Introduction

This book is the result of works dedicated to specific applications of metaheuristics in smart electrical grids. From electric transmission, distribution networks to electric microgrids, the notion of intelligence refers to the ability to propose acceptable solutions in an increasingly more restrictive environment. Most often, it refers to decision-making assisting tools designed to support all human action.

Optimization techniques and, in particular, metaheuristics, due to their diversity, their faculty to reproduce natural processes and their good accuracy/execution speed compromise, do enjoy a growing success in the energy world where the diversity of problems and requirements often requires one to intervene and quickly develop acceptable and attractive solutions.

Although development in industrial environments is always constrained by the time factor, value creation continues to be a target and differentiation factors must always be identified. The precise acknowledgment of physical problems remains the unifying element that, coupled with the fields of optimization and statistics, allows for the definition of innovative tools. Furthermore, this is the blueprint that is promoted and that finds its place in the field of "data science".

The chapters in this book are independent but always follow the same approach. A state-of-the-art of metaheuristics is presented with, in particular:

– path-based heuristics;

– solution population-based methods;

– performance evaluation of metaheuristics.

Applications specific to power systems follow with:

– the optimal placement of FACTS (Flexible Alternative Current Transmission System) to manage reactive power;

– the optimization of the internal topology of a wind farm.

Two examples of the interaction of disciplines are addressed, on the one hand, by introducing the topological complexity of networks and, on the other hand, by getting involved in statistical estimation:

– topological study of electric networks;

– estimation of the parameters of an α-stable distribution.

The application domain of the metaheuristics will expand through the development of electric smart networks (*SmartGrid* and *MicroGrid*). A presentation of the future challenges is the subject of Chapter 8:

– extension to *SmartGrids* and *MicroGrids*.

1

Single Solution Based Metaheuristics

1.1. Introduction

In daily life, optimizing is a common activity for both individuals and professionals. For example, the process of optimizing involves minimizing production time and expenditure, and maximizing profit and performance. As a result, optimization has become a discipline in itself to solve various problems, particularly in the economic sector [SAM 69], in the field of biology [GOT 82] and in various industries [YOS 00]. To solve these problems, technology is used to implement algorithms that simulate real problems in order to achieve results that will subsequently be used according to the intended purpose. These simulations can be simple but also very complex. The developed algorithms can be accurate or approximated, leading to the global optimum or to a solution closed to the global optimum. The objective of optimization is to find the global and/or the local optimum or optima. Depending on the optimization problem being addressed, one or more methods can be applied, and one of them may be more suitable than the others.

These methods include the class of path-based methods also called single-solution metaheuristics. These methods are algorithms in which the search for the optimum is achieved by manipulating a single solution throughout the progression of the algorithm. From an initial solution, the latter evolves throughout the algorithm following a certain mechanism until the stopping criterion is reached. Furthermore, the acceptance of a solution instead of another is carried out by means of various ways based on the proposed model. The principal characteristic of pattern-search heuristics is reflected by the fact that they mainly favor the use of exploitation by focusing their search in a given region of the search space.

In this chapter, we are going to introduce a number of path-based methods starting with most common algorithms, notably descent methods, simulated annealing, microcanonical annealing and even tabu search. We will proceed with exploratory local search algorithms that incorporate other path-based methods such as the Greedy Randomized Adaptive Search (GRASP) method, variable neighborhood search, guided local search and iterated local search. We are also going to present other methods such as Nelder and Mead's simplex method, the noising method and smoothing methods.

1.2. The descent method

The descent method (called "hill climbing" in maximization problems) is based on a randomly initialized solution or initialized with a greedy method. It then selects a solution in its neighborhood that strictly improves the current solution. This selection can be done in a number of different ways. The retained solution may be the first feasible solution that improves the objective function or the best feasible solution of the entire neighborhood. Depending on this choice, the method is, respectively, called simple descent method or steepest descent method.

Algorithm 1.1: The steepest descent method

---

1 **Generate** a random initial solution s
2 **Generate** the neighborhood $N(s)$ of s
3 **For each** *Neighbor s' in $N(s)$* **Do**
4   **Evaluate** s'
5   **If** s' *improves* s **Then**
6   **Update** s^* with s'
7   **End**
8 **End**
9 **Return** s^*

The descent method is one of the simplest methods found in the literature; however, it presents a significant limitation. It may find itself easily trapped in a local minimum and therefore encourages exploitation and not exploration. In order to overcome this problem and be able to visit different regions of the search space, a variant called the restarted descent method has been implemented and involves executing the algorithm several times, thus allowing that various regions of the search space be visited. Nonetheless, another technique can be applied in order to escape from local minima, notably by accepting a degrading solution with a certain probability, a technique that can be found in simulated annealing.

1.3. Simulated annealing

Simulated annealing [KIR 84] is known for being the first metaheuristic to propose a process to escape local optima, and so by implementing the Metropolis algorithm proposed in 1953 [MET 53]. It is a method inspired from the annealing process practiced in metallurgy, which consists of melting metal at high temperature to be then cooled to a stable condition, called thermodynamic equilibrium, is obtained. This stable state may be "good" or "bad", that is with minimal energy or not. Indeed, when the metal is quickly cooled, deformations can arise, whereas a "perfect" metal is achieved if the cooling process is adequate. The temperature corresponds to the control parameter of the metal stability.

By analogy, based on a random solution s, a solution s' is generated in the neighborhood of s. If this neighbor solution improves the current solution, s is updated. Otherwise, i' can also be accepted following the probability $\exp(-\Delta f / T)$. This probability makes it possible to accept a degrading solution in the case where the solution s' presents a small degradation Δf with respect to s or when the temperature T is large enough. Therefore, exploration is preferred. However, this probability becomes smaller when knowing that the temperature follows a decreasing function and is updated at each iteration, thereby making exploitation more suitable.

Algorithm 1.2: Simulated annealing

---

1 **Initialize** the initial temperature T
2 **Generate** a random initial solution s
3 **While** *the stopping criterion is not satisfied* **Do**
4   **Generate** a neighbor s' of s
5   **Evaluate** s'
6   **If** $f(s') \leq f(s)$ *or* $\exp(-\Delta f/T) > rand(0,1)$ **Then**
7 | **Update** s with s'
8   **End**
9   **Update** the temperature T
10 **End**
11 **Return** s

Simulated annealing therefore depends on the temperature and its evolution. If it follows a strongly decreasing function, the algorithm is trapped in a local optimum. This is then referred to as premature convergence. Otherwise, the global optimum can be reached but optimality remains unguaranteed.

On the other hand, simulated annealing implements the Metropolis algorithm proposed in 1953 [MET 53], which may require a quite significant computation time hence microcanonical annealing.

1.4. Microcanonical annealing

Microcanonical annealing was introduced in 1987 by Bernard [BAR 87] and its model is described by algorithm 1.3. This method has similarities with the principles implemented in simulated annealing. Microcanonical annealing involves reducing the total energy based on a total high energy by decreasing the kinetic energy between two levels. This reduction follows a given decreasing function and allows the algorithm to converge toward optimal solutions. This method utilizes the algorithm proposed by Creutz in 1983 [CRE 83] whose objective was to maximize the entropy for a constant total energy by means of a succession of transitions.

Algorithm 1.3: Microcanonical annealing

---

1 **Set** total energy E_t
2 **Generate** an initial random solution s
3 **Calculate** the energy E of s
4 **Define** the maximal number of iterations it_{int} between two levels of the total energy
5 **While** *the number of accepted solutions is non-zero* **Do**
6   **While** it_{int} *is not reached* **Do**
7   **Generate** a transition from s to s'
8   **Calculate** the energy variation ΔE between s and s'
9   **If** $\Delta E \leq E_t - E$ **Then**
10   **Accept** the transition toward s'
11   **End**
12   **If** $\Delta E \leq 0$ **Then**
13   **Update** the best solution found
14   **End**
15   **End**
16   **Update** E_t
17 **End**
18 **Return** the best solution found

In general, starting from a randomly drawn initial state s_0 with a high energy E_0 and a demon energy initialized with a value of 0, an energy reduction with a fixed percentage is applied followed by the Creutz algorithm until it reaches a thermodynamic equilibrium state. These two operations are executed until there is no more improvement.

Microcanonical annealing is known to be similar to simulated annealing. This method is just as effective as its predecessor in terms of results except that it is simpler and faster in terms of computational times [HER 93]. This speed is due to the implementation of the Creutz algorithm. However, it still remains possible to find the same local optimum repeatedly during the search, even if we have escaped from it previously. This is what tabu search tries to take into consideration by making use of the notion of memory.

1.5. Tabu search

Tabu search, introduced by Glover in 1986 [GLO 86a], is based on the principle of human memory. This algorithm makes it possible to memorize previously encountered solutions by storing them in what we call a tabu list.

Tabu search consists of exploring the neighborhood starting from a given position, and selecting the best solution encountered not being included in the tabu list. Consequently, it is possible to keep a degrading solution that therefore allows escaping from local minima and the fact of prohibiting a move to already encountered solutions avoids falling back into these local minima.

Algorithm 1.4: Tabu search

---
1   **Generate** a random initial solution s
2   **Initialize** an empty tabu list T
3   **While** *the stopping criterion is not satisfied* **Do**
4   **Generate** N non-tabu neighbors of s **Evaluate** the N neighbors
5   **Select** the best neighbor s'
6   **Update** the best solution found s^*
7   **Insert** s' into T
8   **Update** s with s'
9   **End**
10 **Return** s^*

The size of this tabu list thus represents the major parameter of this method. By increasing the size of this list, the exploration mechanism is favored. On the other hand, by decreasing the size of the tabu list, the exploitation mechanism is favored. This list can have a variable size during the search [TAI 91] or be reactive [BAT 94] depending on the solutions obtained; in other words, if the same solution is often obtained, the size of the list is increased or decreased if the current solution is only rarely improved.

1.6. Pattern search algorithms

In this section, we are going to present more recent path-based algorithms, in particular the GRASP method, variable neighborhood search, guided local search and iterated local search.

1.6.1. *The GRASP method*

The GRASP method was proposed by Feo and Resende [FEO 95] and is one of the simplest methods in metaheuristics. This is an iterative method that at each iteration undergoes a step constructing the solution, followed by a step involving a local search to return the best workable solution to the given problem, as described in algorithm 1.5.

Algorithm 1.5: The GRASP method

---
1 **Generate** an initial random solution s
2 **Initialize** the maximal number of iterations k_{max}
3 **For** k *ranging from* 1 *to* k_{max} **Do**
4   **Construct** solution s with an incremental cost
5   **Apply** a local search on s
6   **Update** the best solution found s^*
7 **End**
8 **Return** s^*

The construction step (algorithm 1.6) inserts an element at each iteration in the workable solution. The choice of this element is carried out randomly based on a restrictive list of candidates comprising only the best ones. The quality of a candidate is obtained based on the benefits that it brings to the solution under construction and is updated during the following iterations. Therefore, the result is a solution in which local optimality cannot be guaranteed. A local search method is then applied, which brings us to the second step of the algorithm. Based on the solution obtained during the construction phase, a local search method such as the descent method, simulated annealing or even tabu search is applied in order to improve this solution.

The GRASP method is a simple method that executes with a relatively small computation time and which leads to good results. It can therefore easily be integrated among other metaheuristics.

Algorithm 1.6: The construction step of the solution

---

1 **Based** on an empty solution s:
2 **Evaluate** the incremental cost of each candidate element
3 **While** *solution s is not comprehensive* **Do**
4   **Build** the restrictive list of candidates (RLC)
5   **Select** randomly an element e of the RLC
6   **Insert** e into s
7   **Reevaluate** the incremental costs
8 **End**
9 **Return** solution s

1.6.2. *Variable neighborhood search*

Variable neighborhood search [MLA 97] is based on the systematic change in the neighborhood during the search.

We start by selecting a set of neighborhood structures N_k where $k = 1, 2, ..., k_{max}$ and determine an initial solution s. Then, three steps are applied: perturbation, local search and the move or continuation starting from s. Perturbation consists of randomly generating a solution s' in the neighborhood of s defined by the kth neighborhood structure. From s', a local search method is applied which returns s''. The move makes it possible to refocus the search around s''. As a matter of fact, if s'' improves the best known solution, then s is updated with s'' and the algorithm is restarted from the first neighborhood, otherwise the following neighborhood is considered. This method then allows the exploration of several types of neighborhoods until the current solution is improved. Once at this stage, the neighborhoods of the new solution are explored and so on until a stopping criterion is satisfied.

Thus, when the variable neighborhood search is performed, it is necessary to determine the number and type of neighborhood to utilize, the exploration order of the neighborhood during the search (in general, in an increasing manner depending on the size of the neighborhood), the strategy for changing neighborhood, the local search method and the stopping criterion.

Algorithm 1.7: Variable neighborhood search

---

1 **Generate** a random initial solution s
2 **Define** the number of neighborhoods k_{max}
3 **Define** the set of neighborhoods $N_k(k = 1, 2, ..., k_{max})$
4 **For** k *ranging from* 1 *to* k_{max} **Do**
  /* perturbation   */
5   **Generate** a ncighbor s' of s in the kth neighborhood. /* Local
      search   */
6   **While** *the stopping criterion is not satisfied* **Do**
7   **Generate** a neighbor $v_{s'}$ of s'
8   **If** $v_{s'}$ *improves* s' **Then**
9       $s'' = v_{s'}$
10   **End**
11 **End**
    /* move   */
12 **If** s'' *improves* s^* **Then**
13    $s = s''$
14    $k = 1$
15 **Else**
16    $k = k + 1$
17 **End**
18 **End**
19 **Return** the best solution s

Variants of this method have been proposed such as variable neighborhood descent [HAN 01a], variable neighborhood search and decomposition [HAN 01b] and biased variable neighborhood search [HAN 00].

Variable neighborhood descent makes use of the steepest descent method during the local search and we stop if the solution is improved, otherwise the following type of neighborhood is considered.

Search and variable neighborhood decomposition utilize the same steps as the variable neighborhood search except that one selects a neighbor s' of s and its neighborhood is generated following the same type of neighborhood such that the intersection of the neighborhoods of s and s' be empty and the steepest descent method is applied. As a result, the local optimum s'' is obtained. The intersection of the neighborhood of s and s' is taken, s'' is inserted and once again the steepest descent method is applied. The move is then carried from the last local optimum obtained.

Biased variable neighborhood search is capable of keeping the best solution s_{opt} found throughout the whole search and in order to encourage the exploration of the search space, the refocusing of the search is done by using a parameter α and a function ρ that calculates the distance between two solutions s and s'. In effect, based on a solution s, a neighbor s' is selected by employing the first type of neighborhood, then the local search method is applied thereto yielding the local optimum s''. If s'' improves s_{opt}, then s_{opt} is updated with s''. Then, the search is refocused on s'' if $f(s'') - \alpha * \rho(s, s') < f(s)$, the search is restarted from the first neighborhood with s'' as a starting solution; otherwise, the next neighborhood is addressed.

1.6.3. *Guided local search*

To escape local optima, some methods use several neighborhood structures such as variable neighborhood search while others addtionally employ some memory to avoid revisiting a solution such as tabu search. Introduced by Voudouris, guided local search [VOU 99] utilizes a technique whose solution set and neighborhood structure remains identical throughout the search, but that dynamically modifies the objective function. This technique makes it possible to orientate the search toward another region of the search space, thus encouraging exploration.

In the case of minimization problems, equation [1.1] represents this modification that is reflected in the increase in the objective function with a set of penalizations.

$$h(s) = g(s) + \lambda . \sum_{i=1}^{M} p_i . I_i(s) \qquad [1.1]$$

where:

  – $g(s)$ is the objective function of a given problem;

  – λ is the regularization parameter;

– p_i are the penalization parameters;

– M is the number of attributes defining the solutions;

– $I_i(s)$ allows specifying whether the solution s contains the attribute i and therefore takes 1 or 0 as values.

The regularization parameter λ enables us to determine the significance of the variation in the objective function and to control the influence of the information related to the search.

The penalization parameters p_i correspond to the weights of the constraints of each attribute i with respect to the solution. At each iteration, only the attributes trapped in a local optimum that maximize the utility are penalized by incrementing p_i by 1. This utility is calculated according to the expression [1.2] based on the cost of this attribute c_i and its penalization parameter p_i.

$$u_i(s^*) = I_i(s^*) \frac{c_i}{1 + p_i} \qquad [1.2]$$

Algorithm 1.8: Guided local search

---

1 **Generate** an initial random solution s
2 **Initialize** penalization parameters p_i with 0
3 **Apply** a local search on s
  /* Let s^* be the solution obtained   */
4 **While** *the stopping criterion is not satisfied* **Do**
5   **For each** *attribute i of s^** **Do**
6   **Calculate** the utility u_i
7   **End**
8   **Determine** the maximum u_j of the utilities
9   **Penalize** the attribute j
10 **End**
11 **Return** the best solution found

1.6.4. *Iterated local search*

Iterated local search, proposed by Lourenço in 2001 [LOU 01, LOU 03], is the most general model of exploratory algorithms. In effect, from a solution s, an intermediate solution s' is selected by applying a perturbation, then a local search is performed culminating in a local optimum (s'') that can be kept based on the acceptation criterion.

Algorithm 1.9: Iterated local search

---

1 **Generate** an initial random solution s
2 **Apply** a local search method on s
3 **While** *the stopping criterion is not satisfied* **Do**
4   **Generate** s' following the perturbation function of s
5   **Apply** a local search method on s'
6   **Update** the best solution found s^*
7 **End**
8 **Return** s^*

It should be noted that the perturbation is intended to direct the search toward another basin of attraction. Thus, it significantly impacts the search, it must be neither too small nor too large. A value that is too small will not make it possible to explore more solutions and the algorithm will quickly stagnate. On the other hand, a large value will give the algorithm a character similar to "random-restart" algorithms, which will bias the search. As a result, non-deterministic perturbation is a means to avoid going through the same cycles again. It is characterized by the so-called "perturbation force" that can be fixed or variable, random or adaptive. If the force is adaptive, exploration and exploitation criteria can be controlled. By increasing this force, exploration is preferred and by decreasing it, exploitation is preferred.

The objective of the acceptance criterion is to determine the conditions that the new local optimum must satisfy in order to replace the current solution. This criterion thus enables the implementation of an equilibrium by keeping the newly found local optimum or by restarting from the previously found local optimum.

1.7. Other methods

In this section, we will introduce other path-based algorithms, in particular the Nelder–Mead simplex method, smoothing methods and the noising method.

1.7.1. *The Nelder–Mead simplex method*

Initially proposed by Spendley in 1962 [SPE 62], then improved by Nelder and Mead in 1965 [NEL 65], the simplex method aims at solving unconstrained optimization problems by utilizing a succession of simplex transformations.

Initially, a set of $(n + 1)$ vertices $\vec{x}_i$ in a n-dimensional space is initialized therefore constituting the current simplex. This initialization can be achieved by generating a point $\vec{x}_0$, then by defining the other points around it toward each of the directions $\vec{e}_i$ of the space with an amplitude a:

$$\vec{x}_i = \vec{x}_0 + a.\vec{e}_i \qquad\qquad [1.3]$$

Until the stopping condition is reached, the simplex is transformed with reflection α, expansion γ and contraction β operators applied to the worst vertex $\vec{x}_h$ defined by equations [1.5]–[1.8], the goal being to replace the vertex with the highest cost with another having a lower cost.

In the following, vector $\vec{c}$ represents the centroid with respect to all vertices of the simplex except $\vec{x}_h$:

$$\vec{c} = \frac{1}{n} \sum_{j \neq h} \vec{x}_j \qquad\qquad [1.4]$$

– Reflection operator:

The reflection operator is applied on $\vec{x}_h$ whose cost is f_h in order to obtain $\vec{x}_r$ with cost f_r. If $f_l \leq f_r < f_s$, vertex $\vec{x}_h$ is replaced by vertex $\vec{x}_r$, with f_l the cost of the best vertex $\vec{x}_l$ and f_s the cost of vertex $\vec{x}_s$ classified in the second position.

$$\vec{x}_r = \vec{c} + \alpha(\vec{c} - \vec{x}_h) \qquad\qquad [1.5]$$

– Expansion operator:

If $f_r < f_l$, the expansion operator is applied on vertex $\vec{x}_r$ obtaining vertex $\vec{x}_e$ of cost f_e. In the case where $f_e < f_r$, vertex $\vec{x}_e$ is accepted otherwise vertex $\vec{x}_r$ is.

$$\vec{x}_e = \vec{c} + \gamma(\vec{x}_r - \vec{c}) \qquad [1.6]$$

– Contraction operator:

If $f_r \geq f_s$, the contraction operator is applied and vertex $\vec{x}_c$ of cost f_c is obtained. If $f_s \leq f_r < f_h$, vertex $\vec{x}_c$ is obtained with equation [1.7] and if $f_c \leq f_r$, vertex $\vec{x}_c$ is accepted. On the other hand, if $f_r \geq f_h$, vertex $\vec{x}_{c'}$ is obtained with equation [1.8] and if $f_{c'} \leq f_h$, vertex $\vec{x}_{c'}$ is accepted.

$$\vec{x}_c = \vec{c} + \beta(\vec{x}_r - \vec{c}) \qquad [1.7]$$

$$\vec{x}_{c'} = \vec{c} + \beta(\vec{x}_h - \vec{c}) \qquad [1.8]$$

If no vertex is accepted during the previous steps, all vertices $\vec{x}_i$ are updated:

$$\vec{x}_i = \frac{\vec{x}_i + \vec{x}_l}{2} \qquad [1.9]$$

Just like all path-based algorithms, this method leads to a convergence toward a local optimum and in order to overcome this limitation of the conventional method, it is possible to restart it once a local optimum is reached, reinitializing $\vec{x}_0$ every time.

1.7.2. *The noising method*

Introduced by Charon in 1993 [CHA 93], the noising method is a single-solution metaheuristic based on the descent approach. From an initial solution and at each iteration, noise is added to the objective function such that the values of the objective function be directed toward a descent. The noise added to the current solution changes from a given initial value and decreases at each iteration until the value is zero or a minimal value. The variation of this noise can be defined in various ways. Algorithm 1.10 summarizes the approach of the noising method.

Algorithm 1.10: The noising method

---

1 **Generate** an initial random solution s
2 **Initialize** noise r
3 **Repeat**
4 | **Add** noise r to the value of the objective function of s
5 | **Apply** a local search method on s according to r
6 | **Update** r
7 **Until** $r = r_{min}$;
8 **Return** the best solution found

In this method, two parameters have to be determined, the noise rate and the decreasing rate of this noise. The first consists of defining the values of r_{max} and r_{min} with r_{min} usually set to 0 while the second parameter may follow the geometric decreasing function defined by equation [1.10] or other more advanced methods [CHA 06]. However, the choice of these parameters has a significant impact on the performance of this method.

$$r = r.\alpha \text{ with } \alpha \in]0, 1[\qquad\qquad [1.10]$$

1.7.3. *Smoothing methods*

The main goal of smoothing methods is to reduce the number of local optima as well as the depth of the basins of attraction by modifying the objective function yet without changing search space [GLO 86b, JUN 94]. Once this smoothing operation is performed, any path-based method or metaheuristic can generally be utilized.

First, this approach involves subdividing the problem being considered into several successive instances relating to a specific search space. First of all, the simplest instance is dealt with and a local search method is then applied as a second step. The solution obtained is kept as an initial solution of the problem related to the next instance, which becomes increasingly more complex at each iteration and therefore enables this solution to be improved.

Algorithm 1.11: The smoothing method

---

1 **Generate** an initial random solution s
2 **Initialize** the smoothing factor α
3 **Repeat**
4 $\quad$ **Apply** the smoothing operation on the instance I
5 $\quad$ **Apply** a local search method on s according to I
6 $\quad$ **Update** α
7 **Until** $\alpha < 1$;
8 **Return** the best solution found

The smoothing makes it possible to decrease the likelihood of being trapped in a local optimum. In addition, this technique can reduce the complexity of the algorithm that implements it. Moreover, the computational time of the algorithm can prove considerable.

1.8. Conclusion

All the methods presented in this chapter are considered to be local searches, because they are based on intensification that allows a good quality solution to be obtained. Furthermore, to improve the results obtained, the fact of distributing the search over a larger number of regions happens to be a complementary method as a means to span several regions of the search space by generating multiple solutions [XU 14].

2

Population-based Methods

2.1. Introduction

Metaheuristics, also known as stochastic algorithms, are characterized by the introduction of the notion of randomness. Contrary to exact methods that explore the search space by making use of different techniques such as enumeration and tree-based methods, stochastic algorithms visit only part of the search space in a random fashion, therefore reaching a satisfactory approximated solution in a reasonable time. Exact methods guarantee, under certain conditions, the optimality of the solution obtained, which is not the case for metaheuristics.

The term "solution population-based metaheuristics" refers to algorithms that manipulate a set of solutions whose size is predefined. Indeed, after initializing the starting population, the different solutions communicate with each other and evolve throughout iterations, generating a new population until the stopping criterion is satisfied. The search for the optimum is thereby achieved by manipulating a number of solutions that travel through the search space according to their own information as well as the information that other solutions transmit with a very specific mechanism. Moreover, metaheuristics based on populations of solutions are characterized by the fact that these favor exploration, that is that they broaden their search over several regions of the search space.

In this chapter, we describe a selection of algorithms based on populations of solutions by separating them into two large families: evolutionary algorithms and swarm intelligence based algorithms. More specifically, we will first present genetic algorithms, evolution strategies, coevolutionary algorithms, cultural algorithms, differential evolution, biogeography-based optimization and a hybrid approach. Thereafter, we are going to introduce particle swarm optimization (PSO), ant colony optimization, cuckoo search, the firefly algorithm and the fireworks algorithm.

2.2. Evolutionary algorithms

Evolutionary algorithms are inspired by biological evolution. In effect, the principle of survival and reproduction of the fittest individuals is applied at each generation within a population of individuals. This principle is based on natural selection and on the modification of certain genetic characteristics in these individuals in a random manner according to a certain probability. In the case of a unary modification, this modification is called mutation; otherwise, it is referred to as crossover. Evolutionary algorithms are a large family of metaheuristics among which we are going to consider genetic algorithms, evolution strategies, coevolutionary algorithms, cultural algorithms, differential evolution, biogeography-based optimization and Bayesian approach based metaheuristics.

Algorithm 2.1: Evolutionary algorithms

---

1 **Initialize** population P
2 **Evaluate** the μ individuals of P
3 **While** *the stopping criterion is not satisfied* **Do**
4   **Select** ρ individuals of P for reproduction
5   **Apply crossover** on the ρ selected individuals
6   **Apply mutation** on the λ children obtained
7   **Evaluate** the λ children obtained
8   **Select** μ individuals of the population P'
9   **Replace** population P with population P'
10 **End**
11 **Return** the best solution

2.2.1. *Genetic algorithms*

Genetic algorithms, introduced by Holland [HOL 92] and developed in detail by Goldberg [GOL 89], are part of evolutionary algorithms because they are inspired by the theory of evolution. Furthermore, they bring forward genetic crossover and mutation operators as well as selection and replacement operators, thus providing a means to shift from one generation to another. The choice of these operators is performed according to the problem [ROW 04]. In addition to these operators, the coding or data representation is also an important parameter that can have a direct impact on the solution returned [RON 97]. Among other things, this encoding may be binary, real or defined according to the Gray code [ROW 04].

2.2.1.1. *Selection operator*

The selection operator enables the choice of individuals upon which the crossover will be applied. These individuals thus represent the "parent individuals". There are several ways to perform this selection such as making use of biased selection or roulette, tournament selection, rank-based selection or Boltzmann selection [GOL 91, BAC 00, HAU 04].

2.2.1.2. *Crossover operator*

The objective of the crossover operator is to provide a recombination of the information of the genetic material of a set of individuals, usually two parents, giving birth to children individuals whose validity must be ensured. Therefore, generated children individuals inherit certain characteristics from their parents. However, a crossover rate of p_c is defined beforehand in order to determine the proportion of parents that could be recombined. In general, this crossover rate $p_c \in [0, 45, 0, 95]$.

There are several types of crossovers, namely one-point crossover, multipoint crossover, uniform crossover, linear crossover and barycentric crossover [POO 95, BAC 00, HAU 04].

2.2.1.3. *Mutation operator*

The mutation operator allows for random change in part of the information of the genetic material of the descendants. This operator has the characteristic of guaranteeing the exploration of the search space [MA 10, NOL 98]. However, a mutation probability p_m is defined beforehand in order to control the change in an element of the solution. In general, this probability takes a very small value $p_m \in [0.001; 0.01]$.

The choice of this operator must follow three main characteristics, namely ergodicity, the validity of the generated solutions and locality. Ergodicity is the characteristic that provides a guarantee that all the solutions of the search space can be reached, whereas locality allows for the control of the size of the mutation by ensuring that it remains quite small [RAD 91].

2.2.1.4. Replacement operator

The role of this operator is to identify individuals that will be part of the new generation. There are various ways to achieve this replacement including stationary replacement, generational replacement and elitist replacement. The last method is the simplest and makes it possible to retain the best individuals among the population [BAC 00, HAU 04].

2.2.2. Evolution strategies

Evolution strategies are part of the family of evolutionary algorithms and have been proposed by Rechenberg in 1973 [REC 73]. As the basis, the first method introduced is called "two-membered ES" or "$(1 + 1) - ES$". This algorithm has the peculiarity of manipulating a single individual at a time. More exactly, starting from a parent individual, a child individual is generated by means of the mutation operator, the best of them is then selected as a new parent.

Next, the "multi-membered ES" algorithm or "$(\mu + 1) - ES$" was proposed that incorporates the notion of communication between the individuals of the population [REC 73]. This method enables a child individual to be generated from μ parent individuals, with $\mu \geq 1$, by utilizing recombination in addition to mutation. Based on this method, Schweffel [SCH 81] has proposed two other "multi-membered ES" methods called "$(\mu + \lambda) - ES$" and "$(\mu, \lambda) - ES$". The difference lies in the process for the selection of the next generation. In effect, from μ parent individuals, λ children individuals are generated. In the "$(\mu + \lambda) - ES$" method, the selection of the next generation is achieved among the μ parent individuals and the λ children individuals while in the "$(\mu, \lambda) - ES$" the selection is among the λ children individuals. Two other strategies can be cited, "$(\frac{\mu}{\rho} + \lambda) - ES$" and "$(\frac{\mu}{\rho}, \lambda) - ES$" with ρ corresponding to the number of parent individuals that are involved in the generation of a child individual.

In 1995, Hansen [HAN 95] suggested the algorithm called the Covariance Matrix Adaptation Evolution Strategy. This method is characterized by the fact that the covariance matrix of the multinormal distribution is self-adaptive and is relative to the mutation operator that allows new individuals to be generated. This method has met with huge success and remains among the most cited methods.

2.2.3. *Coevolutionary algorithms*

Coevolutionary algorithms have been proposed by Hillis in 1990 [HIL 90]. They are inspired from species interacting with each other, such as parasites and their hosts, and evolving in a dependent manner, unlike evolutionary algorithms that only take into account the evolution of a single species.

This dependence is reflected at the evaluation level of an individual from a population (of a given species), which takes into consideration the evaluations of the individuals from the other populations (of other species). This evaluation is therefore subjective.

Among coevolutionary algorithms two strategies can be distinguished, competitive and cooperative:

– Regarding competitive coevolutionary algorithms [ROS 97] such as the prey–predator model [NOL 98], the different populations independently evolve and then start competing with each other. Furthermore, each population searches for the local optimum by means of the so-called local objective function, then the competition between them results in a state of equilibrium. Thus, an individual from a population is in competition with the individuals of the other populations that evolve within their own species and each population benefits from the failure of others.

– Regarding cooperative coevolutionary algorithms [POT 94], each population addresses part of the problem and the assembly of these partial solutions leads to a global solution. As a result, the collaboration between these different populations, independent from each other, has a direct impact on the quality of the solution. In other words, the evaluation of an individual is related to its ability to cooperate with individuals from other populations.

2.2.4. *Cultural algorithms*

Cultural algorithms were introduced by Reynolds in 1994 [REY 94] and are inspired by the cultural evolution principle. In this approach, the selection of individuals does not happen according to the evolution of the genetic material but according to the cultural evolution that comprises two levels: the microevolutionary and the macroevolutionary level. The microevolutionary level is the space describing the population of solutions. The macroevolutionary level corresponds to the knowledge space or belief space.

At the microevolutionary level, there are three operators:

– the evaluation operator of each individual of the population via the objective function;

– the selection operator determining the individuals of the next generation;

– the evolution operator able to make the population evolve based on the influence function.

At the macroevolutionary level, one can find the update operator of the knowledge set. There are five main knowledge sources: normative knowledge, situational knowledge, the knowledge of the territory, temporal knowledge and knowledge related to the domain of the problem [REY 05].

These two spaces interact according to a communication protocol materialized by the acceptance and influence functions:

– the acceptance function provides a means for selecting the individuals that will contribute to the development of the knowledge;

– the influence function makes it possible to make the population evolve according to the data recorded in the knowledge space.

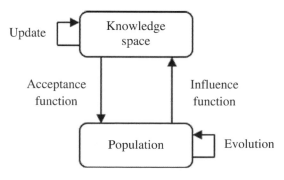

Figure 2.1. *The cultural algorithm model*

2.2.5. *Differential evolution*

Introduced by Storn and Price in 1995 [STO 95], differential evolution is an evolutionary algorithm initially proposed to solve continuous and unconstrained optimization problems. Similarly to any evolutionary algorithm, the differential evolution method consists of making a population of individuals evolve using the mutation, crossover and selection operators.

At a generation G (or iteration), an individual is represented by a vector of dimension D such that:

$$x_{i,G} = (x_{1i,G}, x_{2i,G}, ..., x_{Di,G}) \text{ with } i = 1, 2, ..., N \qquad [2.1]$$

where N is the size of the population.

After the random initialization of the population following a uniform distribution and covering all the parameter space, the process called *evolution* is applied at each iteration or generation. This *evolution* process provides a means of making changes to individuals by applying a succession of operators: mutation, crossover and selection.

2.2.5.1. *Mutation*

From a common vector $x_{i,G}$, a mutant vector $x_{i,G}$ is generated based on a strategy given by the following equations:

– *Rand/1*:

$$v_{i,G} = x_{r_1,G-1} + F.(x_{r_2,G-1} - x_{r_3,G-1}) \qquad [2.2]$$

– *Best/1*:

$$v_{i,G} = x_{best,G-1} + F.(x_{r_1,G-1} - x_{r_2,G-1}) \qquad [2.3]$$

– *Current to best/1*:

$$v_{i,G} = x_{i,G-1} + F.(x_{r_1,G-1} - x_{r_2,G-1}) + F.(x_{best,G-1} - x_{i,G-1}) \qquad [2.4]$$

– *Best/2*:

$$v_{i,G} = x_{best,G-1} + F.(x_{r_1,G-1} - x_{r_2,G-1}) + F.(x_{r_3,G-1} - x_{r_4,G-1}) \qquad [2.5]$$

– *Rand/2*:

$$v_{i,G} = x_{r_1,G-1} + F.(x_{r_2,G-1} - x_{r_3,G-1}) + F.(x_{r_4,G-1} - x_{r_5,G-1}) \qquad [2.6]$$

with:

– r_1, r_2, r_3, r_4 and r_5, randomly selected indices, non-identical and different from i;

– $x_{best,G-1}$, the best individual found in the $(G-1)th$ generation;

– $F \in [0.2]$, a constant influencing the differential variation in the vectors.

2.2.5.2. *Crossover*

In order to favor the intensification of the perturbated parameter vector and following mutation, crossover is achieved between the parent vector $x_{i,G-1}$ and the mutant vector $v_{i,G}$ generating the trial vector $u_{i,G}$ obtained by:

$$u_{ji,G} = \begin{cases} v_{1i,G} & \text{if } randb(j) \leq CR \text{ or } j = rnbr(i) \\ x_{ji,G-1} & \text{if } randb(j) > CR \text{ and } j \neq rnbr(i) \end{cases} \quad j = 1, 2, ..., D \quad [2.7]$$

where:

– *randb(j)* is the jth randomly generated value according to the uniform distribution on $[0, 1]$;

– $CR \in [0, 1]$ corresponds to the crossover coefficient;

– *rnbr(i)* corresponds to a randomly chosen index in the set $1, 2, ..., N$.

2.2.5.3. *Selection*

The selection operator is applied to the parent vectors $x_{i,G-1}$ and the trial vectors $u_{i,G}$ obtained during the crossover, thus defining the vectors $x_{i,G}$ of the next generation with the rule:

$$x_{i,G} = \begin{cases} u_{i,G} & \text{if } f(u_{i,G}) < f(x_{i,G-1}) \\ x_{i,G-1} & \text{otherwise} \end{cases} \qquad [2.8]$$

Following the version of the differential evolution proposed by Storn, a number of variations have been introduced which can be distinguished by their adaptive and self-adaptive character [LIU 05, QIN 05, QIN 09a].

2.2.6. *Biogeography-based optimization*

Biogeography-based optimization is an evolutionary algorithm introduced by Simon in 2008 [SIM 08] inspired by the geographical distribution of biological organisms, whose mathematical model had been proposed in 1967 by MacArthur and Wilson [MAC 67]. This study describes the phenomenon of migration of a species from one island or habitat to another and the phenomenon of emergence of a new species or of extinction of an old one.

Faced with an empty habitat, species migrate and inhabit this habitat. Subsequently, these species may compete, implying the extinction of a given species in this habitat. Each habitat has a Habitat Suitability Index (HSI) and Suitability Index Variables (SIV). The HSI depends directly on the habitat and makes it possible to determine if the latter is suitable for a given species. On the other hand, SIVs are variables independent of the habitat such as temperature, precipitation or even plant diversity. Several models representing the migration of species are proposed in [MAC 67], comprising linear models and other more complex nonlinear ones. A study about several models has been carried out by Ma [MA 10], where it has been shown that nonlinear models are more effective. In the following, we consider the linear model proposed by Simon in 2008 [SIM 08].

Biogeography-based optimization considers a population of individuals as a habitat. Each habitat is represented by SIV variables and its evaluation corresponds to its HSI index. These habitats are described by two parameters depending on the number S of species present, namely the immigration rate λ and the emigration rate μ. λ represents the arrival of species in a given habitat, whereas μ represents the departures of species from this habitat. A habitat with a low HSI is a habitat populated by several species S, that is, with a low immigration rate λ and a high emigration rate μ. Therefore, a habitat with a low HSI constitutes a "good" solution.

Consequently, as the number of species in a habitat increases, the immigration rate of individuals of another species λ decreases and vice versa. The immigration rate of a habitat with S species is given by:

$$\lambda_s = I(1 - \frac{S}{S_{max}}) \tag{2.9}$$

where I is the maximum immigration rate reached when the habitat is empty and S_{max} is the maximal number of species that this habitat can accommodate.

As the number of species in a habitat increases, so does the emigration rate of individuals of other species μ. The immigration rate of a habitat with S species is given by:

$$\mu_s = E(\frac{S}{S_{max}}) \tag{2.10}$$

where E is the maximal emigration rate reached when all species are located in the habitat.

The evolution of the number of species during a time interval $[t, t + \Delta t]$ is carried out according to the following equation:

$$
\begin{aligned}
P_S(t + \Delta t) \quad = \quad & P_S(t)(1 - \lambda_S \Delta t - \mu_S \Delta t) \\
& + P_{S-1} \lambda_{S-1} \Delta t + P_{S+1} \mu_{S+1} \Delta t
\end{aligned}
\tag{2.11}
$$

with P_S the probability that a habitat shelters exactly S species, obtained according to the number of species already present in the habitat and the arrival and departure frequencies of the species. Moreover, in order for a habitat to accommodate S species at iteration $i+1$, one of the following conditions must be met:

– there are S species at iteration i without any immigration and emigration between iterations i and $i + 1$;

– there are $S - 1$ species at iteration i and one species has immigrated;

– there are $S + 1$ species at iteration i and one species has emigrated.

As a result, the variation in time Δt is considered to be very small and tends to 0 so that there be no more than one immigration or emigration at the same time. From equation [2.11], the following system of equations is obtained:

$$P_s = \begin{cases} -(\lambda_S + \mu_S)P_S + \mu_{S+1}P_{S+1}, S = 0 \\ -(\lambda_S + \mu_S)P_S + \lambda_{S-1}P_{S-1} + \mu_{S+1}P_{S+1}, 1 \leq S \leq S_{max} - 1 \\ -(\lambda_S + \mu_S)P_S + \lambda_{S-1}P_{S-1}, S = S_{max} \end{cases}$$

$$[2.12]$$

The main characteristic of migration is the exchange of information between the habitats that causes a change to a solution with a certain probability P_{mod} uniformly distributed between 0 and 1, unlike evolutionary algorithms that generate new solutions. This exchange is done through the immigration and emigration rates of a given habitat and the best solution is always kept from one generation to another.

A natural disaster, such as a storm or fire, may occur and abruptly change the HSI of a habitat, which is reflected in the mutation of a habitat at the algorithmic level with a rate defined by:

$$m_s = m_{max}\left(1 - \frac{P}{P_{max}}\right) \qquad [2.13]$$

where m_{max} is the predefined parameter and $P_{max} = \max_S P_S$ $(S = 1, 2, ..., S_{max})$. Thus, if a habitat is selected for the mutation the latter is performed on an SIV chosen in a random manner and replaced by a random value generated in its definition domain.

2.2.7. *Hybrid metaheuristic based on Bayesian estimation*

The Bayesian approach based metaheuristic is a very recent method for solving continuous problems, proposed in 2015 by Nakib [NAK 15], and is a part of hybrid evolutionary algorithms. This method utilizes crossover and mutation operators except that the operator is chosen dynamically at each iteration, contrary to conventional methods in which this choice is made during the design of the algorithm. The particularity of this metaheuristic lies in the fact that it solves the problem of the choice of operators by means of dynamic exploration strategies. It also aims at solving the problem of reduced performance related to large-sized problems. As a matter of fact, when the size grows too large, the performance of a stochastic algorithm decreases.

The principle of this Bayesian approach based metaheuristic is to define m crossover operators and n mutation operators. It then yields $m \times n$ possible strategies. The best strategy is then chosen using the Bayes rule:

$$p(x|z) = \frac{p(z|x) \times p(x)}{p(z)} \qquad [2.14]$$

where x is the state corresponding to an exploration strategy and z is the observation obtained through the utilized metric that evaluates the quality of the exploration strategy. The metric considered in this case is the Euclidean distance defined by:

$$Dist = \sum_{j=1}^{P-1} \sum_{j'=j+1}^{P} \sum_{i=1}^{D} |G_{ij} - G_{ij'}| \qquad [2.15]$$

where P corresponds to the size of the population, D to the size and G to the gene.

By using this approach to evaluate several exploration strategies, the complexity of the algorithm increases but its performance remains stable.

Algorithm 2.2: Bayes rule based evolutionary algorithm

---

1 **Initialize** population P
2 **Initialize** the likelihood of each strategy with a metric on T generations
3 **While** *the stopping criterion is not satisfied* **Do**
4   **Choose** the best strategy with the Bayes rule
5   **Select** the chromosomes
6   **Apply the crossover** on the selected parents
7   **Apply the mutation** on the selected individuals
8 **End**
9 **Return** the best solution

2.3. Swarm intelligence

Swarm intelligence is a family of metaheuristics inspired by natural phenomena and more specifically by the behavior of a group or a population of agents that communicate between themselves and interact with their environment in order to survive. These interactions allow the population of agents to perform complex tasks in an organized way. We address PSO, ant colony optimization, cuckoo search, the firefly algorithm and the fireworks algorithm.

2.3.1. *Particle Swarm Optimization*

PSO, proposed by Kennedy and Eberhart in 1995 [EBE 95], is inspired by the social behavior of birds as well as that of fish and, notably, by their travels. It utilizes the metaphor of the grouped flight of birds and that of fish shoals described by Reynolds [REY 87] and by Heppner and Grenander [HEP 90], who introduced the mathematical models of these natural phenomena.

The particle swarm is represented by a population of particles or solutions that travel in the search space in order to eventually find the global optimum. These particles exchange information between themselves related to a position of the space that proves promising. This information is taken into account during displacements in addition to their own data. Three components will thus influence the movement of a particle from one position to another:

– the physical component or component of inertia influences the movement towards the current direction of the particle;

– the cognitive component attracts the particle towards the best position through which it has passed up to the current iteration;

– the social component directs the particle to the best position found by the swarm during the search.

Each particle is characterized by the position vector $\vec{X}_i$ and velocity vector $\vec{V}_i$ which direct the movement of the particle in the space. It also keeps in memory the best position which it has passed through, denoted as $\vec{P}_i$, and the best position achieved by all the swarm, denoted as $\vec{P}_g$. The vector $\vec{V}_i$ represents the velocity of the movement of the particle and thus takes into account the different components presented above, which are updated at each iteration.

In the original version of the PSO algorithm, $\vec{V}_i$ is written as follows:

$$\vec{V}_i(t+1) = \vec{V}_i(t) + c_1 r_1 [\vec{P}_i(t) - \vec{X}_i(t)] + c_2 r_2 [\vec{P}_g(t) - \vec{X}_i(t)] \quad [2.16]$$

where $i = 1, 2, ..., N$ and N is the size of the swarm; c_1 and c_2 are the acceleration coefficients making it possible to favor the influence of the cognitive component or that of the social component, respectively; r_1 and r_2 are random values between $[0; 1]$.

Once the velocity is updated, the positions $\vec{X}_i$ [2.17], $\vec{P}_i$ [2.18] and $\vec{P}_g$ [2.19] are also updated at each iteration.

$$\vec{X}_i(t+1) = \vec{X}_i(t) + \vec{V}_i(t+1) \qquad\qquad [2.17]$$

$$\vec{P}_i(t+1) = \begin{cases} \vec{P}_i(t) & , \text{if} f(\vec{X}_i(t+1)) \geq \vec{P}_i(t) \\ \vec{X}_i(t+1)) & , \text{otherwise} \end{cases} \qquad [2.18]$$

$$\vec{P}_g(t+1) = \arg\min_{\vec{P}_i} f(\vec{P}_i(t+1)), 1 \leq i \leq N \qquad [2.19]$$

Algorithm 2.3: Particle swarm optimization

---

1 **Define** the swarm size. **Initialize** parameters ω, c_1 and c_2
2 **For each** *particle p_i* **Do**
3   **Initialize** position x_i
4   **Initialize** velocity v_i
5   **Initialize** the best position of particle P_i
6 **End**
7 **Determine** the best position of the swarm P_g
8 **While** *the stopping criterion is not satisfied* **Do**
9   **For each** *particle p_i* **Do**
10   **Update** velocity v_i
11   **Update** position x_i
12   **Update** the best position of particle P_i
13   **End**
14   **Update** the best position of the swarm P_g
15 **End**
16 **Return** the best solution

Since introduction of PSO, many improvements have been proposed. The first was by Eberhart in 1996 [EBE 96] who inserted the concept of maximum travel velocity denoted as $\vec{V}_{max}$, allowing the control of the divergence and avoiding the tendency for particles to come out of the search space. The displacement is limited to a given iteration of each particle by $\vec{V}_{max}$ on each dimension, which results in balancing the exploration and the exploitation between them. In addition, strategies for containing the particles have been proposed in order to gather them back within the search space [CLE 06]. For example, particles are brought back to the border with a non-zero velocity or with a velocity $\vec{V}_i(t) = \vec{V}_i(t)c$, where $c \in [-1, 0]$. The choice of $\vec{V}_{max}$ is however decisive, at the risk of leading to bad results.

A few years later, Shi and Eberhart [SHI 98] introduced a new parameter called the coefficient of inertia as a means of balancing exploration and exploitation in a general manner. This coefficient of inertia ω provides a way of controlling the influence of the current velocity on that of the next iteration. In the proposal of Shi [SHI 98], the coefficient of inertia is dynamic and follows a linear variation according to the equation:

$$\omega = \omega_{min} + (\omega_{max} - \omega_{min})\frac{iter}{max_{iter}} \qquad [2.20]$$

with $iter$ corresponding to the current iteration, max_{iter} to the maximal iterations number and ω_{min} and ω_{max} as, respectively, the minimal and maximal values that ω can take ($\omega_{min}, \omega_{max} \in [0, 1]$).

The equation [2.16] defining the velocity thus becomes:

$$\vec{X}_i(t+1) = \omega\vec{V}_i(t) + c_1 r_1[\vec{P}_i(t) - \vec{X}_i(t)] + c_2 r_2[\vec{P}_g(t) - \vec{X}_i(t)] \qquad [2.21]$$

In 2002, Clerc and Kennedy [CLE 02] have presented a different approach to PSO, canonical PSO. This method introduces the constriction coefficient χ that controls velocities during iterations and thereby can overcome the divergence problem. New parameters related to cognitive and social components, ϕ_1 and ϕ_2, have also been introduced. It can be observed, in equation [2.23], that χ is dependent of ϕ_1 and ϕ_2, which allows us to remove a parameter: V_{max} [CLE 02]. As a result, the update of the velocity is done by:

$$\vec{V_i}(t+1) = \chi(\vec{V_i}(t) + \phi_1 r_1 [\vec{P_i}(t) - \vec{X_i}(t)] + \phi_2 r_2 [(\vec{P_g}(t) - \vec{X_i}(t)]) \quad [2.22]$$

with:

$$\chi = \frac{2}{\phi - 2 + \sqrt{\phi^2 - 4\phi}} \quad\quad\quad [2.23]$$

where $\phi = \phi_1 + \phi_2$, $\phi > 4$.

Tests have shown that the optimal constriction coefficient is $\chi = 0.7298844$ with $\phi = 4.1$ and $\phi_1 = \phi_2$. Nonetheless, in some cases the combination of the constriction coefficient χ with a maximum velocity $\vec{V_{max}}$ results in obtaining better performance, particularly with regard to the convergence velocity [SHI 99].

Finally, one last important characteristic relative to the topology of the neighborhood being employed [KEN 02] can significantly influence the performance of the algorithm. In the original algorithm, the defined topology is the star topology in which each particle is connected to all the population and shares global information $\vec{P_g}$. The main disadvantage of this method is that exploration is not encouraged, which may imply premature convergence (this is referred to as the *global version*). Versions called *local versions* have been thus proposed. The essential difference lies in the communication between particles that is no longer achieved via the global information $\vec{P_g}$ but by means of local information $\vec{P_{gi}}$ representing the best solution found in the neighborhood of a given particle. Among them, one can find the version with the ring topology proposed by Eberhart in 1996 [EBE 96].

2.3.2. *Ant colony optimization*

Ant colony optimization was introduced by Dorigo in 1991 [DOR 91] and is inspired by the behavior of ants when searching for food [DEN 90]. Ants share the particularity that they can find the shortest way between their nest and a food source by dropping during their search a volatile chemical substance called pheromone. This chemical communication is a phenomenon of "stigmergy":   ants organize themselves by making use of indirect communication through the modification of the environment in which they evolve by depositing pheromones that evaporate after a while.

Ants begin by exploring the space near their nest, depositing pheromones on their way to the source of food. This allows their fellows to follow the path that leads to this source, thus strengthening the amount of chemical substance on the path. The shorter the way is, the greater the concentration of pheromones that can be found thereon, thus attracting even more ants.

By analogy, artificial ants aim to find the least costly path between the origin site and the destination site by progressively building the solution as they move around and by updating the pheromone traces. Initially, the construction of this solution s is done iteratively based on the exploration of a comprehensive graph $G(V, E)$ composed of a set of nodes V and edges E connecting the nodes. Furthermore, at each iteration m the ants construct m solutions in n steps. Each step involves the insertion of an arc (i, j) to the current partial solution s_k relative to the ant k, corresponding to the transition from the node i to the node j where $j \in N_i{}^k$, where $N_i{}^k$ is the set of feasible neighbors of s^k from the node i. This choice is based on a probability rule defined in general by the equation proposed in the "Ant System" algorithm [DOR 96]:

$$p_{ij}{}^k(t) = \frac{a_{ij}(t)}{\sum_{l \in N_i{}^k} a_{il}(t)} \qquad [2.24]$$

with:

$$a_{ij}(t) = \frac{[\tau_{ij}(t)]^\alpha [\eta_{ij}(t)]^\beta}{\sum_{l \in N_i{}^k} [\tau_{il}(t)]^\alpha \cdot [\eta_{il}(t)]^\beta)} \qquad [2.25]$$

where:

– τ_{ij} is the amount of pheromone that can be found on the arc (i, j) at iteration t;

– η_{ij} is the heuristic value of the move from node i to node j;

– α and β are parameters that control the influence of the pheromone values and the heuristics about the choice of the ant.

When the parameter α tends to 0, the likelihood of selecting the closest node is high. Conversely, when the parameter β tends to 0, the influence of the pheromone rate on the choice for the next node will be stronger resulting in quick stagnation.

The update of the traces of pheromones, represented by equation [2.26] in the case of the "Ant System", is carried out while respecting the natural mechanisms of evaporation and deposition of pheromones. Evaporation (reduction of the pheromone rate) is applied on the paths less visited by the ants, whereas deposition increases the pheromone rate of the most promising or satisfactory pathways.

$$\tau_{ij}(t+1) = (1-\rho)\tau_{ij}(t) + \Delta\tau_{ij}(t) \qquad [2.26]$$

with ρ, the decay coefficient in $[0, 1]$ and $\Delta\tau_{ij}(t)$, the sum of the quantities of pheromones deposited by all the ants on the arc (i, j).

Between these two processes some algorithms are able to insert actions called "demon actions" that are specific to them, such as local searches in order to improve their effectiveness [DOR 99a, DOR 99b].

Algorithm 2.4: Ant colony optimization

---

1 **Define** the colony size
2 **Initialize** pheromone traces
3 **While** *the stopping criterion is not satisfied* **Do**
4   **For each** *ant* **Do**
5   **Build** a solution
6   **End**
7   **Update** the pheromone traces
8 **End**
9 **Return** the best solution

Included among the algorithms implemented in the hypercube framework [BLU 04] are the basic "Ant System" algorithm, the "Ant Colony System" algorithm [DOR 97] and the "Max-Min Ant System" algorithm [STU 00] which are considered to be the best performing in this category [DOR 05].

The "Ant Colony System" algorithm, a variant of the "Ant System" algorithm, presents significant differences:

1) the use of a new transition rule, called the "pseudo-random-proportional rule", which decides whether the transition functions in a deterministic manner or in a probabilistic one;

2) the offline update of pheromone traces, which happens when all the agents have built their solutions and is made at the level of the best solution found during the entire search, thus strengthening exploitation;

3) the online update of pheromone traces, which happens during the construction of a solution by an agent, strengthening the exploration of the search space.

The "Max-Min Ant System" algorithm is also a variant of the "Ant System" algorithm that stands out mainly due to the fact that the pheromone rate is defined in a given interval $[\tau_{min}, \tau_{max}]$ and is initialized at τ_{max}. Being offline, the update of pheromones can be applied to the best solution found during the current iteration or to the best solution found during the search.

2.3.3. *Cuckoo search*

Cuckoo search is a recent method for solving difficult optimization problems. Introduced by Yang in 2009 [YAN 09b], it is based on the reproduction behavior of a certain species of nesting parasitic birds called cuckoos. It turns out that before laying its eggs, the female cuckoo undertakes a search for a host nest of another species and which already contains other eggs from this other species. Once chosen, it lays its eggs in this nest when the other host is absent. In addition to their parasitic qualities, cuckoos have an aggressive character in that, after hatching, the young cuckoos eject the other eggs out of the nest in order to be better fed.

Concerning the algorithm, three assumptions are made:

1) a cuckoo lays one egg at a time in randomly chosen nests;

2) the best nests will be transmitted to the next generation;

3) the number of available nests is fixed and the host bird may discover the egg with a probability of $p_a \in [0, 1]$. In this case, the host bird may abandon its nest and build a new one or throw out the egg. To represent this hypothesis, the

author has chosen to replace a proportion p_a of nests by new nests randomly generated.

Thus, the generation of a new solution or cuckoo i is done with the following equation:

$$x_i^{(t+1)} = x_i^{(t)} \oplus L\acute{e}vy(\lambda) \tag{2.27}$$

where $\alpha > 0$ corresponds to the size of the step related to the size of the problem generally set at 1, and $L\acute{e}vy$ represents the Lévy flight describing bird flights according to their distribution:

$$L\acute{e}vy \sim u = t^{-\lambda}, 1 < \lambda \leq 3 \tag{2.28}$$

Algorithm 2.5: "Cuckoo" search

---
1 **Initialize** the population of n host nests
2 **Define** the maximal number of generations G_{max}
3 **While** G_{max} *or the stopping criterion is not reached* **Do**
4 　　**Randomly select** a cuckoo i with Lévy flights
5 　　**Evaluate** the selected cuckoo
6 　　**Randomly choose** a nest j among the n nests
7 　　**If** *the nest j improves i* **Then**
8 　　　│ **Update** the nest j
9 　　**End**
10 　　**Abandon** a proportion p_a of the worst nests
11 　　**Build** a proportion p_a of new nests
12 　　**Keep** the best solutions
13 　　**Store** the solutions
14 　　**Update** the best solution
15 **End**
16 **Return** the best solution

2.3.4. *The firefly algorithm*

The firefly algorithm has been introduced by Yang in 2008 [YAN 08, YAN 09a, LUK 09, YAN 10] and is once again inspired by observing nature. Fireflies emit an intermittent light to attract their own kind. These luminous signals are emitted by female fireflies in order to attract and feed from male fireflies. Over time, this light diminishes little by little.

At the algorithm level, three rules are defined:

1) fireflies are considered unisex so that they can mutually attract each other;

2) brightness is associated with the objective function and is determined depending on the region of this objective function to be optimized;

3) attractiveness is proportional to the intensity of the light: the brightest firefly attracts those which are less bright. In cases in which two fireflies emit light with the same intensity, the move choice is done randomly.

In the case of a maximization problem, the light intensity of a firefly located at position x can be defined in the simplest case by a proportionality relation with the objective function:

$$I(x) \propto f(x) \qquad\qquad [2.29]$$

The variation of this intensity is defined according to the distance r separating this firefly i and another j:

$$I_{ij} = I_0 \exp(-\gamma r_{ij}^2) \qquad\qquad [2.30]$$

where I_0 corresponds to the light intensity at the origin and γ is the light absorption coefficient.

Knowing that attractiveness is proportional to light intensity, its equation is thus defined as follows:

$$\beta_{ij} = \beta_0 \exp(-\gamma r_{ij}^2) \qquad\qquad [2.31]$$

where β_0 is the attractiveness at $r = 0$ and r_{ij} is the distance between two fireflies i and j.

Therefore, the movement of a firefly i attracted by a firefly j is made as follows:

$$x_i = x_i + \beta_0 \exp(-\gamma r_{ij}^2)(x_j - x_i) + \alpha\epsilon_i \qquad [2.32]$$

where the second term corresponds to the attractiveness and the third term corresponds to the random aspect of the move with α being a random value that can be constant and ϵ_i a vector of random values following the Gaussian distribution.

Algorithm 2.6: The firefly algorithm

---

1   **Initialize** the population of fireflies
2   **Define** the maximal number of generations G_{max}
3   **For each** *firefly* l_i **Do**
4   **Determine** the light intensity I_i
5   **End**
6   **Define** the light absorption coefficient γ
7   **While** G_{max} *is not reached* **Do**
8   **For each** *firefly* l_i **Do**
9   **For** j *ranging from* 1 *to* i **Do**
10   **If** $I_j > I_i$ **Then**
11   **Move** l_i towards l_j
12   **End**
13   **Update** the attractiveness
14   **Evaluate** the new solutions
15   **Update** light intensity
16   **End**
17   **End**
18   **Update** the best solution
19   **End**
20   **Return** the best solution

2.3.5. *The fireworks algorithm*

The fireworks algorithm proposed by Tan in 2010 [TAN 10] is inspired by the observation of the explosion of fireworks. In effect, when a firework is activated, the explosion generates a set of sparks around it.

At the beginning of the fireworks algorithm, n fireworks are randomly selected in the search space. Following the explosion, a set of sparks are generated around each firework x_i and evaluated. Among the fireworks and the sparks generated, n elements are selected corresponding to the n fireworks of the next iteration. This procedure is repeated until the stopping criterion is met.

There are two types of behavior in an explosion called "good explosion" and "bad explosion":

– a "good explosion" is described by a significant number of sparks that surround the center of the explosion, which shows that this region is promising;

– a "bad explosion" is described by a small number of sparks scattered in the search space, which shows that the search is moving away from the optimum. It is necessary to increase the search radius.

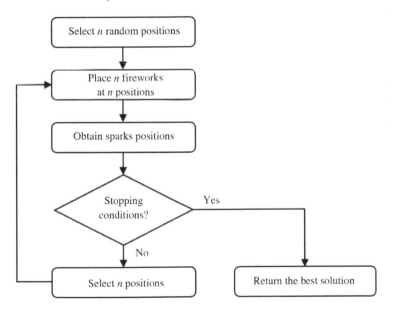

Figure 2.2. *The fireworks algorithm model*

In this algorithm, three characteristics have to be determined, namely the number of sparks, the amplitude of the explosion and the generation of sparks.

In a first stage, the number of sparks generated by the fireworks x_i is defined by means of the following equation:

$$s_i = m \frac{y_{max} - f(x_i) + \xi}{\sum_{i=1}^{n}(y_{max} - f(x_i)) + \xi}$$

[2.33]

where:

– m is a control parameter related to the total number of sparks generated by the n fireworks;

– y_{max} corresponds to the evaluation of the worst solution among the n fireworks;

– ξ is the smallest value of the computer in order to avoid division by 0.

The number of sparks is controlled in order to avoid the generation of too large a number of sparks and this is done according to the following equation:

$$s_i = \begin{cases} round(am) & \text{if } s_i < am \\ round(bm) & \text{if } s_i < bm, a < b < 1 \\ round(s_i) & \text{otherwise} \end{cases}$$

[2.34]

where a and b are constant parameters.

In a second stage, the amplitude of the explosion is defined by:

$$A_i = \hat{A} \frac{f(x_i) - y_{min} + \xi}{\sum_{i=1}^{n} f(x_i) - y_{min} + \xi}$$

[2.35]

where $\hat{A}$ is the maximum explosion amplitude and y_{min} is the evaluation of the best solution among the n fireworks. Thus, the amplitude of a good explosion is smaller than that of a bad explosion.

In a third stage, the generation of sparks is achieved following random directions z that are obtained with:

$$z = round(d.rand(0,1))$$

[2.36]

where d is the dimension of the position x and $rand(0.1)$ is a random value in the interval $[0, 1]$ following the uniform distribution. The positions of the sparks are then obtained with algorithm 2.7. Another algorithm has been proposed using a Gaussian distribution (algorithm 2.8) in order to keep the diversity of sparks [TAN 15].

Algorithm 2.7: Obtain the position of a spark

1 **Initialize** the position $\tilde{x}_j$ of a spark
2 **Initialize** z
3 **Randomly select** z dimensions of $\tilde{x}_j$
4 **Calculate** the move $h = A_i.rand(-1, 1)$
5 **For each** *dimension* $\tilde{x}_k^j$ *selected in* $\tilde{x}_j$ **Do**
6 $\quad$ $\tilde{x}_k^j = \tilde{x}_k^j + h$
7 $\quad$ **If** $\tilde{x}_k^j < x_k^{min}$ *or* $\tilde{x}_k^j > x_k^{max}$ **Then**
8 $\quad\quad$ **Carry out the projection** of $\tilde{x}_k^j$ in the potential space:
$$\tilde{x}_k^j = x_k^{min} + |\tilde{x}_k^j|\%(x_k^{max} - x_k^{min})$$
9 $\quad$ **End**
10 **End**

Algorithm 2.8: Obtain the position of a specific spark

1 **Initialize** the position $\hat{x}_j$ of a spark
2 **Initialize** z
3 **Randomly select** z dimensions of $\hat{x}_j$
4 **Calculate** the coefficient of the Gaussian explosion $g = Gaussian(1, 1)$
5 **For each** *dimension* $\hat{x}_k^j$ *selected in* $\hat{x}_j$ **Do**
6 $\quad$ $\hat{x}_k^j = \hat{x}_k^j.g$
7 $\quad$ **If** $\hat{x}_k^j < x_k^{min}$ *or* $\hat{x}_k^j > x_k^{max}$ **Then**
8 $\quad\quad$ **Achieve the projection** of $\hat{x}_k^j$ in the potential space:
$$\hat{x}_k^j = x_k^{min} + |\hat{x}_k^j|\%(x_k^{max} - x_k^{min})$$
9 $\quad$ **End**
10 **End**

The selection of the positions for the generation of the following fireworks is performed according to the probability defined by:

$$p(x_i) = \frac{R(x_i)}{\sum_{j \in K} R(x_j)}$$ [2.37]

where $R(x_i)$ is the distance between position x_i and the other positions (Euclidean distance or Manhattan distance) and K is the set of the positions of the fireworks and the sparks.

2.4. Conclusion

All these methods are based on the evolution of a population of solutions that communicate with each other and exchange information during the search. They thus favor exploration. Furthermore, the balance between the notions of exploration and exploitation provides a means to achieve good results, which gave birth to the hybrid metaheuristics methods. This hybridization can be done:

– by integrating local search methods in a solution population-based method such as mimetic algorithms (evolutionary algorithms with an integrated local search method);

– through the cooperation of metaheuristics communicating between themselves at varying levels;

– through the integration of metaheuristics and systemic methods.

Performance Evaluation of Metaheuristics

3.1. Introduction

Metaheuristics have been introduced with the objective of solving difficult optimization problems in a reasonable time. These methods make use of a number of parameters that can be adjusted according to the problem to be solved. Since their introduction, several have been proposed in the literature. Since these methods are of a stochastic nature, the evaluation of their performance must take this aspect into consideration.

The first evaluation can be performed by means of theoretical study through the calculation of complexity [KAR 72]; nevertheless, this study remains insufficient to define the effectiveness of a stochastic algorithm. However, an experimental evaluation must be achieved by means of simulations. Regarding the comparison of different metaheuristics, statistical tests must be conducted. Moreover, an experimental model must be established in order to clarify the objectives as well as the choice of instances implemented, which can be real and/or simulated.

In this respect, several tools are available for the evaluation of metaheuristic performance and the choice of the best tool is not trivial. Accordingly, in this chapter, we are going to present the different performance measures that can be used. Then, we will review tools for statistical analysis. Finally, we will describe a few benchmarks used in the literature which aim to compare the performance of metaheuristics.

3.2. Performance measures

In this section, we present the different performance measures of metaheuristics. In the case of exact methods, the execution time of the algorithm is a sufficient criterion for its evaluation because the optimality of the solution is guaranteed. On the other hand, any optimization algorithm with stochastic characteristics is evaluated following specific indicators such as the quality of the solutions obtained, the computational effort necessary for its execution and its robustness.

3.2.1. *Quality of solutions*

The quality of a solution is defined by its cost or its *fitness* obtained by evaluating the objective function. This quality corresponds to a numerical value that makes it possible to indicate to what extent the solution obtained is satisfactory.

For some problems, the global optimum is known. In this case, the quality of a solution is determined by the distance between this solution and the global solution, called the absolute difference. The closer to zero this distance is or, in general, the smaller the error between these two solutions is, the better the solution will be.

This absolute difference can be defined with the expression $|f(s) - f(s^*)|$ or $|f(s) - f(s^*)|/f(s^*)$, where s is the solution obtained and s^* is the optimal global solution. However, knowing that these measures are variable at different scales, an absolute approximation can also be employed and obtained by means of $|f(s) - f(s^*)|/|f_{worst} - f(s^*)|$ or even $|f(s) - f(s^*)|/|E_{unif}(f) - f(s^*)|$, where f_{worst} is the worst cost of the objective function and $E_{unif}(f)$ is the average value of a uniform distribution of the solutions [ZEM 81, ZLO 02].

For other problems, the optimal solution is not known in advance. In this case, several methods are proposed so as to define a reference with respect to the quality of the solution. In this sense, the reference solution might be the best solution found after the algorithm has stopped. The latter will be updated once a better solution is found. Nonetheless, this does not guarantee the optimality of the solution under consideration and informs us even less about the existence of an optimal solution or even several optimal solutions. Another alternative to the global solution can be determined with the definition of lower bounds. As a matter of fact, several techniques have been developed to this effect, including relaxation techniques among which the conventional continuous relaxation technique and the Lagrangian relaxation technique can be highlighted [GEO 74, MAR 04]. Thereby, the quality of a solution is defined according to this lower bound. Concerning real problems, the quality of the final solution may be fixed in advance and consequently becomes a benchmark with respect to the quality of the other solutions.

3.2.2. *Computational effort*

For any optimization algorithm, the computational analysis can be performed according to a theoretical or empirical analysis. The theoretical analysis is carried out by means of the study of the worst-case complexity of the algorithm. There are two types of complexities: asymptotic and average-case. Generally, asymptotic complexity is not sufficient to define the performance of metaheuristics. Average-case complexity may therefore be more representative in the case where the distribution of input instances is known *a priori*.

The empirical study can be done through various measures related to the computational time. In effect, this latter either corresponds to the time of the central processing unit, which is the processor, or to the time related to the internal clock of the machine. In addition, the computational time may take into consideration input/output operations, as well as the preprocessing/ postprocessing time.

The main drawback of these empirical study measures lies in the fact that they remain dependent on the characteristics of the machine. These features are linked to the performance of the machine from a physical point of view; notably the processor, RAM memory, cache memory but also the operating system, to the programming language and to the compiler used for the execution of the metaheuristic.

To compensate for this limitation, other measures or indicators independent of the machine have been proposed such as the number of evaluations of the objective function. This metric is acceptable for constant or *time-intensive* objective functions. However, this latter can present a limitation when it comes to problems with a small number of evaluations of the objective function or when they are not constant in time. For example, this problematic is perceived at the level of dynamic optimization problems and algorithms which have representations with varying sizes such as in genetic programming and robotics.

Several stopping criteria can be employed such as the number of iterations, the time required to obtain a given solution and the time necessary to obtain a solution with a certain proportion of a reference solution [TAL 09].

3.2.3. *Robustness*

Several definitions for sensitivity or robustness analysis have been proposed in the literature. It is carried out through the study of the variation of the results achieved by the metaheuristic with respect to its parameters. In fact, the smaller this variation is, the more robust or insensitive the algorithm is [MON 84]. In other words, the sensitivity analysis corresponds to the insensitivity of the metaheuristic with regard to a small deviation of the instances applied as input or of the parameters of the algorithm.

Moreover, the performance of a metaheuristic is determined by applying it to different problems and/or by varying the instances of the problem. Afterward, all of the results obtained are considered to define the robustness of the algorithm.

Therefore, by considering the parameters of the algorithm as being the sensitivity analysis input values and its performances as output values, several indicators can be taken into account in order to evaluate the sensitivity among which can be found the sensitivities related to a parameter and to the performance. The first consists of measuring the impact of a given parameter on performance by maintaining the other parameters constant, while the second enables the measurement of the average impact of a parameter on a set of output values relative to a set of instances [NAK 13].

3.3. Statistical analysis

Once the experimental results for different indicators are obtained, statistical analysis methods can be utilized to estimate the performance of the metaheuristics. The first two indicators that can be used are the mean and the standard deviation of the results obtained by each metaheuristic. Next, several statistical tests can be used to compare the different algorithms. These statistical tests are used to estimate the confidence that can be attributed to the results obtained. Hereafter, the choice of statistical tests as well as of the procedure to follow will be presented.

3.3.1. *Data description*

To start, it is necessary to establish a description of the results that will therefore represent the inputs in this analysis. This description takes into account two aspects, the first corresponds to the performance measure to be considered and the second to the variability measure of these data.

According to the problem being addressed, the measurement of the performance is performed according to one of the following two methods:

– the mean of n observations calculated according to equation [3.1];

– the median that corresponds to the central value of the observations when they are ordered:

$$\bar{X} = \frac{\sum_{i=1}^{n} X_i}{n} \qquad [3.1]$$

In general, the mean is the most utilized measure because it has significant mathematical properties, and it is the most representative with respect to the distributions of the symmetrical data. On the other hand, the use of the mean when the data assume very large or very small values is not recommended, it is advisable to employ the median as measure of performance.

Concerning the variability measure, it can be achieved by using different methods [WHI 01] and determining:

– the range obtained with the difference between the largest and the smallest value in the data set;

– the interquartile range corresponding to the difference between the third and the first quartile, which are obtained by dividing the data set ordered in four groups of equal size;

– the standard deviation calculated by expression [3.3]:

$$V(X) = \frac{1}{n} \sum_{i=1}^{n} (X_i - \bar{X})^2 \qquad\qquad [3.2]$$

$$\sigma = \sqrt{V(X)} \qquad\qquad [3.3]$$

In general, when the size of the data increases, all distributions tend toward a Gaussian (normal) distribution. Thus, the most commonly used variability measure is the standard deviation with a confidence interval. This confidence interval is a means to define the reliability of the experiments carried out: the smaller it is, the more reliable the results are.

Other measures can be calculated such as success rate TS and performance rate TP following, respectively, expressions [3.4] and [3.5]. In effect, the success rate is equal to the ratio between the number of successes achieved $NbSucces$ and the total number of executions carried out $NbExec$. Moreover, the performance rate also takes into account the computational effort that makes it possible to find the solution through the total number of evaluations of the objective function ($NbFoncEval$).

$$TS = \frac{NbSucces}{NbExec} \qquad\qquad [3.4]$$

$$TP = \frac{NbSucces}{NbExec * NbfoncEval} \qquad\qquad [3.5]$$

However, a success corresponds to finding a solution equal to the expected solution, in other words the optimal solution.

3.3.2. *Statistical tests*

Based on the different assumptions previously stated, a set of statistical tests called hypothesis tests can be applied depending on the problem. In effect, these tests consist of performing comparisons between the results obtained and those expected, that is, the outcomes defined by the assumptions. Statistical tests also provide a means to perform a comparison between several metaheuristics and to determine the reliability of the results obtained.

In the case where the normality test is verified, the t-test is the most recommended test [HSU 08]. Nonetheless, in other cases, a non-parametric analysis is carried out by means of the Wilcoxon test [GEH 65b, GEH 65a], the permutation test [LIN 96, KIM 00] or even the Mann–Whitney test [RUX 06], which are valid to compare two results. In effect, these latest statistical tests allow two methods to be compared based on the P-value and the metric under consideration. On the other hand, to achieve a comparison between several algorithms, the analysis of variance (ANOVA) models [FRE 81] as well as multivariate ANOVA models are recommended. These enable a simultaneous analysis of different performance measures to be made.

3.4. Literature benchmarks

There are several benchmarks to test a metaheuristic whose goal is to evaluate the performance of a stochastic algorithm as well as its convergence. Among these benchmarks, the best known are those of the IEEE CEC competition (*Congress on Evolutionary Computation*) and the *Black-Box Optimization Benchmarking*.

These benchmarks contains a set of test functions each characterized by certain characteristics described in the section.

3.4.1. *Characteristics of a test function*

Test functions can evaluate the different characteristics of optimization algorithms. Therefore, each one of them has a number of properties. In fact, these are especially related to modality, separability, roughness and symmetry [HAN 09].

– *Modality*: Modality corresponds to the number of spikes that can be found in the definition space of the objective function. Unimodality refers to the objective function when it only has a single optimum and multimodality when the objective function comprises several local optima.

– *Separability*: Separability is a characteristic of functions whose variables or parameters are independent of one another. Thus, several optimization processes can be independently launched in parallel thereby facilitating the solution of the basic problem. On the other hand, non-separable functions are more difficult to solve due to the dependence of decision variables.

– *Roughness*:   Roughness or regularity is a property describing the representation of the objective function. As a point of fact, when roughness is high, it is reflected by a large number of variations, whereas when it is small, it is the opposite that is expressed. Thereby, for a local search method, this roughness provides information about the difficulty that will be met in order to solve the problem.

– *Symmetry*: A function is said to be symmetric when it does not vary after a rotation of the coordinate system. As previously stated, stochastic search methods utilize Gaussian distributions in order to generate new solutions. As a result, the search for the global optimum is relatively biased for symmetric functions.

3.4.2. *Test functions*

Hereafter, we are going to present the most commonly used test functions with their respective descriptions [QIN 09b, LIA 13].

Next, we consider the dimension d of the problem.

3.4.2.1. *The sphere function*

Known under the name of the *De Jong function*, its global optimum is located at the point $\vec{x}^* = \vec{0}$ with $f(\vec{x}^*) = \vec{0}$ in the recommended search space $\vec{x} \in [-100; 100]^d$:

$$f(x) = \sum_{i=1}^{d} x_i^2 \qquad\qquad [3.6]$$

Properties:

– unimodal;

– separable;

– symmetric.

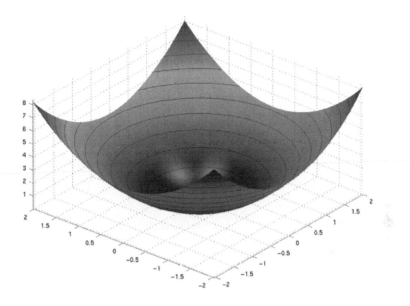

Figure 3.1. *Representation of the sphere function. For a color version of this figure, see www.iste.co.uk/heliodoro/metaheuristics.zip*

3.4.2.2. *The Rosenbrock function*

Also called *Rosenbrock's valley function* or *Rosenbrock's banana function*, its global optimum is $f(\vec{x}^*) = \vec{0}$ at point $\vec{x}^* = \vec{1}$, in the search space $\vec{x} \in [-30; 30]^d$ and a and b are parameters whose recommended values arc couples $(100; 1)$, $(2; 1)$, $(1; 1)$, $(0.5; 1)$ or $(1; 100)$.

$$f(x) = \sum_{i=1}^{d-1} [a(x_{i+1} - x_i^2)^2 + b(x_i - 1)^2] \tag{3.7}$$

Properties:

– unimodal;

– non-separable;

– asymmetric.

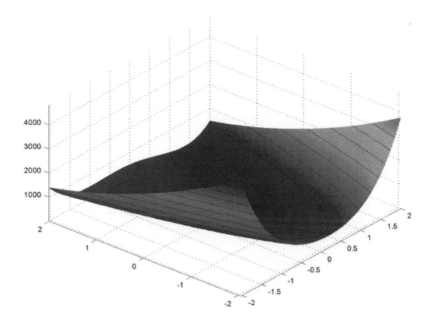

Figure 3.2. *Representation of the Rosenbrock function. For a color version of this figure, see www.iste.co.uk/heliodore/metaheuristics.zip*

3.4.2.3. *The Rastrigin function*

Its global optimum corresponds to the point $\vec{x}^* = \vec{0}$ with $f(\vec{x}^*) = \vec{0}$ and the search space generally considered corresponds to the hypercube described by $\vec{x} \in [-5, 12; 5, 12]^d$:

$$f(x) = 10d + \sum_{i=1}^{d} [x_i^2 - 10\cos(2\pi x_i)] \qquad [3.8]$$

Properties:

– multimodal;

– separable;

– symmetric.

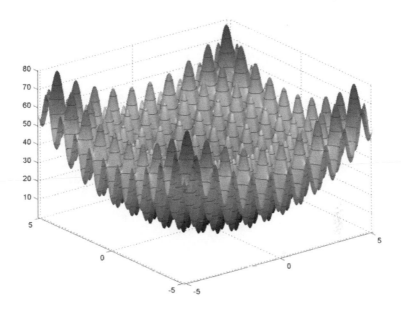

Figure 3.3. *Representation of the Rastrigin function. For a color version of this figure, see www.iste.co.uk/heliodore/metaheuristics.zip*

3.4.2.4. *The Schwefel function*

This function is usually evaluated on the hypercube $x_i \in [-500; 500]$ with $i = 1, ..., d$ and its global optimum is $f(\vec{x}^*) = \vec{0}$ for $\vec{x}^* = 420, \vec{9}687$:

$$f(x) = 418.9829d - \sum_{i=1}^{D} x_i \sin(\sqrt{|x_i|}) \qquad [3.9]$$

Properties:

– multimodal, large number of local optima with the second best optimum far away;

– non-separable;

– asymmetric.

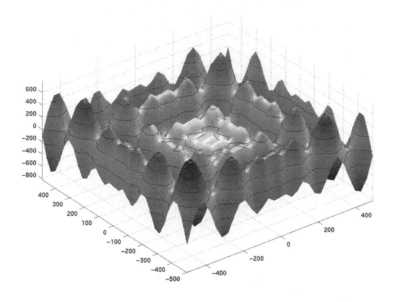

Figure 3.4. *Representation of the Schwefel function. For a color version of this figure, see www.iste.co.uk/heliodore/metaheuristics.zip*

3.4.2.5. *The Ackley function*

Its global optimum is $f(\vec{x}^*) = \vec{0}$ at the point $\vec{x}^* = \vec{0}$, the search space is $\vec{x} \in [-32; 32]^d$ and a, b and c are parameters whose recommended values are 20, 0.2 and 2π, respectively:

$$f(x) = -a\exp(-b\sqrt{\frac{1}{d}\sum_{i=1}^{d} x_i^2} - \exp(\frac{1}{d}\sum_{i=1}^{d}\cos(cx_i)) + a + \exp(1) \quad [3.10]$$

Properties:

– multimodal;

– non-separable;

– symmetric.

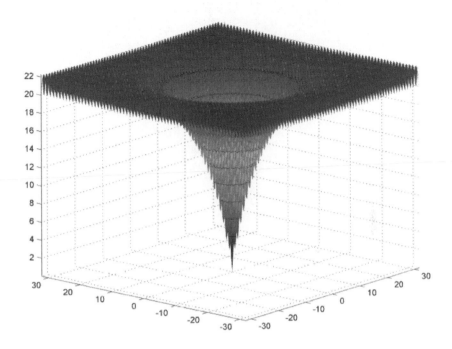

Figure 3.5. *Representation of the Ackley function. For a color version of this figure, see www.iste.co.uk/heliodore/metaheuristics.zip*

3.4.2.6. *The Griewank function*

Its global optimum is $f(\vec{x}^*) = \vec{0}$ at the point $\vec{x}^* = \vec{0}$, the search space is defined by $\vec{x} \in [-600; 600]^d$. On a large scale, this function is similar to the sphere function previously described, as can be seen in Figure 3.6.

$$f(x) = \sum_{i=1}^{d} \frac{x_i^2}{4000} - \prod_{i=1}^{d} cos(\frac{x_i}{\sqrt{i}}) + 1 \qquad [3.11]$$

Properties:

– multimodal;

– non-separable;

– asymmetric.

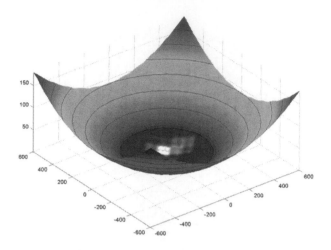

Figure 3.6. *Representation of the large-scale Griewank function. For a color version of this figure, see www.iste.co.uk/ heliodore/metaheuristics.zip*

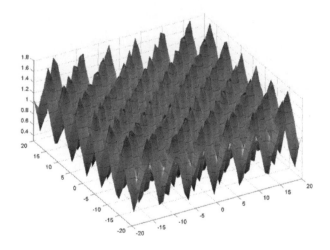

Figure 3.7. *Representation of the small-scale Griewank function. For a color version of this figure, see www.iste.co.uk/ heliodore/metaheuristics.zip*

3.4.2.7. *The Michalewicz function*

In general, the evaluation of this function is done on the hypercube defined by $x_i \in [0; \pi]$ of which m is a parameter whose recommended value is 10. Moreover, the global optimum of this function and its performance depend on the chosen dimension:

$$f(x) = -\sum_{i=1}^{d} \sin(x_i) \sin^{2m}\left(\frac{i x_i^2}{\pi}\right) \qquad [3.12]$$

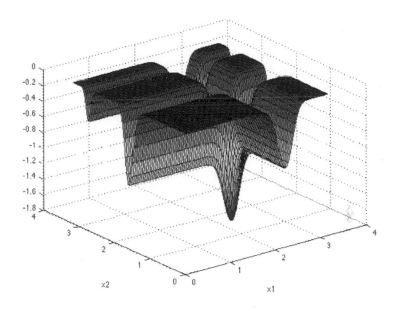

Figure 3.8. *Representation of the Michalewicz function. For a color version of this figure, see www.iste.co.uk/heliodore/metaheuristics.zip*

Properties:

– multimodal, very large number of local optima;

– separable;

– asymmetric.

3.5. Conclusion

In this chapter, we have described the methods and tools for the validation of a metaheuristic applied to a given problem and for the comparison of performances.

Statistical analysis provides a means to validate a metaheuristic applied to a given type of problem and also to compare it with other metaheuristics to determine which is most suitable. Bearing this point in mind, there are multicriteria support methods for decision making such as the *ELECTRE (ELimination Et Choix Traduisant la REalité or ELimination and Choice Expressing REality)* methods initially proposed by Roy in 1968 [ROY 68, FIG 05] and the *PROMETHEE (Preference Ranking Organization METHod for Enrichment Evaluations)* method introduced by Brans in 1985 [BRA 85]. Therefore, in our study, these methods can be utilized in order to assist in the choice of the metaheuristic to solve a given optimization problem.

4

Metaheuristics for FACTS
Placement and Sizing

4.1. Introduction

In recent years, the interconnection of networks and the deregulation of energy markets have strongly modified the operating conditions of electric energy transport networks. Networks operators (*transmission system operator* [TSO]) have to find the most efficient manner to manage energy exchanges (*power flow* [PF]) between increasingly more numerous and varied producers (introduction of decentralized production), and consumers increasingly further away from production facilities (interconnected networks), while taking into account the physical constraints of networks operating increasingly closer to their operating limits. Such management requires that increasingly higher performance means are made available to control power transits in transport lines, on the one hand, to optimize the PF (for example to reduce congestion nodes) and, on the other hand, to increase the stability of the network. In this sense, *flexible alternative current transmission system* (FACTS), by mainly acting on the distribution of reactive power in the network, emerge as devices offering a great flexibility of control. Thus, they allow, in steady state, the "optimization" of the PF and a better control of the voltage in the nodes of the network as well as, in a transient state, a significant improvement of network stability.

The objective is then to determine the optimal distribution of reactive power with respect to the optimal localization and sizing of FACTS in order to improve the performance of an electric network. Since reactive power acts at the local level, can it have an influence on the overall behavior of the network? Can we then deduce the area of influence of a reactive node? Furthermore, the localization and the sizing of reactive power must provide a means to identify if its management can be distributed or if it should be localized. In other words, the questions that emerge are as follows:

– where can FACTS be placed in the network?

– how many FACTS?

– what power (size) can be assigned to these FACTS?

– what type(s) of FACTS?

– at what price?

This chapter addresses these questions. Here, we will only consider the case of the network operating in steady state, without taking into account the transient state (that is network transient stability). To this end, three major novelties have been introduced:

– in the free choice (achieved by the algorithm) of the four decision variables (the number of FACTS, their positioning, their setpoint and their type). In point of fact, to our knowledge, little (or no) work addresses these four variables at the same time;

– in the hybridization of the algorithm through the proposed coding;

– the last contribution consists of the application of a new algorithm (α-*stable Lévy particle swarm optimization* [α-SLPSO]). This chapter is organized into four sections.

Section 4.3 is a brief reminder of the PF model and its solution. It also presents the modifications of the network model introduced by implanting FACTS. It concludes with a quick review of a few criteria to be optimized through the placement of the FACTS, related, in particular, to the security of the network and the increase in its capacity for energy transportation.

Section 4.4 of the chapter will review some discrete particle swarm optimization (PSO) methods implemented to solve the optimal placement and sizing problem of FACTS. In this section, we also give the codes of the particles used to achieve these problems.

In this section, we propose a new agent population based algorithm (α-SLPSO) and a Lévy local search (*α-stable Lévy local search* [α-SLLS]) based on the scaling invariance properties of Lévy α-stable distributions. We test these two algorithms on test functions by comparing them to other variants of the PSO.

Finally, section 4.5 of the chapter presents simulation results obtained with an application to the case of IEEE 30 and IEEE 57 networks, respectively, in the single-objective and multiobjective cases.

4.2. FACTS devices

For a few years, the electric power supply market has been open to competition in order to decrease the price of energy. This change has reflected the separation between production, transport and distribution activities. Although customers may choose their producer, the carrier remains unchanged. As a matter of fact, the transportation activity keeps its monopoly and this network is managed by an independent network management: the TSO. This manager's main function is to coordinate power exchanges in order to ensure the good functioning and sustainability of the network. The possibility of building new transport routes, in order to increase the performance and robustness of the network, is becoming increasingly difficult under the pressure of environmentalists and the slow pace of administrations. This drives the network manager to acquire means to control power transits in lines so that the existing network can be operated most efficiently and in the safest way possible.

FACTS devices can be used to control power transits in a continuous manner over the power grid. They operate by providing or absorbing reactive power, increasing or decreasing the voltage at the nodes, controlling the line impedance or by modifying voltages phases. An additional advantage is that they allow extending the boundaries of the network.

In steady state, these devices are used in two cases:

– to maintain the voltage by providing reactive power when the load is high and the voltage is too low, conversely they absorb some if the voltage is high;

– to control power transit in order to avoid one line being used more than another, and to avoid reaching its limits. They operate by controlling the reactance of the lines and by adjusting phase differences.

In transient state, they enable the improvement of network stability (reduction of the oscillations of power exchanges).

Several types of FACTS have been developed with different architectures and technologies such as:

– the *static var compensator* (SVC);

– the *static synchronous compensator* (STATCOM);

– the *thyristor controlled series capacitor* (TCSC);

– the *unified power flow controller* (UPFC).

Each has its own characteristics and can be utilized to meet very specific requirements.

4.2.1. *The SVC*

The SVC is a *shunt* device (parallel compensation) that can be connected to the nodes or on a point sectioning a line. It enables the transmissible power in networks to be increased by providing or absorbing reactive power. In steady state, the reactive compensation is used for sectioning lines (which makes it possible to increase the transmittable power of long transmission lines by controlling the voltage at the section point) and for maintaining the voltage at the nodes. In transient state, shunt devices provide a mechanism to dynamically control the voltage for improved transient stability and for damping power oscillations.

Theoretically, the SVC is lossless, which means that the admittance is purely imaginary and is modeled by a switch that switches between a capacitor and an inductor. When the switch is on the capacitor, the current is positively out of phase, which has the effect of injecting reactive power into the system. Conversely, if the switch is on the inductance it creates a negative phase in the current, the reactive power is then absorbed.

4.2.2. *The STATCOM*

The STATCOM (based on the structure of a three-phase voltage converter) is a shunt device primarily used at the nodes of the network for dynamic compensation, in order to facilitate voltage withstand, to increase stability in transient state, and to damp power oscillations. The STATCOM reacts according to the difference between the output voltage of the converter u and the line voltage u_0:

– if $u_0 < u$: the current flows from the converter to the network, the STATCOM then produces reactive power (capacitive behavior);

– if $u_0 < u$: the current flows from the network to the converter, the STATCOM absorbs reactive power (inductive behavior);

– if $u_0 = u$: no current flows and there is no exchange of reactive energy.

Its ability to maintain the voltage of the network is better than that of the SVC and it presents some advantages, such as:

– the space needed for the installation is reduced due to the lack of inductance;

– resorting to harmonic filters is not necessary;

– the performance in dynamic state is better.

4.2.3. *The TCSC*

The TCSC (series compensation device) comprises an inductor controlled by thyristors in parallel with a capacitor. Placed on a line, it can change its reactance and its primary effect is to control the PF that circulates in the line where it is placed. The reactive power produced by the TCSC is proportional to the power flowing through the line. With this device operating on the current in the line, apparent powers vary in the same manner as active powers.

4.2.4. *The UPFC*

The UPFC is a hybrid structure between parallel and series compensation. It is composed of two voltage converters connected by a DC link. It corresponds to the combination of a STATCOM and a *static synchronous series compensator* (SSSC). Its principle is to derive part of the current flowing in the line to reinject it with an appropriate phase.

Its hybrid aspect enables it to perform all the functions of the other FACTS devices:

– voltage regulation;

– active and reactive PF control;

– stability improvement;

– limiting short-circuit currents;

– damping power oscillations.

4.3. The PF model and its solution

The proposed approach is based on the association of a PF-based lattice computation and numerical optimization techniques. This section briefly presents the PF problem and its solution.

4.3.1. *The PF model*

The PF model gives a representation of an electrical network operating in steady state. Its equations rely on the Kirchhoff laws (Kirchhoff's point rule) based on a description of the network in terms of nodes (generators and/or loads) and links between these nodes (energy transport lines). They formalize a state of equilibrium of the network under certain input conditions (for example consumed and generated powers) and certain operation constraints (for example the maximal PF on transport lines).

The state of the network is comprehensively described by state variables which are:

– the node voltage amplitude, that is U_i for node i;

– the node voltage phase, that is θ_i for node i.

The network is subject to various inputs, which are:

– active and reactive powers consumed in "load" nodes, or respectively, at node i: P_{Di} and Q_{Di};

– active and reactive powers generated in "generator" nodes, or respectively, at node i: P_{Gi} and Q_{Gi}.

Network equilibrium is obtained when the state variables U_i and θ_i satisfy active and reactive power equilibrium equations in each of the nodes of the network. For the node i, these equations are, respectively, given by relations [4.1] and [4.2].

$$P_{Gi} - P_{Di} = U_i \sum_{j\in\Omega_i} U_j \left(G_{ij}\cos(\theta_i - \theta_j) + B_{ij}\sin(\theta_i - \theta_j)\right) \qquad [4.1]$$

$$Q_{Gi} - Q_{Di} = U_i \sum_{j\in\Omega_i} U_j \left(G_{ij}\sin(\theta_i - \theta_j) - B_{ij}\cos(\theta_i - \theta_j)\right) \qquad [4.2]$$

where Ω_i is the set of nodes connected to node i, including node i. Variables G_{ij} and B_{ij} are the elements of the admittance matrix Y such that $Y_{ij} = G_{ij} + jB_{ij}$.

The solution of power equilibrium equations [4.1] and [4.2] is subject to a set of operating constraints of the network, corresponding to its physical limitations. These constraints are classified into two families:

– constraints of inequality: inequality constraints relate to the bounds of maximal flow on transportation lines:

$$S_{ij}(U_i, \theta_i) \leq S_{ij_{max}} \qquad [4.3]$$

where S_{ij} is the PF on the line connecting nodes i and j and $S_{ij_{max}}$ is the maximal flow allowed on the same line;

– bound constraints on state and input variables, with:

- upper and lower bounds on active and reactive powers generated at the "generators" nodes:

$$P_{Gi_{min}} \leq P_{Gi} \leq P_{Gi_{max}} \qquad [4.4]$$

$$Q_{Gi_{min}} \leq Q_{Gi} \leq Q_{Gi_{max}} \qquad [4.5]$$

- upper and lower bounds on the amplitude of the voltage at the different nodes of the network:

$$U_{i_{min}} \leq U_i \leq U_{i_{max}} \qquad\qquad [4.6]$$

4.3.2. *Solution of the network equations*

There are two approaches for solving the equations of the PF model:

– an approach known as *PF* where the problem consists of solving power equilibrium equations [4.1] and [4.2] for certain variables (state or input) imposed;

– an approach known as *optimal power flow (OPF)*, where the problem consists of minimizing a given functional, usually with respect to the costs of generated active and/or reactive powers, while on the one hand, satisfying power equilibrium equations [4.1] and [4.2] and, on the other hand, inequality and bound constraints [4.3]–[4.6].

4.3.2.1. *The PF approach*

The examination of power equilibrium equations [4.1] and [4.2], in terms of number of equations ($2N$ where N is the total number of nodes) and number of state and input variables ($4N$), shows that it is necessary to define certain variables in order to be able to solve these equations.

The choice between imposed and varying variables to be determined at each node will depend on the nature of the node considered, in other words:

– for "load" nodes:

- imposed variables: P_{Di} and Q_{Di};

- variables to be determined: U_i and θ_i;

– for "generator" nodes with the exception of the "balance" node (or *swing bus*):

- imposed variables: P_{Gi} and U_i;

- variables to be determined: Q_{Gi} and θ_i;

– for the "balance generator" node:

- imposed variables: U_i and θ_i;

- variables to be determined: P_{Gi}, Q_{Gi} and U_i.

Once imposed variables are defined, the solution of the nonlinear PF problem (that is to say, of the power balance equations [4.1] and [4.2]) is determined using an iterative numerical method (for example, the Newton–Raphson method). This solution gives the state of the network for given operating conditions (imposed variables), which ensures power equilibrium in each of the nodes of the network. However, such a solution will only be valid if it satisfies imposed inequality and bounds constraints, which may not be the case. In case of a non-valid solution, it is then necessary to change the variables imposed at each node and compute a new solution.

4.3.2.2. The OPF approach

The OPF approach differs from the PF approach in the sense that it searches for a solution that, on the one hand, will satisfy all the inequality and bounds constraints of the network and, on the other hand, will optimize (often minimize) a given functional.

Analogously to the PF problem, the determination of a solution involves the imposition of certain input or state variables, namely:

– for "load" nodes:

- imposed variables: P_{Di} and Q_{Di};

- variables to be determined: U_i and θ_i;

– for "generator" nodes with the exception of the "balance" node (or *swing bus*):

- imposed variables: none;

- variables to be determined: P_{Gi}, Q_{Gi}, U_i and θ_i;

– for the "balance generator" node:

- imposed variables: θ_i;

- variables to be determined: P_{Gi}, Q_{Gi} and U_i.

Here, the number of variables to be determined is higher than for the PF problem. In order to solve the problem, it is necessary to add additional constraints. These constraints represent, on the one hand, inequality [4.3] and bound constraints [4.4]–[4.6] and, on the other hand, the functional to be optimized.

For example, a functional relative to the cost of the generated power can be expressed as:

$$J_{eco} = \sum_{i=1}^{N_G} f_i(P_{Gi}, Q_{Gi}, U_i, \theta_i) \qquad\qquad [4.7]$$

where N_G is the total number of "generator" nodes.

The solution to the OPF problem, if it exists, determines a network state that respects all the constraints of the network (namely of equality, inequality and bounds). It has the advantage of being able to integrate energy cost constraints in the placement and sizing problem of FACTS in a network. Naturally, the solution to this problem will strongly depend on the retained cost criteria and parameters and will be "optimal" only for these criteria and given parameters, which may appear as a limitation of the obtained solution of the FACTS placement and sizing problem. However, constraints of the same order do exist in the case of a PF-based solution. In fact, the solution to the PF problem depends on the choice of imposed values (and more particularly of the voltage amplitudes imposed at the "generators" nodes) and the solution of the FACTS placement and sizing problem will be here dependent on the distribution of these imposed variables.

In other words, whether for solving the network equations by means of a PF approach or an OPF approach, the solution of the FACTS placement and sizing problem will be dependent on the imposed variables, that is of a certain configuration of the network in terms of requested powers, generated powers, etc. Overlooking this limitation implies taking into account the variations, within certain boundaries, of the inputs imposed to the PF or OPF problems. The associated optimization problem will then have to resort to optimization techniques in a stochastic environment, which does not fall within the scope of the present study.

As part of the work presented in this chapter, the search for a solution to the FACTS placement and sizing problem is performed based on solving network equations using an OPF approach with constant cost parameters.

4.3.3. *FACTS implementation and network modification*

To implement a FACTS in a node or a line of the electric grid is mainly tantamount to changing the distribution of reactive power within the network. This modification mainly depends on the nature of the FACTS (for example series or parallel) being implemented. For most FACTS in steady state it generally results, at the description level of the network, in modifying either the admittance matrix Y or the reactive power demands in some nodes.

Without being exhaustive, the following list provides indications on these modifications for a few commonly used FACTS:

– parallel FACTS:

- STATCOM: modification of the reactive power at the connection node of the STATCOM;

- SVC: modification of the parallel impedance at the connection node of the SVC, modification of the matrix Y;

– series FACTS·

- TCSC: modification in the impedance of the line where is implemented the TCSC, modification of the matrix Y;

- phase-shifting transformer: modification of the impedance of the line where the transformer is implemented, modification of the matrix Y.

More details on the modeling associated with these different FACTS (and some others) can be found in Gerbex's works [STE 03].

Only examples of STATCOM, SVC and TCSC are addressed here. The modification in the network is thus made in the form of a modification to the reactive power required at the selected nodes or by a form of controlling power transit in the selected lines.

4.3.4. *Formulation of FACTS placement problem as an optimization issue*

For FACTS devices being modeled in steady state, the criteria to be optimized will mainly have a direct relationship with the effect of FACTS on power transits (PF) and on voltages at the nodes of the network under study.

These criteria are in the form of objective functionals to be minimized or maximized according to the cases being considered, namely:

– maximization of the supplied load;

– maximization of the system safety, with:

  - line load balancing;

  - node voltage balancing;

  - operation safety;

– minimization of active losses.

4.3.4.1. *Supplied load maximization*

The maximization of the supplied load (*system loadability*) consists of determining the maximum power that can be supplied to consumers, while satisfying the constraints of the network. The associated functional, to be maximized, is expressed as:

$$J_1 = \sum_{i=1}^{N_L} P_{L_i} \qquad [4.8]$$

where P_{L_i} is the power consumed at the node i and N_L is the total number of network nodes.

4.3.4.2. *System safety maximization*

In this case, FACTS should make it possible to exploit the network with a maximal safety margin. To this end, two criteria can be retained, namely, line load balancing and node voltage balancing. These two criteria may also be associated with defining a criterion for operation safety.

4.3.4.2.1. Line load balancing

This balancing consists of distributing loads between the various lines of the network in the most uniform possible manner. The associated functional to be minimized is then expressed as:

$$J_2 = \sum_{j=1}^{N_B} (\frac{S_j}{S_{j_{max}}})^2 \qquad [4.9]$$

where S_j is the power transiting in the line j, $S_{j_{max}}$ is the maximal power allowed in the line j and N_B is the total number of lines.

4.3.4.2.2. Node voltage balancing

This balancing consists of distributing the voltages at the various nodes of the network in the most uniform possible manner. The associated functional to be minimized is then expressed as:

$$J_3 = \sum_{i=1}^{N_L} (\frac{U_i - U_{i_N}}{U_{i_N}})^2 \qquad [4.10]$$

where U_i is the voltage at node i, U_{i_N} is the nominal voltage at the node i and N_L is the total number of nodes of the network.

In the case where voltages are expressed per unit, the nominal voltage $U_{i_N} = 1$ and the criterion J_3 are expressed as:

$$J_3 = \sum_{i=1}^{N_L} (U_i - 1)^2 \qquad [4.11]$$

4.3.4.2.3. Operation safety

Operation safety combines line load balancing and node voltage balancing. The associated functional to be minimized is given by:

$$J_4 = \sum_{j=1}^{N_B} \omega_j (\frac{S_j}{S_{j_{max}}})^{2p} + \sum_{i=1}^{N_L} \omega_i (\frac{U_i - U_{i_N}}{U_{i_N}})^{2q} \qquad [4.12]$$

where ω_j and ω_i are weights that make it possible to give importance to certain critical lines or certain critical nodes of the network. Variables p and q are exponents that provide a means to weigh penalization between line overloads and voltage deviations.

4.3.4.3. *Minimization of active losses*

The main objective here is to minimize active losses in network lines. Apart from a degradation in lines due to their heating by Joule energy dissipation, decreasing active losses provides an assured economic advantage, the associated cost being charged to consumers. The associated functional to be minimized, is given by:

$$J_5 = \sum_{j=1}^{N_B} R_j I_j^2 \qquad \qquad [4.13]$$

where R_j is the resistance of the line j and I_j is the current flowing through the same line.

In the context of the present report, the retained criterion concerns balancing the voltages at the nodes of the network. The associated functional, to be minimized, is then given by equation [4.11].

4.4. PSO for FACTS placement

We present the different techniques used to solve the FACTS placement and sizing problem. Because of its ability to solve a broad class of difficult problems, PSO will be applied and adapted to the problem of placement and sizing of FACTS. As we will see further, the latter is addressed in the form of a hybrid problem (continuous/discrete variables). We begin by indicating the manner in which the particles are coded in the two case studies:

– special case: the number of FACTS is set to 2 of the STATCOM type. This case study is justified by a desire for a good validation of the algorithms applied (as well as of parametrization) in section 4.5. To this end, the standard variant of PSO 2007 and the *velocity likelihoods* method (section 4.4.2) are, respectively, applied on the continuous and discrete variables;

– general case: the number and type of the FACTS are left open. Discrete variables are processed by the "velocity likelihoods" method. Comparatively, continuous variables are manipulated by means of two algorithms: the PSO standard 2007 and the α-SLPSO algorithm (see section 4 4.4.3.1). The main motivation for the introduction of the new PSO (α-SLPSO) approach lies in the desire for improvement of the results obtained by the PSO standard 2007.

In the following, we detail the *velocity likelihoods* method applied to address the discrete character (the placements of FACTS) of our optimization problem. We have slightly modified this method in order to make improvements in the results obtained.

Finally, in the last part of this section we present a new algorithm (α-SLPSO), which will be validated based on 15 test functions.

4.4.1. *Solutions coding*

Taking all the decision variables into account in the PSO algorithm calls for a deep reflection on how to best represent a solution (good coding of particles). As a matter of fact, the manipulation of numerous variables, separately considered, results in poor results due to the non-synchronization of the convergence of the different decision variables (that is to say, a decision variable can converge slowly or converge toward a local optimum), which leads to local optima and possibly to the non-convergence of the algorithm.

In order to address this problem, two types of coding have been proposed. The first is appropriate in the case of the placement and sizing of two FACTS of the same type (special case) and the second is appropriate for the case of the placement and sizing of several FACTS of different types (general case).

4.4.1.1. *Placement and sizing case of two FACTS of the same type*

In this type of coding, a particle i is represented by a vector:

$$\overrightarrow{X_i} = (e_1...e_{n_f}; t_1...t_{n_f}; v_1...v_{n_f})$$

and designating by:

$- e_i \in \{1, .., Number\ of\ nodes\}$, $e_i \neq e_j$ for every $j \neq i$: the locations of the FACTS;

$- t_i \in \{STATCOM, SVS, TCS\}$: the types of FACTS;

$- v_i \in [Q_{min}, Q_{max}]$: setpoint values of the FACTS;

$- n_f \in N$: the number of FACTS (fixed) to be placed.

A solution (or particle) can thus be represented as follows:

v_1	v_2	...	v_{n_f}
t_1	t_2	...	t_{n_f}
e_1	e_2	...	e_{n_f}

As we have already pointed out, this type of encoding is suitable in the case of the optimal placement and sizing of n_f FACTS of the same type, that is to say:

– the FACTS type is fixed (here STATCOM);

– the number of FACTS n_f is fixed (two in our case).

4.4.1.2. *Placement and sizing case of several FACTS of different types (general case)*

In this type of encoding, the shape of the particle is modified as hereafter in order to clarify decision variables. This type of encoding is appropriate to the general case where the type of the FACTS is left open (STATCOM, SVC and TCSC), the number of FACTS is free but also in the special case where the type of the FACTS is fixed.

A particle is represented by a vector:

$$V = (e_1...e_n e_{n+1}...e_{2n} e_{2n+1} e_{2n+b}; v_1...v_n v_{n+1}...v_{2n} v_{2n+1} v_{2n+b})$$

and designating by:

– $e_i \in \{0, 1\}$, 0 if there are no FACTS placed at the node i and 1 otherwise;

– n, the number of nodes in the network;

– b, the number of branches in the network;

– $v_i \in [Q_{min}, Q_{max}]$, the setpoint values of the FACTS.

Furthermore, as a table:

e_1	e_2	...	e_{2n+b}
v_1	v_2	...	v_{2n+b}

REMARK 4.1.– The two decision variables "type" and "number" are explicit in this type of encoding. In effect, in order to know the number of FACTS to

be placed, the sum over the e_i has to be carried out and to know the type of the FACTS placed at node i, we proceed in the following way:

- if $i \in \{1, .., n\}$, the FACTS is of the STATCOM type;

- if $i \in \{n+1, .., 2n\}$, the FACTS is of the SVC type;

- if $i \in \{2n+1, .., 2n+b\}$, the FACTS is of the TCSC type.

4.4.2. *Binary particle swarm optimization*

The discrete PSO method, so-called *velocity likelihoods*, has been introduced by Correa Freitas and Johnson from the University of Kent in the UK [COR 06]. The basic principle is briefly presented here and illustrated by a simple example. A modification of the method will be subsequently introduced for better exploration of the whole search space.

4.4.2.1. *Variables definition*

Let a particle denoted by di whose position $\overrightarrow{X_{di}}$, of dimension M, is defined at iteration k by:

$$\overrightarrow{X_{di}}(k) = [x_{di1} \ x_{di2} \ ... \ x_{diM_i}]$$
[4.14]

with $x_{dim} \in [1 \cdots N]$, $m = 1, ..., M$ and $x_{dim} \neq x_{diq} \ \forall m, q$. and N, the total number of possible positions for the particle di.

In the case of a FACTS placement problem, the dimension M of the particle is identified to the number of FACTS to be implemented in the network. By choosing particles of different sizes, it will then be possible to introduce the number of FACTS to be implemented as an optimization parameter. However, a different hybridization approach taking into account the number and types of the FACTS as optimization variables will be presented further.

The elements x_{dim} being identified to the nodes of the network to choose $x_{dim} \neq x_{diq} \ \forall m, q$ is tantamount to forbidding that several FACTS be positioned at a same node. At iteration $(k-1)$, the best position of the particle di is given by:

$$\overrightarrow{P_{best}^{di}}(k-1) = [p_{di1} \ p_{di2} \ ... \ p_{diM}]$$
[4.15]

with $b_{dim} \in [1 \cdots N]$, $m = 1, ..., M_i$ and $b_{dim} \neq b_{diq} \ \forall m, q$.

Each particle di has a set $\Omega_{inform_{di}}$, of size $N_{inform_{di}}$, of informant particles that communicate with it by transmitting it their respective best positions. Let then the best position of the set of informant particles of the particle di be defined at iteration $(k-1)$ by:

$$\overrightarrow{G_{best}^{di}}(k-1) = [g_{di1} \, g_{di2} \cdots g_{diL}] \tag{4.16}$$

with $g_{dil} \in [1 \cdots N], l = 1 \cdots L$ and $g_{dil} \neq g_{diq} \; \forall \, l, q$.

Let the displacement velocity of the particle di defined, at iteration k, be:

$$\overrightarrow{V_{di}}(k) = \begin{bmatrix} v_{di1} & v_{di2} & \cdots & v_{diN} \\ p_{di1} & p_{di2} & \cdots & p_{diN} \end{bmatrix} \tag{4.17}$$

with $p_{dij} \in [1 \cdots N], j = 1 \cdots N$ and $p_{dij} \neq p_{diq} \; \forall \, j, q$.

The first line of $\overrightarrow{V_{di}}$ contains weights associated with the positions contained in the second line of $\overrightarrow{V_{di}}$.

4.4.2.2. Algorithm description

The discrete PSO *velocity likelihoods* algorithm is based on the following steps:

– from the position $\overrightarrow{X_{di}}(k)$, the fitness function is calculated, at iteration k, $J(\overrightarrow{X_{di}}(k))$;

– knowing $J(\overrightarrow{X_{di}}(k))$, we update, if necessary $\overrightarrow{P_{best}^{di}}(k)$ and $\overrightarrow{G_{best}^{di}}(k)$;

– knowing $\overrightarrow{V_{di}}(k)$, $\overrightarrow{X_{di}}(k)$, $\overrightarrow{P_{best}^{di}}(k)$ and $\overrightarrow{G_{best}^{di}}(k)$, we update the velocity $\overrightarrow{V_{di}}(k+1)$;

– knowing $\overrightarrow{V_{di}}(k+1)$ and $\overrightarrow{X_{di}}(k)$, the position $\overrightarrow{X_{di}}(k+1)$ is updated.

4.4.2.3. Computation of $J(\overrightarrow{X_{di}}(k))$

The determination of the objective function $J(\overrightarrow{X_{di}}(k))$ is achieved from an OPF-based solution of the network model under study. The state variables thus obtained are then used to determine $J(\overrightarrow{X_{di}}(k))$. As a reminder, the equations of the PF model (equations [4.1]–[4.6]) form a nonlinear equation system.

4.4.2.4. *Update of* $\overrightarrow{P_{best}^{di}}$ *and* $\overrightarrow{G_{best}^{di}}$

Similarly to the standard PSO described in Chapter 2, the best personal positions $\overrightarrow{P_{best}}$ and those of the informants of the particles $\overrightarrow{G_{best}}$ are updated using the conventional operation procedure of a PSO algorithm. In other words, the update of $\overrightarrow{P_{best}^{di}}(k)$ and $\overrightarrow{G_{best}^{di}}(k)$ of the particle di at iteration k is done as follows:

– if $J(\overrightarrow{X_{di}}(k)) < J(\overrightarrow{P_{best}^{di}}(k-1))$, then $\overrightarrow{P_{best}^{di}}(k) = \overrightarrow{X_{di}}(k)$, otherwise, $\overrightarrow{P_{best}^{di}}(k) = \overrightarrow{P_{best}^{di}}(k-1)$;

– let $J(\overrightarrow{P_{best}^{dr}}(k)) = \min_{j \in \Omega_{inform_{di}}} J(\overrightarrow{P_{best}^{dj}}(k))$:

if $J(\overrightarrow{P_{best}^{dr}}(k)) < J(\overrightarrow{G_{best}^{di}}(k-1))$, then $\overrightarrow{G_{best}^{di}}(k) = \overrightarrow{P_{best}^{dr}}(k)$, otherwise, $\overrightarrow{G_{best}^{di}}(k) = \overrightarrow{G_{best}^{di}}(k-1)$.

4.4.2.5. *Velocity update of particle* di

The different stages of the updating process of the velocity V_{di} are described in algorithm 4.1, where $\alpha_{di}(k) > 0$, $\beta_{di}(k) > 0$ and $\gamma_{di}(k) > 0$ are real positive.

The parameters $\alpha_{di}(k)$, $\beta_{di}(k)$ and $\gamma_{di}(k)$ reflect the "degree of attractiveness", respectively, given at position $\overrightarrow{X_{di}}$, best position $\overrightarrow{P_{best}^{di}}$ and best global position $\overrightarrow{G_{best}^{di}}$, associated with the particle di, in the process of updating the velocity. In the basic version of the algorithm, they are chosen as being constant. They play similar roles to those played by the parameters $w_{ci}(k)$, $c_{i1}(k)$ and $c_{i2}(k)$ in the continuous PSO case. They increase the relative weight of some positions contained in the velocity vector $\overrightarrow{V_{di}}$ according to whether or not these positions belong to $\overrightarrow{X_{di}}$. $\overrightarrow{P_{best}^{di}}$ and $\overrightarrow{G_{best}^{di}}$.

A stochastic component is introduced in the update process of the velocity in the following way:

$$\overrightarrow{V_{di}}(k)\,[1, 1 : N_i] = \overrightarrow{V_{di}}(k)\,[1, 1 : N_i] * \varphi_{di}(k) \qquad [4.18]$$

where $*$ represents the Hadamard product (that is component wise) of two matrices and $\varphi_{di}(k)$ is a vector of N random variables uniformly distributed between 0 and 1.

Algorithm 4.1: Update of the velocities of the particles using the *velocity likelihoods* method

1 **For** $j = 1 \cdots N$ **Do**
2 　**For** $m = 1 \cdots M$ **Do**
3 　　**If** $\overrightarrow{V_{di}}(k)\,[2, j] = \overrightarrow{X_{di}}(k)\,[m]$ **Then**
4 　　　$\overrightarrow{V_{di}}(k)\,[1, j] = \overrightarrow{V_{di}}(k)\,[1, j] + \alpha_{di}(k)$
5 　　**End**
6 　　**If** $\overrightarrow{V_{di}}(k)\,[2, j] = \overrightarrow{P_{best}^{di}}(k)\,[m]$ **Then**
7 　　　$\overrightarrow{V_{di}}(k)\,[1, j] = \overrightarrow{V_{di}}(k)\,[1, j] + \beta_{di}(k)$
8 　　**End**
9 　**End**
10 　**For** $l = 1 \cdots L$ **Do**
11 　　**If** $\overrightarrow{V_{di}}(k)\,[2, j] = \overrightarrow{G_{best}^{di}}(k)\,[l]$ **Then**
12 　　　$\overrightarrow{V_{di}}(k)\,[1, j] = \overrightarrow{V_{di}}(k)\,[1, j] + \gamma_{di}(k)$
13 　　**End**
14 　**End**
15 **End**

Let the elementary component $\overrightarrow{V_{di_j}}(k)$ of the velocity be defined as:

$$\overrightarrow{V_{di_j}}(k) = \left[\begin{array}{c} v_{di_j}(k) \\ p_{di_j}(k) \end{array} \right] = V_{di}(k)\,[1 : 2, j]$$

The velocity $\overrightarrow{V_{di}}(k + 1)$ is then determined by a reorganization of the velocity $\overrightarrow{V_{di}}(k)$ according to a descending sort of the weights $v_{di_j}(k)$ associated with the elementary components $\overrightarrow{V_{di_j}}(k)$:

$$\overrightarrow{V_{di}}(k + 1) = tri_{v_{di_j}(k)\, descending} \left[\overrightarrow{V_{di}}(k)\,[1 : 2, j] \right] \quad for\ j = 1 \cdots N \quad [4.19]$$

4.4.2.6. *Update of the velocity*

The update of the position $\overrightarrow{X_{di}}$ consists of selecting as a new position the M components of the second line of the velocity vector $\overrightarrow{V_{di}}(k+1)$ associated with the M strongest weights of the first line of the same vector, namely the M first components of the second line of $\overrightarrow{V_{di}}(k+1)$

$$\overrightarrow{X_{di}}(k+1) = \overrightarrow{V_{di}}(k+1)\,[2,1:M] \qquad\qquad [4.20]$$

4.4.2.6.1. Example

Consider a study case in which the number of nodes $N = 5$. Let a particle di be of size $M = 3$. The position and the velocity of the particle, at iteration k, are, respectively, given by:

$$\overrightarrow{X_{di}}(k) \;=\; \begin{bmatrix} 3 & 4 & 1 \end{bmatrix}$$

$$\overrightarrow{V_{di}}(k) \;=\; \begin{bmatrix} 1.25 & 1,10 & 1.02 & 0.95 & 0.87 \\ 3 & 4 & 1 & 5 & 2 \end{bmatrix}$$

Assume that, after updating, the best position and the best global position associated with the particle di are, respectively, given by:

$$\overrightarrow{P_{best}^{di}}(k) \;=\; \begin{bmatrix} 2 & 5 & 3 \end{bmatrix}$$

$$\overrightarrow{G_{best}^{di}}(k) \;=\; \begin{bmatrix} 1 & 2 \end{bmatrix}$$

Let then the weight parameters be $\alpha_{di} = 0,1$, $\beta_{di} = 0,2$ and $\gamma_{di} = 0,4$, the first step for updating the velocity consists of determining the change in weights associated with each position according to [4.4], [4.7] and [4.12], such that:

$$\overrightarrow{Vdi}(k) = \begin{bmatrix} (1.25+0.10+0.20) & (1.10+0.10) & (1.02+0.10+0.4) \\ 3 & 4 & 1 \\ (0.95+0.20) & (0.88+0.20+0.40) & \\ 5 & 2 & \end{bmatrix}$$

$$\overrightarrow{V_{di}}(k) = \begin{bmatrix} 1.55 & 1.20 & 1.52 & 1.15 & 1.48 \\ 3 & 4 & 1 & 5 & 2 \end{bmatrix}$$

Introducing the vector:

$$\varphi_{di}(k) = \begin{bmatrix} 0.71 & 0.500.95 & 0.20 & 0,70 \end{bmatrix}$$

The velocity is modified according to [4.18]:

$$\overrightarrow{V_{di}}(k) * \varphi_{di}(k) = \begin{bmatrix} 1.10 & 0.60 & 1.44 & 0.23 & 1.04 \\ 3 & 4 & 1 & 5 & 2 \end{bmatrix}$$

Taking [4.19] into account, the velocity is then updated as:

$$\overrightarrow{V_{di}}(k+1) = \begin{bmatrix} 1.44 & 1.10 & 1.04 & 0.60 & 0.23 \\ 1 & 3 & 2 & 4 & 5 \end{bmatrix}$$

The position of the particle di is then updated, according to [4.20], by selecting the $M = 3$ first components of the second line of $\overrightarrow{V_{di}}(k+1)$, that is:

$$\overrightarrow{X_{di}}(k+1) = \overrightarrow{V_{di}}(k+1)[2, 1:3] = \begin{bmatrix} 1 & 3 & 2 \end{bmatrix}$$

4.4.2.7. Modification of the method

In order to better explore the whole of the search space and thus avoiding becoming eventually trapped in a local optimum, the original algorithm has been modified in the following way:

– a variation of the parameters $\alpha_{di}(k)$, $\beta_{di}(k)$ and $\gamma_{di}(k)$. Here, by modulating these parameters, the underlying idea is to avoid that the position of the particle di does not get stuck too quickly in its best position, $\overrightarrow{P_{best}^{di}}$, or the best position of its informants, $\overrightarrow{G_{best}^{di}}$. To this end, the parameters $\alpha_{di}(k)$, $\beta_{di}(k)$ and $\gamma_{di}(k)$ $\gamma_{di}(k)$ are adapted depending on iteration k in the following manner:

$$\alpha_{di}(k) = \alpha_{dii} + (\alpha_{dif} - \alpha_{dii})\frac{k}{N_{iter}} \tag{4.21}$$

$$\beta_{di}(k) = \beta_{dii} + (\beta_{dif} - \beta_{dii})\frac{k}{N_{iter}} \tag{4.22}$$

$$\gamma_{di}(k) = \gamma_{dii} + (\gamma_{dif} - \gamma_{dii})\frac{k}{N_{iter}} \qquad [4.23]$$

where N_{iter} is the total number of iterations, α_{dii} and α_{dif} are the initial (for $k = 0$) and final values (for $k = N_{iter}$) of $\alpha_{di}(k)$, β_{dii} and β_{dif} are the initial and final values of $\beta_{di}(k)$, and at last γ_{dii} and γ_{dif} are the initial and final values of $\gamma_{di}(k)$;

– the introduction of an additional random contribution $\varphi_{di_3}(k) \cdot va_{di}$ in the update phase of the velocity of particle di. This contribution, by randomly modifying the respective weight of each possible positions, must be able to allow certain positions, of smaller weight, to be "upgraded" and thus to be retained again. In order to assign an importance, which can be variable, to this random contribution, it is defined by

$$\varphi_{di_3}(k) \cdot va_{di}(k) = \varphi_{di_3}(k) \cdot (va_{dii} + (va_{dif} - va_{did})\frac{k}{N_{iter}}) \qquad [4.24]$$

where va_{dii} and va_{dif} are the initial and final values of $va_{di}(k)$ and $\varphi_{di_3}(k)$ is a vector of N_i random variables uniformly distributed between 0 and 1.

In light of these changes, the first line of the velocity vector of particle di then becomes:

$$\begin{aligned}
\overrightarrow{V_{di}}(k) &= \varphi_{di_1}(k) * \overrightarrow{V_{di}}(k) + \varphi_{di_2}(k) * f(\alpha_{di}(k), \beta_{di}(k), \gamma_{di}(k)) \\
&\quad + \varphi_{di_3}(k) \cdot va_{di}(k) \qquad [4.25]
\end{aligned}$$

where $f(\alpha_{di}(k), \beta_{di}(k), \gamma_{di}(k))$, a vector of size N, only represents the sum of the contributions of $\alpha_{di}(k)$, $\beta_{di}(k)$ and $\gamma_{di}(k)$ to the update of the velocity $\overrightarrow{V_{di}}(k)$, respectively, determined by equations [4.4], [4.7] and [4.12]. $\varphi_{di_1}(k)$ and $\varphi_{di_2}(k)$ are vectors of N random variables uniformly distributed between 0 and 1.

It should be noted that imposing $\varphi_{di_1}(k) = \varphi_{di_2}(k)$ and $va_{di}(k) = 0$ in equation [4.25] amounts to applying equation [4.18] during the updating process of the velocity of the particle di, that is to applying the non-modified method.

REMARK 4.2.– It should be noted that in fixing the positions and the FACTS type, it is possible to launch a PSO algorithm to optimize the "FACTS setpoints" variable (in other words, their FACTS placement and sizing problem is transformed into a *bilevel* problem). However, the computing time explodes depending of the number of particles considered. In effect, at each iteration and for each particle, an optimization subproblem has to be solved.

4.4.3. *Proposed Lévy-based hybrid PSO algorithm*

The two basic mechanisms that characterize metaheuristics are the diversification mechanism and the intensification mechanism. These two "non-contradictory" upstream processes must allow the downstream optimization process to reach an equilibrium state (which is usually an optimum of a functional to achieve). This dynamic, which is different from one metaheuristic to another, is all the more delicate as it can lead the optimization process toward a local optimum. The PSO is no exception to this rule [ELA 09].

This premature convergence characteristic of the PSO algorithm has prompted several researchers from different areas to develop different theories to reconcile these two dynamics and therefore to avoid a premature convergence of the PSO algorithm. A large number of these works consist of changing the rules for updating the velocity $\vec{v}$, the position $\vec{x}$ and/or the topology of informant particles [DAS 08].

As part of the improvement of the basic PSO algorithm initiated by Clerc *et al.* [CLE 07], we propose a new PSO algorithm designated by α-SLPSO. Basically, this algorithm has been designed to solve the FACTS placement and sizing problem. Nevertheless, after finding that α-SLPSO indeed competed with the standard PSO 2007, we have proposed extending its domain of application by comparing it with other PSO algorithms.

Moreover, a Lévy local search designated by *SLLS* or by analogy to α-*SLPSO*, α-SLLS will also be presented in this part of the book. Its operating principle inherits from the same mechanism as the α-SLPSO algorithm, with the exception that this local search relies on a single agent only (that is, one evaluation per iteration) rather than a population of agents. We wanted to present it because, despite being decorrelated from the objective of "FACTS optimal placement", it constitutes an excellent optimization method and opens new perspectives.

4.4.3.1. *Description of the α-SLPSO algorithm*

What is the fastest way to find a hidden target? This sensitive question is of vital importance for animals that thrive to survive. Furthermore, searching for a hidden object is one of the most frequent tasks of living species, for example to find food, a sexual partner or shelter, etc. In these examples, the search time is usually a limiting factor that must be optimized for the survival of the species. Therefore, determining the best search strategy is a crucial problem, which has inspired numerous experimental and theoretical works in different areas (applied mathematics, stochastic processes, molecular biology, etc.). An optimization problem is no exception to these rules. In effect, by analogy, the objective function to be optimized $\vec{f}$ (the object searched for) can be greedy in terms of computational time, which drives more and more engineers and decision makers to define algorithms which are less greedy in terms of computational time.

Experimental works and observations on the search strategy of living species (including humans) reveal that the latter is generally intermittent [BEN 05], namely that active (local) search phases alternate randomly with fast ballistic search phases (jumps) (Figure 4.1).

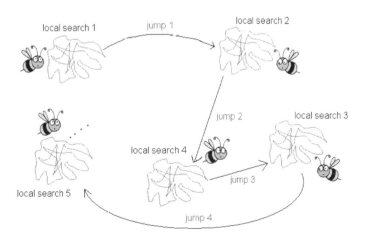

Figure 4.1. *Operating principle of the stable Lévy PSO (α-SLPSO) algorithm*

This means that, in metaheuristics jargon and in particular in PSO techniques, at any iteration t of the optimization process, every particle must be able, when these informants are not present, to exploit promising areas of the search space other than those that have been promised by the intensification stage. In other words, each particle $\overrightarrow{P_i}$ must actually alternate intensive search stages and ballistic jumps intermittently. It will therefore be necessary to formally and truthfully transmit this behavior to each particle of the swarm. One of the most effective and widely employed means to reproduce intermittency consists of introducing the concept of α-stable distributions (also called Lévy α-stable). As a matter of fact, we distinguish Brownian motion of Levy flights by the lack of a characteristic scale in the latter: the second-order moment of the Lévy distribution is infinite. This means that rare events are possible or in our case, very large jumps are possible.

Therefore, we propose to update the positions of the particles by making use of the α-stable distribution as follows:

$$\overrightarrow{x_i(t+1)} = S_\alpha(\beta, \gamma, \Delta) \tag{4.26}$$

where α, β, γ and Δ are, respectively, the stability index, the asymmetry parameter, the scaling parameter and the positioning parameter of the Lévy α-stable distribution. Although the parameter α can be adapted to every optimization problem, in our optimization algorithm it will be set to $\frac{1}{2}$. In other words, the particles positions will be updated using the Lévy distribution that corresponds to the case where $\alpha = \frac{1}{2}$. It should be noted that the Lévy distribution is a special case of Lévy α-stable distributions.

Referring to equation [4.26] to [CHA 76], the computation of the new position of the particle $\overrightarrow{x_i(t+1)}$ at iteration $t+1$ is achieved by means of equations [4.27], [4.28] by defining $\gamma = K \times |r_1\overrightarrow{G_{best_i}(t)} - r_2\overrightarrow{P_{best_i}(t)}|$ and $\Delta = \left(\frac{\overrightarrow{G_{best_i}(t)} + \overrightarrow{P_{best_i}(t)}}{2} \right)$.

$$\overrightarrow{x_i(t+1)} = \left(\frac{\overrightarrow{Gbest_i(t)} + \overrightarrow{Pbest_i(t)}}{2} \right) + K$$

$$\times |r1\overrightarrow{Gbest_i(t)} - r2\overrightarrow{Pbest_i(t)}| \times y \tag{4.27}$$

$$y = \frac{\pi}{2} * \left[bphi * tan(\phi) - \beta * log \left[\frac{\pi}{2} * w * \left(\frac{cos(\phi)}{bphi} \right) \right] \right] + z \quad [4.28]$$

and designating by:

$$w = -log(u)$$

$$\phi = (u - 0.5) * \pi$$

$$z = \beta * tan(\pi * \frac{\alpha}{2})$$

$$bphi = \frac{\pi}{2} + \beta * \phi$$

and r_1, r_2 and u uniform variables between 0 and 1, $K \in]0, 1]$ a real positive, $\overrightarrow{P_{best_i}(t)}$ and $\overrightarrow{G_{best_i}(t)}$, respectively, the best position of particle $\overrightarrow{x_i}$ and that of its best informant at time t. Equations [4.27] and [4.28] are obtained from [CHA 76] by analogy to the simulation of Lévy α-stable distributions.

Unlike conventional PSO methods, this method does not use velocity in an explicit manner. However, velocity is implicitly taken into account in the parameter γ of the random variable S_α, namely the term $|r_1\overrightarrow{G_{best_i}(t)} - r_2\overrightarrow{P_{best_i}(t)}|$ of equation [4.27]. In effect, the farther the best position of particle i, $\overrightarrow{P_{best_i}(t)}$, moves away from the best position of its informants, G_{best}^{di}, the larger the parameter γ will be, which as result will increase the dispersion of the particles (the velocity of the particle in question will be greater). To avoid that a particle be frozen when γ is equal to 0 and to increase the diversity of the optimization process, we have added two random components r_1 and r_2. Thereby, the quantity $|r_1\overrightarrow{G_{best_i}(t)} - r_2\overrightarrow{P_{best_i}(t)}|$ converges more slowly to zero and it avoids the particle getting stuck when $\overrightarrow{P_{best_i}(t)} \rightsquigarrow \overrightarrow{G_{best_i}(t)}$.

As we can observe, the α-SLPSO algorithm has two main parameters, K and β. The K parameter makes it possible to renormalize the scaling parameter γ with respect to the search space. This parameter has an important property which is that of regulating the intensification stage. In effect, $|r_1\overrightarrow{G_{best_i}(t)} - r_2\overrightarrow{P_{best_i}(t)}|$ tends toward 0 when $K \rightsquigarrow 0$. As a result, the realizations of the random variable S_α will be concentrated on a point of the search space. However, when $K \succ 0$, the realizations of the random variable

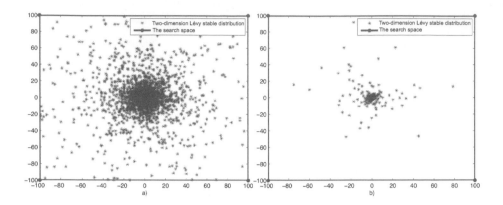

Figure 4.2. *Two-dimension Lévy α-stable distribution for a) $\gamma = 1$, b) $\gamma = 0.001$, the other parameters are fixed as follows: $\alpha = 0.5$, $\beta = 0$ and $\triangle = 50$. The search space is fixed to $[-50, +50]$*

S_α will be sparser (Figure 4.2). In other words, the parameter K controls the length of the jumps achieved by particles.

As we noted earlier, this parameter depends on the extreme values X_{max} and X_{min} of the search space. In summary, we propose calculating the parameter $K^- j$ relative to the dimension $D^- j$ of the particle in the following manner (equation [4.29]) :

$$K^j = (X^j_{max} - X^j_{min})/100 \qquad [4.29]$$

where X^j_{max} and X^j_{min} are, respectively, the maximal and minimal values of the component $D^- j$ of the particle j.

Figure 4.3 shows that it makes sense to simulate a variable S_α asymmetric (namely, $\beta \neq -1$) at the boundaries of the search space. As a point of fact, it is preferable for particles to remain in the search space rather than leave it. Therefore, in order to avoid particles leaving the search space more often, we propose computing (at each iteration of the optimization process) the parameter $\beta^j_i(t + 1)$ corresponding to the component j of the particle i at iteration $t + 1$ in the following manner (equation [4.30]):

$$\beta^j_i(t + 1) = -\frac{m}{2(X^j_{max} - X^j_{min})} \qquad [4.30]$$

with:

– m the positioning parameter Δ which is equal to: $\left(\frac{\overrightarrow{G_{best_i}}+\overrightarrow{P_{best_i}}}{2}\right)$;

– X_{max}^j and X_{min}^j are, respectively, the maximal and minimal value of the component D^j of the particle j.

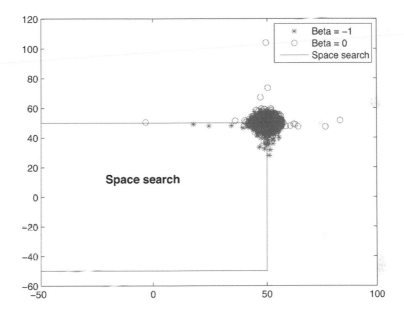

Figure 4.3. *Lévy α-stable distribution in two dimensions for $\alpha = 1,95$, $\beta = -1$ (star) and $\beta = 0$ (circle), the scale parameter $\gamma = 15$ and the positioning parameter $\Delta = 50$. The search space is set to $[-50, +50]$*

In order to ensure that the asymmetry parameter β lies between $[-1, 1]$, we have divided m by 2.

4.4.3.2. *Design of a Lévy local search (α-SLLS)*

In almost all areas, whether in engineering sciences (biology, mathematics, physics, etc.) or in social science and humanities (history, sociology, etc.), the concept of scale distribution could contribute greatly to the understanding of certain phenomena (chaos, for example). This concept of scale distribution (or scale relativity [NOT 11]) introduces a scale space, which is the space of the solutions and their transformations (that is of the transformations between scales).

In this section, we will focus on Lévy local search : α-SLLS.

A local search method is essentially characterized by a notion of neighborhood and a mechanism for exploiting the latter [DRE 03]. These methods are known as *"descent methods"*.

In general, the concept of a local search algorithm is the following: the algorithm starts its search from an arbitrary point in the space of possible solutions. Then, in a "local" area around this departure point, it searches for one or several solutions. In other words, the algorithm improves the solution of the problem by strolling in the search space from one neighbor to another, often slightly modifying the current solution until it can no longer improve the solution and/or a certain stopping criterion is reached (algorithm 4.2).

Algorithm 4.2: Local search

```
/* j, j':  current and next selected solutions      */
/* S:  search space                                  */
/* V(j):  neighbor of j in S                         */
/* val(j):  fitness of j                             */
```
1 $j \leftarrow$ initial solution in S
2 $i \leftarrow j$
3 **While** *stopping conditions are not reached* **Do**
4   **Choose** $j' = V(j)$
5      $j \leftarrow j'$
6   **If** $val(j) < val(i)$ **Then**
7          $i \leftarrow j'$
8   **End**
9 **End**
10 **Return** i

To build our α-SLPSO algorithm, we have assumed that the optimal search strategy of living species is generally intermittent and that (local) active search phases alternate randomly with fast ballistic search phases (jumps).

Algorithm 4.3: Lévy local search (LLS)

```
   /* S_α(β,γ,s):   random Lévy variable of parameters α, β,
      γ and s                                                      */
   /* s, s':  current solution and selected neighbor
      solution                                                     */
   /* f(s) and f(s'):  Fitness of s and s', respectively          */
   /* x_min, x_max:  the search space                             */
1 ./* t:  iteration t                                             */
```

2 **Generate** an initial solution s

3 $\alpha \leftarrow \alpha_{max}$

4 $\gamma \leftarrow \left(\frac{x_{max} - x_{min}}{2} \right)$

5 $\beta \leftarrow -\frac{s}{2(X_{max} - X_{min})}$

6 $\triangle\alpha \leftarrow \frac{\alpha_{max} - \alpha_{min}}{Number of iterations}$

7 $\triangle T \leftarrow \frac{T_{max} - T_{min}}{Number of iterations}$

8 **While** *stopping conditions are not reached* **Do**

9   **Generate** randomly a solution $s' = S_\alpha(\beta, \gamma, s)$ **If** $f(s') < f(s)$ **Then**

10 | $s \leftarrow s'$

11 | $\beta \leftarrow -\frac{s'}{2(X_{max} - X_{min})}$

12   **End**

13     $\alpha \leftarrow \alpha_{min} + \triangle\alpha * t$

14     $\gamma \leftarrow \left(\frac{x_{max} - x_{min}}{2} \right) e^{\left(\frac{-\triangle f}{T_{max} - \triangle T * t} \right)}$

15     $t \leftarrow t + 1;$

16 **End**

17 **Return** s

Based on what has been described in section 4.4.3.1, the Lévy local search α-SLLS method can be implemented in the following manner (algorithm 4.3):

– initially, a point s is randomly generated in the search space. This point s constitutes the solution to the problem raised at iteration 0. In addition, as described in Chapter 7, the Lévy probability distribution has four main parameters that are initialized as follows:

- $\alpha = \alpha_{min}$ (scale parameter);

- for each dimension D^j of s, we set $\beta_i^j(0) = -\frac{s(j)}{2(X_{max}^j - X_{min}^j)}$ (symmetry parameter);

- $\gamma^j = \frac{(X^j_{max} - X^j_{min})}{2}$ (the scale parameter) with X^j_{max} and X^j_{min} the bounds of the search space corresponding to the dimension D^j;

- the positioning parameter of the distribution $\Delta = s$ (the initial solution) and finally $T = T_{max}$ (search temperature by analogy to the temperature of the system in simulated annealing);

– at iteration t, a random Lévy variable is generated with parameters:

- $\alpha = \alpha_{min} + \Delta\alpha * t$, with $\Delta\alpha = \frac{\alpha_{max} - \alpha_{min}}{Number\,of\,iterations}$;

- $\gamma \leftarrow \left(\frac{x_{max} - x_{min}}{2}\right) e^{\left(\frac{-\Delta f}{T_{max} - \Delta T * t}\right)}$ with $\Delta f = f(s') - f(s)$ and $f(s')$, the fitness obtained by s' at iteration t, $\Delta T = \frac{T_{max} - T_{min}}{Number\,of\,iterations}$. This formula is known as the Metropolis algorithm;

– the algorithm is stopped if one or several stopping criteria are met. The best solution s is then returned.

As in simulated annealing [KIR 83], the temperature variation T from T_{max} to T_{min} ensures that the equilibrium of the system, described in algorithm 4.3, will only be reached when $\frac{-\Delta f}{T_{max} - \Delta T * t} \rightsquigarrow -\infty$. Moreover, contrary to the α-SLPSO algorithm destined to propose global optimal solutions, α-SLLS is dedicated to propose local optimal solutions. For this reason, we have decided to vary the parameter α (rather than to fix it at $\frac{1}{2}$) from α_{min} to α_{max} such that the last iterations of the optimization process focus on the intensification phase. In fact, when $\alpha \rightsquigarrow 2$, the random variable distribution S_α becomes a Gaussian distribution. In other words, the big jumps become increasingly more unlikely.

The algorithm α-SLLS differs from the general operating principle of a local search (algorithm 4.2) from two perspectives:

– the neighbors s' of the current solution s are randomly chosen according to a Lévy α-stable distribution;

– a solution that degrades the fitness of the objective function is not retained and that, contrary to simulated annealing, regardless of the value of this fitness.

By doing so, we expect that we will not become trapped in a local optimum and that the algorithm will be able to perform large jumps (that is to visit promising search areas).

4.4.3.3. *Results and discussions*

After having documented the operating principle of the α-SLPSO algorithm and its local search α-SLLS, in this section we present the performance obtained using these two algorithms. Although the α-SLPSO algorithm has originally been designed to solve the FACTS placement and sizing problem in electric networks, it is appropriate to compare it with other PSO algorithms in order to quantify its ability to solve different problems. In order to test the α-SLPSO and α-SLLS algorithms, we will use test functions, introduced in Appendix 1.

As a first step, we validate the α-SLPSO algorithm by comparing it to five other PSO algorithms, namely PSO-2 S, EPUS-PSO, CLPSO, CPSO-H and the standard SPO2007. The results of the α-SLPSO algorithm and the α-SLLS are obtained by programs coded in Python. The results of all the other approaches are taken from the literature [ELD 12b, ELD 12a, HSI 09]. Moreover, it should be noted that every algorithm is executed 30 times with each test function. The mean and standard deviation of each algorithm are therefore assessed from each test function. In the end, we achieve the same experimental analysis with the α-SLLS and compare with α-SLPSO and SPO2007 algorithms.

4.4.3.4. *Performance of the α-SLPSO algorithm*

In order to compare the α-SLPSO algorithm to the other variants of PSO, 30 executions of each algorithm are performed in 10-D and 30-D. We record the mean and standard deviation for each method with each test function in a table. A stop criterion common to all algorithms is fixed, namely that optimization processes stop when a maximum number of evaluations Max_{Fes} is reached. Referring to the standards of the CEC2005 conference, Max_{Fes} is a function of the size of the problem to be solved namely, $Max_{Fes} = 10,000 \times D$. Therefore, the stopping criterion Max_{Fes} is set to $40,000$ and $150,000$ in 10-D and 30-D, respectively.

The parameters of the PSO-2S, EPUS-PSO, CLPSO, CPSO-H algorithms and the standard PSO2007 are extracted from [HSI 09]. The parameters of our α-SLPSO algorithm are fixed as follows:

– the number of particles $Nb_{particles}$ is set to 20;
– the number of informants $N_{informants}$ is set to 3;

– the topology of the particles is a social model. That is to say that at each iteration of the algorithm, the informants of each particle are randomly chosen;

– the parameter α is fixed at $\frac{1}{2}$;

– the parameter K is taken according to equation [4.29];

– in the event of leaving the search space, the particles are randomly replaced within the space.

4.4.3.4.1. Results of 10-D problems

Tables 4.1 and 4.2 present the results obtained by α-SLPSO, PSO-2 S, EPUS-PSO, CLPSO, CPSO-H and the standard PSO2007 in terms of mean errors and standard deviations for 30 executions of 11 test functions among 15 presented in Appendix 1. In all cases, the dimension of the function used is equal to 10. The best results among the six algorithms are presented in red. In addition, the α-SLPSO algorithm is tested with three additional functions but not compared due to lack of results from other algorithms. The performance in the last line of each table indicates the number of times (of functions) where the α-SLPSO algorithm exceeds all other algorithms.

The review of these experimental results in the case of 10-D problems brings about the following comments:

– the α-SLPSO, PSO-2S and EPUS-PSO algorithms seem to yield better results than the rest of the variants of PSO. In fact, α-SLPSO, PSO-2S and EPUS-PSO surpass the remaining PSO algorithms with the majority of test functions. Particularly, α-SLPSO, PSO-2S and EPUS-PSO obtain significantly better results than the rest of the algorithms with f_5, f_6 and f_{14};

– the PSO-2S algorithm seems to surpass all other algorithms. In effect, the score of the latter is 6/11 and 8/11 with regard to α-SLPSO and EPUS-PSO, respectively;

– PSO-2S and EPUS-PSO seem to surpass our α-SLPSO algorithm. The score of the α-SLPSO is 5/11 compared to PSO-2S and 4/11 compared to EPUS-PSO;

– finally, we notice that α-SLPSO is surpassed by PSO-2S and EPUS-PSO in the totality of the unimodal test functions (f_1, f_2 and f_{10}).

4.4.3.4.2. Results of 30-D problems

The experimental results for 30-D problems are presented in Tables 4.3 and 4.4. As with 10-D, we compare the algorithms with respect to the mean error and standard deviation from 30 executions, using of the same functions as in the 10-D case.

The examination of these experimental results brings about the following comments:

– as in the 10-D case, PSO-2S and EPUS-PSO algorithms seem to yield better results than the other variants of the PSO. In addition, PSO-2S surpasses all the algorithms except α-SLPSO in the majority of test functions;

– unlike the previous case (10-D), α-SLPSO obtains better results than all the other algorithms. As a matter of fact, its score is 7/11 compared to the two algorithms PSO-2S and EPUS-PSO;

– as in the previous case, α-SLPSO is surpassed by PSO-2S and EPUS-PSO with the totality of unimodal test functions (f_1, f_2 and f_{10});

– α-SLPSO seems to be less sensitive to the increase in dimension D, in particular, in the multimodal functions f_4, f_5, f_6, f_8, f_{10}, f_{13} and f_{15}.

In summary, α-SLPSO gives very good results with all of the test functions in 10-D and 30-D (Table 4.5). These results show us that the algorithm is more efficient when the dimension D of the function to be optimized increases. In other words, α-SLPSO seems to be more suitable to large-sized problems (Table 4.6), which is the case of the FACTS placement and sizing problem.

To consolidate these experimental analyses and to avoid making hasty conclusions, we propose performing a multicriteria analysis of the various results presented in Tables 4.1–4.4. As a matter of fact, if we assume that the α-SLPSO algorithm surpasses the PSO-2S algorithm in six test functions out of 11, that PSO-2S outperforms EPUS-PSO in eight functions out of 11 and that EPUS-PSO in turn surpasses α-SLPSO in 6 out of 11, it is difficult to make a decision between the three methods.

For this purpose, the decision support method ELECTRE II is applied to the results achieved by each algorithm for each test function. Its operating principle consists of calculating a concordance and discordance matrix to then "outclass" (weakly and strongly) the alternatives between them [ROY 68]. Due to the lack of data on the results from the PSO-2S, EPUS-PSO, CLPSO, CPSO-H algorithms and the PSO2007 standard, we will retain only the fitness mean as a classification criterion, namely, 22 criteria (six standard functions and five pivoted functions in dimension 10 and 30). Furthermore, although the functions do not have the same complexity, we have decided to assign a common weight for each of them.

f	α-SLPSO	PSO-2S	EPUS-PSO	CLPSO	CPSO-H	SPSO2007
f_1	$2.73e - 113$ $\pm$ $1.23e - 112$	$1.05e - 086$ $\pm$ $3.10e - 086$	$5.55e - 153$ $\pm$ $2.44e - 134$	$4.02e - 021$ $\pm$ $6.49e - 021$	$9.01e - 010$ $\pm$ $1.38e - 009$	$4.00e - 101$ $\pm$ $1.80e - 100$
f_2	$7.66e - 003$ $\pm$ $1.24e - 002$	$6.18e - 028$ $\pm$ $2.13e - 027$	$9.32e - 012$ $\pm$ $4.16e - 011$	$5.04e + 002$ $\pm$ $1.99e + 002$	$1.62e + 003$ $\pm$ $9.35e + 002$	$1.83e - 027$ $\pm$ $4.03e - 027$
f_3	$1.41e + 000$ $\pm$ $3.95e - 001$	$2.35e - 002$ $\pm$ $1.56e - 002$	$9.13e - 002$ $\pm$ $1.05e - 001$	$2.84e + 000$ $\pm$ $1.05e + 000$	$1.08e + 000$ $\pm$ $1.18e + 000$	$3.10e - 001$ $\pm$ $9.95e - 001$
f_4	$0.00e + 000$ $\pm$ $0.00e + 000$	$4.12e - 015$ $\pm$ $1.21e - 015$	$2.72e - 015$ $\pm$ $1.50e - 015$	$1.78e - 011$ $\pm$ $1.63e - 011$	$7.02e - 006$ $\pm$ $5.77e - 006$	$3.85e - 001$ $\pm$ $2.07e - 001$
f_5	$3.19e - 014$ $\pm$ $1.46e - 013$	$0.00e + 000$ $\pm$ $0.00e + 000$	$0.00e + 000$ $\pm$ $0.00e + 000$	$2.35e - 009$ $\pm$ $2.72e - 009$	$3.83e - 010$ $\pm$ $7.36e - 010$	$5.11e + 000$ $\pm$ $2.29e + 000$
f_6	$0.00e + 000$ $\pm$ $0.00e + 000$	$5.85e - 003$ $\pm$ $2.35e - 002$	$3.21e - 002$ $\pm$ $8.11e - 002$	$2.06e + 000$ $\pm$ $4.80e - 001$	$4.12e + 000$ $\pm$ $1.72e + 000$	$4.04e - 002$ $\pm$ $1.78e - 001$
f_8	$6.68e - 002$ $\pm$ $5.47e - 002$	$-$ $\pm$ $-$	$-$ $\pm$ $-$	$-$ $\pm$ $-$	$-$ $\pm$ $-$	$-$ $\pm$ $-$
Performance	$\frac{3}{6}$	$\frac{2}{6}$	$\frac{6}{6}$	$\frac{5}{6}$		$\frac{4}{6}$

Table 4.1. *Comparison of the different algorithms in 10-D: standard functions*

In order to classify the different variants of PSO, we programmed the ELECTRE II method in Matlab and applied it to our classification problem for different sets of parameters c_1 and c_2 ($c_1 > c_2$ are concordance thresholds in the ELECTRE II method). Figure 4.4 shows the classification results obtained for the different sets of parameters. This figure clearly shows that

α-SLPSO outperforms – in the majority of cases – all other methods. For some values of c_1 and c_2, this figure also shows that α-SLPSO, PSO-2S and EPUS-PSO are indistinguishable.

f	α-SLPSO	PSO-2S	EPUS-PSO	CLPSO	CPSO-H	SPSO2007
f_s	$9.67e-113$ $\pm$ $2.70e-112$	- $\pm$ -	- $\pm$	- $\pm$ -	- $\pm$ -	- $\pm$ -
f_{10}	$2.99e-003$ $\pm$ $4.79e-003$	$3.38e-009$ $\pm$ $9.02e-009$	$3.99e-007$ $\pm$ $1.63e-006$	$8.27e+002$ $\pm$ $3.35e+002$	$2.15e+003$ $\pm$ $1.19e+003$	$1.02e-007$ $\pm$ $4.12e-007$
f_{11}	$3.73e+000$ $\pm$ $1.65e+000$	$4.21e-001$ $\pm$ $7.77e-002$	$8.96e-001$ $\pm$ $2.15e+000$	$6.44e+000$ $\pm$ $4.56e+000$	$3.01e+000$ $\pm$ $2.52e+000$	$5.73e-001$ $\pm$ $1.05e+000$
f_{12}	$1.62c+000$ $\pm$ $4.17e+000$	$1.56e+001$ $\pm$ $2.28e+000$	$2.61e-015$ $\pm$ $1.57e-015$	$8.45e-008$ $\pm$ $2.97e-007$	$1.31e+000$ $\pm$ $9.68e-001$	$2.03e+001$ $\pm$ $8.54e-002$
f_{13}	$1.3e+000$ $\pm$ $4.60e+000$	$2.65e-001$ $\perp$ $9.93e-001$	$7.26e+000$ $\pm$ $4.31e+000$	$8.85e+000$ $\pm$ $3.07e+000$	$2.81e+001$ $\pm$ $1.39e+001$	$1.26e+001$ $\pm$ $7.00e+000$
f_{14}	$4.32e-001$ $\pm$ $3.56e-001$	$6.43e-001$ $\pm$ $3.45e-001$	$1.12c+000$ $\pm$ $1.36e+000$	$1.98c+000$ $\pm$ $5.38e-001$	$3.48e+000$ $\pm$ $1.41e+000$	$4.20e+000$ $\pm$ $1.50e+000$
f_{15}	$4.53e-001$ $\pm$ $2.51e-001$	$-$ $\pm$ $-$	$-$ $\pm$ $-$	- $\pm$ -	- $\pm$ -	- $\pm$ -
Performance	$\frac{2}{5}$	$\frac{2}{5}$	$\frac{4}{5}$	$\frac{3}{5}$	$\frac{3}{5}$	

Table 4.2. *Comparison of the various algorithms in 10-D: shifted functions*

4.4.3.5. *Performance of α-SLLS local search*

In order to present the results of our α-SLLS local search and to compare them to the standard PSO2007 algorithm, 100 executions of the local search are performed in 10-D and 30-D. As in the previous case, we record the mean and standard deviation of each method with each test function in a table. The stop criterion common to all algorithms, Max_{Fes}, is always the same: $40,000$ and $150,000$ in 10-D and 30-D, respectively.

f	α-SLPSO	PSO-2S	EPUS-PSO	CLPSO	CPSO-H	SPSO2007
f_1	$2.36e-135$ $\pm$ $1.19e-134$	$3.02e-119$ $\pm$ $1.56e-118$	$8.50e-263$ $\pm$ $1.02e-262$	$1.34e-025$ $\pm$ $1.71e-025$	$1.57e-010$ $\pm$ $2.99e-10$	$3.36e-107$ $\pm$ $1.79e-106$
f_2	$1.20e-001$ $\pm$ $2.71e-001$	$6.18e-011$ $\pm$ $2.63e-011$	$1.97e+002$ $\pm$ $4.69e+000$	$2.41e+004$ $\pm$ $6.78e+003$	$8.36e+004$ $\pm$ $6.58e+004$	$8.25e-008$ $\pm$ $9.00e-008$
f_3	$5.50e+000$ $\pm$ $7.77e+000$	$9.75e+000$ $\pm$ $9.59e-001$	$2.55e+001$ $\pm$ $3.53e-001$	$2.01e+001$ $\pm$ $3.37e+000$	$1.03e+001$ $\pm$ $1.37e+001$	$1.23e+001$ $\pm$ $1.47e+000$
f_4	$3.12e-015$ $\pm$ $8.61e-016$	$1.63e-001$ $\pm$ $3.85e-001$	$3.91e-015$ $\pm$ $1.07e-015$	$9.90e-014$ $\pm$ $3.80e-014$	$3.90e-006$ $\pm$ $5.98e-006$	$1.36e+000$ $\pm$ $1.13e+000$
f_5	$5.92e-017$ $\pm$ $3.18e-016$	$1.00e+000$ $\pm$ $1.18e+001$	$0.00e+000$ $\pm$ $0.00e+000$	$1.87e-009$ $\pm$ $5.34e-009$	$3.15e-010$ $\pm$ $1.05e-009$	$4.88e+001$ $\pm$ $1.44e+001$
f_6	$0.00e+000$ $\pm$ $0.00e+000$	$3.63e-001$ $\pm$ $2.79e-001$	$4.08e-001$ $\pm$ $1.22e+000$	$1.49e+001$ $\pm$ $1.69e+000$	$1.36e+000$ $\pm$ $3.38e+000$	$1.55e+001$ $\pm$ $1.09e+000$
f_8	$6.97e-003$ $\pm$ $8.99e-003$	- $\pm$ -	- $\pm$ -	- $\pm$ -	- $\pm$ -	- $\pm$ -
Performance	$\frac{5}{6}$	$\frac{4}{6}$	$\frac{6}{6}$	$\frac{6}{6}$	$\frac{6}{6}$	$\frac{5}{6}$

Table 4.3. *Comparison of the various algorithms in 30-D: standard functions*

The parameters of our α-SLLS local search algorithm are fixed as follows:

– the maximal T_{max} and minimal T_{min} temperatures are fixed to 10 and 0, respectively;

– the scale parameters α_{max} and α_{min} are fixed to 2 and $\frac{1}{2}$, respectively;

– in the event of leaving the search space, random replacing inside the space is performed.

f	SLPSO	PSO-2S	EPUS-PSO	CLPSO	CPPSO-H	SPSO2007
f_s	$6.87e - 072$ $\pm$ $3.28e - 071$	- $\pm$ -	- $\pm$ -	- $\pm$ -	- $\pm$ -	- $\pm$ -
f_{10}	$1.95e + 000$ $\pm$ $2.73e + 000$	$7.80e - 005$ $\pm$ $9.25e - 005$	$1.20e + 001$ $\pm$ $2.46e + 001$	$2.38e + 004$ $\pm$ $6.49e + 003$	$3.87e + 004$ $\pm$ $1.71e + 004$	$1.09e - 001$ $\pm$ $1.80e - 001$
f_{11}	$1.56e + 001$ $\pm$ $1.02e + 000$	$1.39e + 001$ $\pm$ $1.48e - 001$	$1.96e + 001$ $\pm$ $2.91e + 001$	$3.04e + 001$ $\pm$ $1.32e + 001$	$3.03e + 001$ $\pm$ $2.59e + 001$	$2.77e + 001$ $\pm$ $1.31e + 001$
f_{12}	$3.12e + 000$ $\pm$ $3.33e + 000$	$1.69e + 001$ $\pm$ $1.66e + 000$	$6.81e - 001$ $\pm$ $1.02e + 000$	$2.22e - 006$ $\pm$ $8.29e - 006$	$1.52e + 000$ $\pm$ $8.30e - 001$	$2.09e + 000$ $\pm$ $1.31e + 000$
f_{13}	$3.19e - 010$ $\pm$ $1.68e - 009$	$1.40e + 000$ $\pm$ $2.73e - 001$	$3.76e + 001$ $\pm$ $1.48e + 001$	$4.70e + 001$ $\pm$ $6.85e + 000$	$9.52e + 001$ $\pm$ $2.93e + 001$	$9.04e + 001$ $+$ $4.03e + 001$
f_{14}	$5.00e + 000$ $\pm$ $3.13e + 000$	$3.34e + 000$ $\pm$ $1.22e + 000$	$4.26e + 000$ $\pm$ $2.97e + 000$	$1.51e + 001$ $\pm$ $1.93e + 000$	$1.36e + 001$ $\pm$ $3.56e + 000$	$3.27e + 001$ $\pm$ $3.19e + 000$
f_{15}	$1.83e - 002$ $\pm$ $2.41e - 002$	- $\pm$ -	- $\pm$ -	- $\pm$ -	- $\pm$ -	- $\pm$ -
Performance	$\frac{2}{5}$	$\frac{3}{5}$	$\frac{4}{5}$		$\frac{4}{5}$	$\frac{3}{5}$

Table 4.4. *Comparison of the various algorithms in 30-D: shifted functions*

f	PSO-2S	EPUS-PSO	CLPSO	CPPSO-H	SPSO2007
10D	$5/11$	$4/11$	$10/11$	$8/11$	$8/11$
30D	$7/11$	$7/11$	$10/11$	$10/11$	$8/11$

Table 4.5. *Comparison of the various algorithms*

4.4.3.5.1. Results of 10-D and 30-D problems

The experimental results for the 10-D and 30-D problems of our α-SLLS Lévy local search are presented in Table 4.7. These results show us that the α-SLLS obtains very encouraging results, in particular, for unimodal functions f_1 and f_2 and in all multimodal functions except the function f_5. Moreover, we notice that the α-SLLS surpasses the two algorithms in the function f_3 in 30-D.

f	f_{21}	f_{22}	f_{23}	f_{24}	f_{25}
50-D	$1.32e - 004$ $\pm$ $4.43e - 005$	$5.16e + 01$ $\pm$ $1.78e + 001$	$2.10e - 003$ $\pm$ $4.07e - 004$	$2.30e + 001$ $\pm$ $4.76e + 000$	$2.67e - 002$ $\pm$ $4.68e - 002$
100-D	$5.52e - 003$ $\pm$ $1.27e - 002$	$1.62e + 002$ $\pm$ $4.54e + 001$	$8.22e - 003$ $\pm$ $3.37e - 003$	$6.11e + 001$ $\pm$ $1.40e + 001$	$1.27e - 002$ $\pm$ $1.80e - 002$
200-D	$1.35e - 001$ $\pm$ $6.04e - 001$	$2.89e + 002$ $\pm$ $6.28e + 001$	$2.86e - 002$ $\pm$ $9.20e - 002$	$1.52e + 002$ $\pm$ $1.76e + 001$	$7.75e - 003$ $\pm$ $1.47e - 002$

Table 4.6. *Results in dimensions 50-D, 100-D and 200-D*

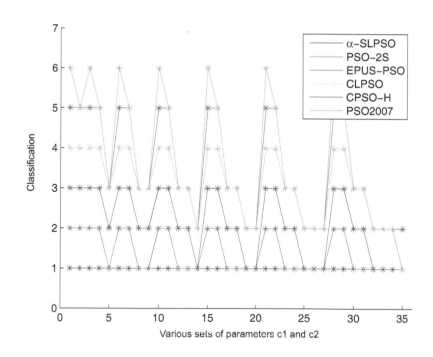

Figure 4.4. *Classification of variants α-SLPSO, PSO-2S, EPUS-PSO, CLPSO, CPSO-H and the PSO2007 standard for a set of concordance parameters c_1 and c_2. For a color version of this figure, see www.iste.co.uk/heliodore/metaheuristics.zip*

f	10-D			30D		
	α-SLLS	α-SLPSO	SPSO2007	α-SLLS	α-SLPSO	SPSO2007
f_1	$6.54e-030$ $\pm$ $2.10e-029$	$2.73e-113$ $\pm$ $1.23e-112$	$4.00e-101$ $\pm$ $1.80e-100$	$4.95e-043$ $\pm$ $1.95e-042$	$2.36e-135$ $\pm$ $1.19e-134$	$3.36e-107$ $\pm$ $1.79e-106$
f_2	$4.3e-004$ $\pm$ $2.15e-004$	$7.66e-003$ $\pm$ $1.24e-002$	$1.83e-027$ $\pm$ $4.03e-027$	$7.41e+000$ $\pm$ $1.01e+000$	$1.20e-001$ $\pm$ $2.71e-001$	$8.25e-008$ $\pm$ $9.00e-008$
f_3	$3.61e+000$ $\pm$ $2.11e+000$	$1.41e+000$ $\pm$ $3.95e-001$	$3.10e-001$ $\pm$ $9.95e-001$	$2.59e+000$ $\pm$ $5.69e+000$	$5.50e+000$ $\pm$ $7.77e+000$	$1.23e+001$ $\pm$ $1.47e+000$
f_4	$1.72e+000$ $\pm$ $8.43e-001$	$0.00e+000$ $\pm$ $0.00e+000$	$3.85e-001$ $\pm$ $2.07e-001$	$4.81e+000$ $\pm$ $2.09e+000$	$3.12e-015$ $\pm$ $8.61e-016$	$1.36e+000$ $\pm$ $1.13e+000$
f_5	$3.15e+001$ $\pm$ $1.19e+001$	$3.19e-014$ $\pm$ $1.46e-013$	$5.11e+000$ $\pm$ $2.29e+000$	$1.23e+002$ $\pm$ $2.42e+001$	$5.92e-017$ $\pm$ $3.18e-016$	$4.88e+001$ $\pm$ $1.44e+001$
f_6	$5.11e+000$ $\pm$ $1.60e+000$	$0.00e+000$ $\pm$ $0.00e+000$	$4.04e-002$ $\pm$ $1.78e-001$	$2.81e+001$ $\pm$ $3.46e+000$	$0.00e+000$ $\pm$ $0.00e+000$	$1.55e+001$ $\pm$ $1.09e+000$
f_8	$4.85e-001$ $\pm$ $3.36e-001$	$6.68e-002$ $\pm$ $5.47e-002$	$-$ $\pm$ $-$	$1.37e-002$ $\pm$ $1.31e-002$	$6.97e-003$ $\pm$ $8.99e-003$	$-$ $\pm$ $-$

Table 4.7. *Results obtained by the α-SLLS local search in 10-D and 30-D with the standard functions*

4.4.4. *"Hybridization" of continuous and discrete PSO algorithms for application to the positioning and sizing of FACTS*

FACTS placement and sizing cannot be decorrelated. In effect, the optimal position of a FACTS is necessarily coupled to its size and vice versa. It thus appears relevant to develop in a coordinated manner the particles associated with the search for the size, namely the continuous particles ci and those associated with the search for the position, i.e. discrete particles di.

The approach retained here is to establish some kind of "hierarchy" between these two types of particles by giving priority to the search for the optimal position. The retained procedure is then based on the following principles:

– the size of a particle di is equal to the number of FACTS, Nb_{FACTS}, to implement;

– the size of the particle ci, associated with the particle di, is equal to the total number of nodes, Nb_{node}, where a FACTS can be placed;

– the modification of the particles follows the following procedure:

- the position of the Nb_{FACTS} FACTS associated with the particle di is determined;

- only the elements of the particles ci (i.e. the nodes) designated by the particle di are modified.

Thus, by linking a variable "FACTS size" to each possible node and changing this variable only when the position of the corresponding node is selected, such an approach is tantamount to fixing a FACTS, whose dimensions will change depending on the positions held in each of the possible nodes of the network and in the end to retain only Nb_{FACTS} nodes (that is Nb_{FACTS} FACTS). In summary, the "hybrid" PSO algorithm based on the principles previously described is based on the steps described in algorithm 4.4.

4.5. Application to the placement and sizing of two FACTS

This section is dedicated to the implementation of the proposed hybrid PSO algorithm in the case of two electrical networks:

– the benchmark network IEEE 30-Bus (or 30 nodes);

– the benchmark network IEEE 57-Bus (or 57 nodes).

Initially, the study based on the 30-node network makes the validation of the algorithm implemented possible. This validation is performed by comparing the optima retained by the PSO with an "optimum" calculated by a systematic exploration of all the search space based on a discretization of the latter.

The application to the 57-node network completes this validation on a more extensive network. The influence of some adjustment parameters of the PSO algorithm on the performance obtained in terms of convergence is illustrated in this network. Similarly, the influence on the optimal solution, of the economic parameters associated with solving the network model using an OPF method, is illustrated.

Algorithm 4.4: Hybrid algorithm for the placement of FACTS.

---

1 **Initialization** of the different parameters associated with the optimization problem

2 **Initialization**, randomly in all the search space of the velocities and positions associated with the $Nb_{particle}$ particles, where $Nb_{particle}$ is the total number of particles

3 **For each** *iteration k* **Do**

4   **Update**, if necessary, the adjustment parameters associated with the optimization problem

5   **For each** *particle i (that is particles di and ci)* **Do**

6   **From** positions $X_{di}(k)$ and $X_{ci}(k)$, computation of the fitness function $J_i(k)$)

7   **Update** $B_{di}(k)$ and $B_{ci}(k)$

8   **End**

9   **For each** *particle i* **Do**

10   **Update** $G_{di}(k)$ and $G_{ci}(k)$

11   **Update** velocity $V_{di}(k+1)$

12   **Update** position $X_{di}(k+1)$

13   **Update** velocity $V_{ci}(k+1)$

14   **Update** position $X_{ci}(k+1)$

15   **End**

16 **End**

17 **Determination** of the best solution among the $Nb_{particle}G_{di}(k)$ and $G_{ci}(k)$

For the two networks, the initial simulation and adjustment parameters of the PSO algorithm are:

– $\alpha_{ii} = 0.2$, $\alpha_{if} = 0.1$ for any particle i;

– $\beta_{ii} = 0.1$, $\beta_{if} = 0.2$ for any particle i;

– $\gamma_{ii} = 0.1$, $\gamma_{if} = 0.5$ for any particle i;

– $va_{ii} = 0.5$, $va_{if} = 0.5$ for any particle i;

– $c_{i1}(k) = c_{i2}(k) = 0.97$ for any particle i and any iteration k;

$- w_i(k) = w_{ii} + (w_{if} - w_{cii})\frac{k}{N_{iter}}$ with $w_{ii} = 1.5$ and $w_{if} = 0.5$ for any particle i;

– bounds on the power of FACTS (position X_i of particles i) :

- $X_{cim_{min}} = -50\,MVAR$ for every component m and every particle i,

- $X_{cim_{max}} = 50\,MVAR$ for every component m and every particle i,

- in the event that the upper or the lower bounds on x_{cim} are exceeded: imposition of $v_{cim} = 0$ and random reinitialization x_{cim} for every component m and any particle i;

– bounds on the velocity $\overrightarrow{V_{ci}}$ of particles ci:

- $V_{cim_{min}} = \frac{(X_{cim_{min}} - X_{cim_{max}})}{2\,\Delta t} = -50$ for every component m and any particle i ($\Delta t = 1$);

- $V_{cim_{max}} = \frac{(X_{cim_{max}} - X_{cim_{min}})}{2\,\Delta t} = 50$ for every component m and any particle i ($\Delta t = 1$);

– number of particles: $Nb_{particles} = 50$;

– number of informant particles: $N_{inform_{ci}} = N_{inform_{di}} = 10$ for any particle i;

– number of iterations: $N_{iter} = 200$;

– number of FACTS to be implemented: $Nb_{FACTS} = 2$;

– type of FACTS to be implemented: STATCOM, that is modification of the demand of reactive power at the connection node of the STATCOM (no modification of the admittance matrix Y);

– economic criterion (equation [4.7]) on active power P when solving the network equations using OPF.

The choice of the weight parameters associated with α_{di}, β_{di} and γ_{di} is carried out in order to give a more significant relative weight to the position of the particle (parameter α_{di}) in early iterations and the best "global" position of the particle (parameter γ_{di}) at final iterations. In addition, a random component, of maximal amplitude $va_{di} = 0, 5$, is introduced in the process of updating the velocity $\overrightarrow{V_{di}}$ of discrete particles $\overrightarrow{X_{di}}$.

4.5.1. *Application to the 30-node IEEE network*

The topology of the 30-node network is given in Figure 4.5. It is composed of 30 nodes including six "generator" nodes. Already having the capability to vary the reactive power injected onto these "generator" nodes by means of alternators, these nodes are eliminated from the search space. This space is thus restricted to 24 "load" nodes among which it is necessary to determine those where the two FACTS will be implemented. The criterion to be minimized is the criterion J_3 (that is, balancing voltages at the nodes, equation [4.10]).

The parameters and bounds associated with the different particles $\overrightarrow{X_{ci}}$ and $\overrightarrow{X_{di}}$ are:

– $Nb_{node} = 24$.

– size of a particle $\overrightarrow{X_{ci}}$: $Z = Nb_{node} = 24$ for any particle i;

– size of a particle $\overrightarrow{X_{di}}$: $M = Nb_{FACTS} = 2$ for any particle i.

In order to systematically determine an "optimal" solution, the search space is discretized as follows:

– examination of all possible pairs of positions, namely 276 couples;

– exploration between $X_{cim_{min}} = -50\,MVAR$ and $X_{cim_{max}} = 50\,MVAR$ with a step of $2\,MVAR$, which yields 51 steps.

The systematic search for the "optimum" is thus based on $276 * 51 * 51 = 717,876$ evaluations of the criterion to be optimized (or in other words, the solutions of the network model using the OPF method).

The PSO being a stochastic-based approach, the evaluation of its performance is made with a set of several trials (algorithm passes). The validation of the proposed algorithm will then be also carried out through its ability to reproduce how is obtained the optimal solution or a solution "close" enough to the optimal solution.

Figures 4.6 and 4.7, respectively, show the optimum obtained, the selected nodes and the reactive power associated with these nodes for 30 passes of the proposed PSO algorithm. By way of comparison, the criterion value obtained without FACTS is also given in Figure 4.6. The examination of these curves leads to the following comments:

– the introduction of FACTS in the network makes it possible to improve voltage balancing in the nodes, and thus increasing the security of the system;

– the optima found by the PSO algorithm are all very close to the "optimum" determined by the systematic approach. Therefore, by showing a very repetitive convergence toward the "optimal" solution, this result highlights the consistency of the PSO algorithm. This aspect is confirmed after examining Figure 4.7 where the positions selected by the PSO approach are very often those corresponding to the systematic "optimal" solution. In particular, the node N°8 is selected by PSO for all the passes. When this is not the case, the nodes selected by PSO are "close" to the "optimal" nodes that, considering the "geographical" numbering of the nodes (Figure 4.5), indicates an action in the same area of influence. Although less obviously "identical" to the power values found by the systematic approach, the powers selected by the PSO algorithm vary around the "optimal" values (Figure 4.7), which indicates a good repeatability of the algorithm;

– the PSO algorithm requires $N_{iter} * Nb_{particle}$, that is $50 * 200 = 10,000$, evaluations of the criterion to be optimized to obtain, at each pass, a solution very close to the systematic "optimal" solution. This number should be related to the $717,876$ evaluations of the criterion required by the systematic approach, thus highlighting the benefit of using an optimization algorithm, here of the PSO-type, for the determination of a satisfactory solution with a large reduction (here 98.6%) of the number of criterion evaluations and therefore of the corresponding computational time.

4.5.2. Application to the IEEE 57-node network

The topology of the 57-node network is given in Figure 4.8. Similarly to the case of the 30-node network, the "generator" nodes (here a total of 7) are removed from the search space.

The parameters and bounds associated with the different particles $\overrightarrow{X_{ci}}$ and $\overrightarrow{X_{di}}$ are as follows:

– $Nb_{node} = 50$;

– size of a particle $\overrightarrow{X_{ci}}$: $Z = Nb_{node} = 50$ for any particle i;

– size of a particle $\overrightarrow{X_{di}}$: $M = Nb_{FACTS} = 2$ for any particle i.

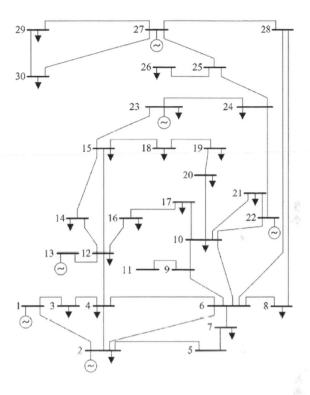

Figure 4.5. *Topology of the IEEE 30-Bus network*

This case study is interesting because the number of possible nodes is double that of the previous case. This results in a much higher number of position pairs (that is 1,225) and thus, a combinatorial search space of larger size. The results obtained must therefore qualify, among other things, the ability of the proposed PSO algorithm to search for an optimum in a wider space. As in the case of the 30-node network, the results obtained are compared with those determined by a systematic approach.

In order to determine this systematic "optimal" solution, the search space is discretized in the following manner:

– examination of all possible pairs of positions, namely 1,225 pair;

– exploration between $X_{cim_{min}} = -50\,MVAR$ and $X_{cim_{max}} = 50\,MVAR$ with a step of $5\,MVAR$, which yields 21 steps.

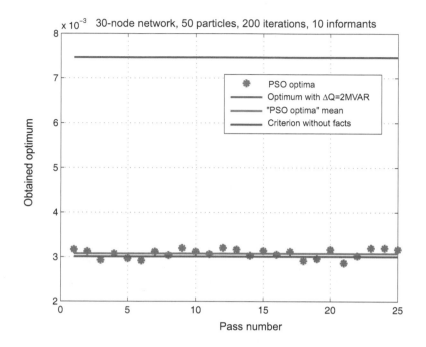

Figure 4.6. *IEEE 30-node network, 50 particles, 200 iterations, 10 informants. Criterion comparison: initial simulation and adjustment parameters*

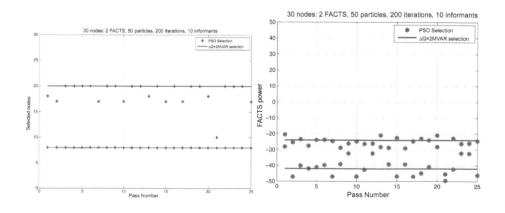

Figure 4.7. *IEEE 30-node network, 50 particles, 200 iterations, 10 informants. Comparison of selected positions and powers: initial simulation and adjustment parameters*

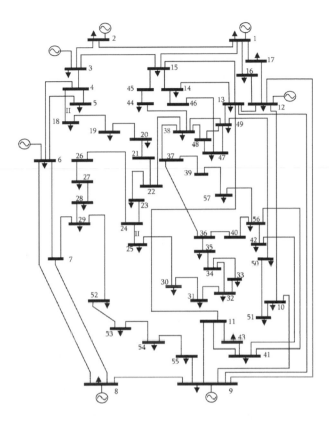

Figure 4.8. *Topology of the IEEE 57-Bus network*

The systematic search for the "optimum" is thus based on 1,225*21*21 = 540,225 evaluations of the criterion to be optimized (or solutions of the network model using the OPF method).

Figures 4.9 and 4.10, respectively, show the optimum obtained, the selected nodes and the reactive power associated with these nodes for 30 passes of the proposed PSO algorithm. By way of comparison, the criterion value obtained without FACTS is also given in Figure 4.9. The examination of these curves brings about the following comments:

– the PSO algorithm proposes very similar, or even "better" optima (67% of cases), than the systematic "optimum" which corresponds only to an "approximation", by means of a discretized approach and with a fairly large "step" of 5 $MVAR$, of a real optimum (Figure 4.9). This result confirms the performance of the PSO algorithm, already validated in the case of the 30-node network;

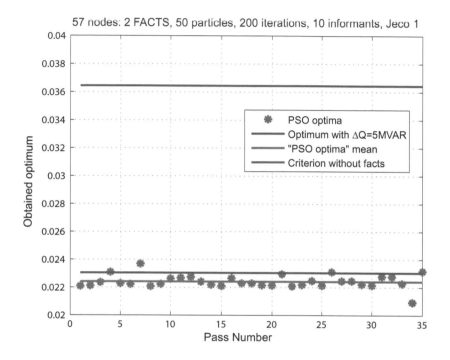

Figure 4.9. *IEEE 57-node network, 50 particles, 200 iterations, 10 informants. Criterion comparison: initial simulation and adjustment parameters*

– the consistency of the proposed PSO algorithm is still highlighted in Figures 4.10 and 4.10 by means of selecting nodes and the "near-constant" associated power, around the systematic "optimal" solution, for 30 passes achieved, and this is achieved inside a more extensive search space;

– the PSO algorithm requires 10,000 evaluations of the criterion to obtain an "optimal" solution. It is worthwhile comparing this figure with the 540,225 evaluations of the criterion that the systematic approach has required through an evaluation of the respective computation time. Therefore, given that the average duration of an evaluation of the criterion is 0.6 s, the search for the systematic solution required 324,135 s, or about 90 h (3.75 days), to approximate the computation time for a PSO pass equal to 6,000 s, that is, 1 h 40 min (which corresponds to an approximately 98% decrease in the computational time).

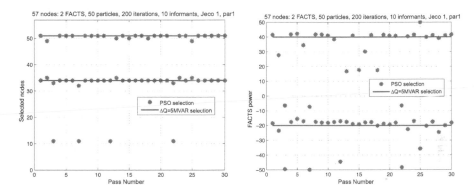

Figure 4.10. *IEEE 57-node network, 50 particles, 200 iterations, 10 informants. Comparison of positions and selected powers: initial simulation and adjustment parameters*

4.5.3. *Significance of the modified* velocity likelihoods *method*

In this section, we present an analysis of the relevance of the *velocity likelihoods* method previously exposed (section 4.4.2.7). Although the continuous PSO approach (associated here with the search for the optimal power of FACTS) is a renowned technique and often utilized, the application of a discrete *velocity likelihoods* PSO method for searching the optimal position of the FACTS can raise issues, in particular regarding the guarantee of a sufficiently comprehensive exploration of the search space. In order to increase the scope of this exploration, a random component va_i has been added during the update of the velocity of the particle $\overrightarrow{V_{di}}$ (equation [4.25]). In order to assess the influence of the component va_i on the performance of the proposed PSO algorithm, it has been removed for a set of 30 algorithm passes.

During these trials, the initial adjustment and simulation parameters are changed, namely $va_{ii} = 0$, $va_{if} = 0$ for any particle i.

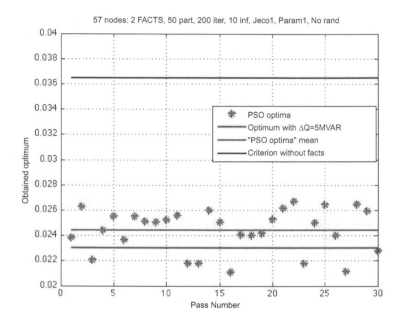

Figure 4.11. *IEEE 57-node network, 50 particles,*
200 iterations, 10 informants. Criterion comparison: cancellation
of the random component va_{di}

Figures 4.11 and 4.12 show the optimum obtained, the selected nodes and the reactive power associated with these nodes for 30 passes achieved.

Figures 4.11 and 4.12 show a greater dispersion of the obtained optima, with only 23% of optima "better" than the systematic optimum. The same dispersion is found in the selected positions and powers. Adding a random component va_i during the updating of velocity $\overrightarrow{V_{di}}$ thus contributes to a significant improvement in the performance of the PSO algorithm implemented. By allowing a better exploration of the search space set, the component va_i avoids becoming trapped in a "local" optimum too quickly and thus results in a better search for a global optimum.

4.5.4. *Influence of the upper and lower bounds on the velocity* $\overrightarrow{V_{ci}}$ *of particles* ci

The previous section demonstrated the importance of a "good" exploration of the search space set associated with the position of FACTS. The same happens for the search for the optimum power to associate with the selected positions. The movement of position $\overrightarrow{X_{ci}}$ of particles ci essentially depends on the velocity $\overrightarrow{V_{ci}}$ of these particles. Several parameters come into play during the evolution of this velocity. More particularly, the amplitude of the upper and lower bounds on this velocity (which are $V_{cim_{max}}$ and $V_{cim_{min}}$) can change the way the search space is explored. Thus, an amplitude that is too large would generate excessively high travel gradients which would yield a "discontinuous" exploration of the search space. *A contrario*, an amplitude that is too low would confine the movement of a particle to a space "too" restricted around its initial position. The influence of these velocity bounds is illustrated through a set of 30 algorithm passes with a reduction of the amplitude bounds on the velocity $\overrightarrow{V_{ci}}$.

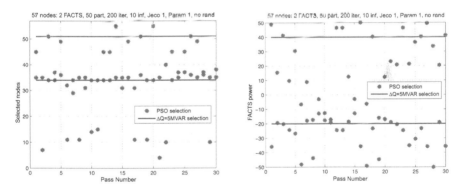

Figure 4.12. *IEEE 57-node network, 50 particles, 200 iterations, 10 informants Comparison of selected positions and powers: cancellation of the random component* va_{di}

During these trials, the initial adjustment and simulation parameters have been modified, more precisely the bounds on velocity $\overrightarrow{V_{ci}}$ of particles ci:

$$- V = \frac{(X_{cim_{min}} - X_{cim_{max}})}{5\,\Delta t} = -20 \text{ for all component } m \text{ and every particle}$$
i $(\Delta t = 1)$;

$$-V = \frac{(X_{cim_{max}} - X_{cim_{min}})}{5\,\Delta t} = 20 \text{ for every component } m \text{ and any particle}$$
$i\,(\Delta t = 1).$

Figures 4.13 and 4.14 show the optimum obtained, the selected nodes and the reactive power associated with these nodes for 30 passes performed. The examination of these curves clearly shows a significant improvement in the performance of the PSO algorithm. Thus, the PSO optimum is better than the systematic optimum in 90% of the cases (compared with the 67% of the first test; see Figure 4.9). Even more remarkable is the consistency of the algorithm with regard to the selection of the positions of the FACTS (see Figure 4.14). An improvement of the same type can be observed in the choice of the powers associated with the selected nodes.

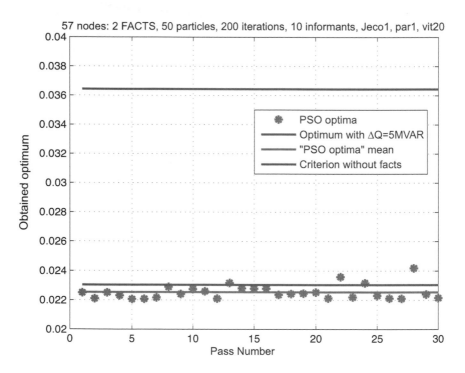

Figure 4.13. *IEEE 57-node network, 50 particles, 200 iterations, 10 informants. Criterion comparison: decrease of max and min boundaries on the velocity $\overrightarrow{V_{ci}}$*

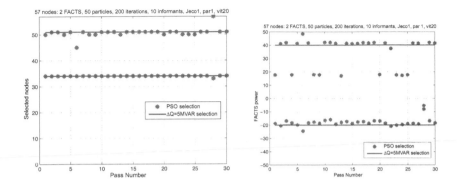

Figure 4.14. *IEEE 57-node network, 50 particles, 200 iterations, 10 informants. Comparison of selected positions: decrease of max and min boundaries on the velocity $\overrightarrow{V_{ci}}$*

The two previous examples for changing the adjustment of the optimization parameters highlight the importance of the choice of the so-called parameters. They also point out the issue of the "optimal" adjustment of these parameters. This issue is, to this day, still open and will have to be the focus of further works. As a general rule, this problem is recurring when implementing a large number of evolutionary-based optimization techniques (PSO, genetic algorithm, etc.) whose behavior is based on a "directed" stochastic exploration of the search space.

4.5.4.1. *Modification of the operating conditions of the electric network*

Solving network equations by means of an OPF method yields a steady-state solution of the network. This solution satisfies the minimization of a power cost functional (equation [4.7]) while satisfying network constraints. It thus represents an "image" of the network in given operating conditions. The result of the FACTS optimal placement and sizing will therefore depend on these operating conditions. In order to illustrate this dependence, a new cost criterion is retained for a set of 30 passes of the PSO algorithm, namely an economic criterion (equation [4.7]) on the active P and reactive powers Q when solving the network equations by means of OPF.

Figures 4.15 and 4.16 show the optimum obtained, the selected nodes and the reactive power associated with these nodes for 30 passes performed. By way of comparison, the value of the criterion obtained without FACTS is also given in Figure 4.15. These results show that the optimal solution, namely nodes 11 and 33, is different from the previous case, thereby clearly bringing forward the dependence of this solution with respect to the network operating conditions. The performance analysis of the PSO algorithm shows that these do not change when modifying operating conditions. As a matter of fact, with the same optimization parameters adjustments, these performances are at the same level as those observed in previous trials (see Figures 4.9 and 4.10) in terms of achieving a PSO optimum better than the systematic "optimum" (67% of performed cases) and reproducibility of the results (that is to say, the consistency of the PSO algorithm).

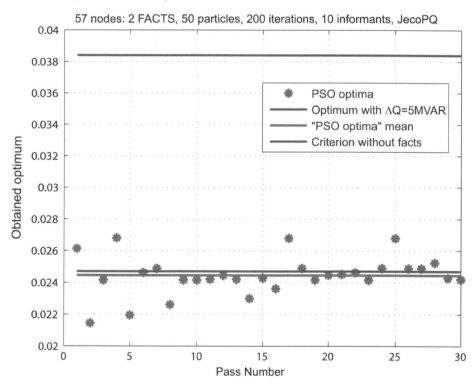

Figure 4.15. *IEEE 57-node network, 50 particles, 200 iterations, 10 informants. Criterion comparison: modification of the economic criterion on P the active and Q the reactive power*

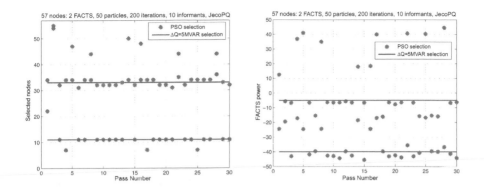

Figure 4.16. *IEEE 57-node network, 50 particles, 200 iterations, 10 informants. Comparison of positions and selected powers: modification of the economic criterion on P the active and Q the reactive power*

4.5.5. *Optimization of the placement of several FACTS of different types (general case)*

We wish now to place and dimension FACTS whose number and type are unknown in the 57-node network in order to minimize the sum of voltage differences in the nodes (criterion J_3). In all cases, unless otherwise stated, the parameters of the algorithm are fixed as follows:

– swarm size: 20;

– number of informants: 3;

– number of iterations: 500.

The results of 15 executions of the PSO2007 and α-SLPSO algorithms are given in Figures 4.17(a)–(d), respectively. These latter show that the two algorithms implemented are consistent (often converging toward a single solution). Nonetheless, a better consistency for the α-SLPSO algorithm should be noted. In fact, the variance obtained by α-SLPSO and PSO2007 is, respectively, equal to 1.39×10^{-7} and 8.19×10^{-7}.

It can be observed that the results obtained by α-SLPSO and PSO2007 are slightly better than in the case in which we have set the FACTS type to two STATCOM (Figure 4.13). As such, the fitness mean is 0.0132 in the general case (that is to say that the type and the number of FACTS are left open), which corresponds to a 65% decrease in the criterion J_3, against 0.0225 when setting the FACTS to two STATCOM, that is nearly 40% decrease in the criterion J_3. Presumably, we might expect that a greater freedom in terms of number, position and type of FACTS allows for a better spatial distribution of the reactive power in the network. This power, acting mainly locally, results in a better uniformity in the voltage profile results thereof.

In addition, it can be observed that the results obtained by PSO2007 are slightly worse than with the α-SLPSO approach. As a matter of fact, the mean of 15 executions of the PSO2007 is 0.0151, which reflects a 59% decrease in the criterion J_3 against a 65% decrease in the criterion J_3 for the α-SLPSO algorithm.

Besides the slightly superior performance in terms of fitness, the major difference between the α-SLPSO and PSO2007 algorithms concerns the convergence of these two algorithms. In effect, Figure 4.18 shows that in the first iterations of the optimization process (the first 120 iterations), the two approaches converge with the same speed. Beyond the 120th iteration, the α-SLPSO approach converges faster than PSO2007. Moreover, the α-SLPSO approach on average converges after 300 iterations, whereas PSO2007, for its part, converges after 500 iterations, which represents a gain of 40% on the convergence speed of the algorithm.

Table 4.9 shows that we use more TCSC-type FACTS. On the other hand, the sum of the power injected by all of the TCSC is just over $7.52\,\mathrm{MVar}$, which represents a fairly low implemented FACTS power reactive value. The same holds for STATCOM- and SVC-type FACTS. This result confirms the "local" action of the reactive power on the behavior of the network. Moreover, Table 4.10 shows that the sum of the installed power is rather large. The associated economical cost can be very significant. For these reasons, it is interesting to address the FACTS placement problem in a multiobjective form associating an economic criterion with the physical criterion. This perspective is initiated and presented in Appendix 2.

	STATCOM	SVC	TCSC
LPD-PSO	85.,54	138.48	7.52
PSO standard 2007	76.31	96.29	12.19

Table 4.8. *Mean from fifteen installed power passes for each FACTS type*

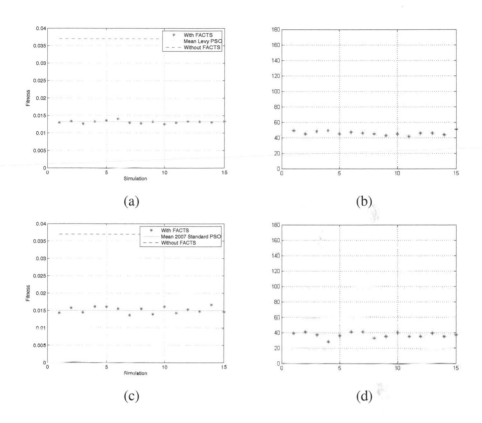

(a)   (b)

(c)   (d)

Figure 4.17. *a) Optimal fitness found based on the α-SLPSO simulations; b) number of optimal FACTS found based on the α-SLPSO simulations, c) optimal fitness found based on PSO2007 simulations and d) number of optimal FACTS found based on PSO2007 simulations*

	STATCOM	SVC	TCSC
LPD-PSO	10.33	15.00	20.73
PSO standard 2007	8.46	10.46	17.86

Table 4.9. *Mean from the fifteen passes of the number of FACTS used for each type of FACTS*

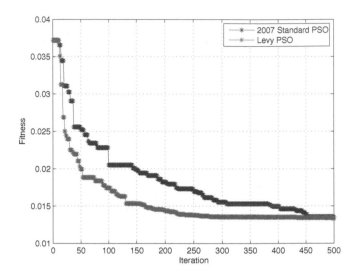

Figure 4.18. *Fitness evolution of the standard PSO2007 algorithm (in blue) and the α-SLPSO PSO algorithm (in red)*

	Fitness	Sum of injected powers	Number of FACTS
LPD-PSO	0.0132	231.54	46.06
PSO standard 2007	0.0151	184.80	36.80

Table 4.10. *Injected powers total sum $(MVar)$, number of installed FACTS and mean of the fitness obtained with algorithms: PSO standard from Clerk 2007 and α-SLPSO*

4.6. Conclusion

FACTS, by mainly acting on the distribution of reactive power in the network, emerge as devices allowing for, on the one hand, in steady state, an "optimization" of power flows and a better control of the voltage in network nodes and, on the other hand, in transient state, a significant improvement in the stability of the network. To be able to select, dimension and place these FACTS in an electrical network is still an open problem today.

In this chapter, the optimization metaheuristics have been applied to provide a solution to this type of problem, within a context of steady-state operation of the network (transient stability problems are not considered here). As part of the applications presented in this report, the FACTS (here STATCOM, SVC and TCSC) are placed and dimensioned to maximize a functional relative to the maximization of the safety of the electric network (voltage balancing in the nodes). The proposed approach combines a solution for the network equations using an OPF method and a search for the optimal solution for the placement and sizing of FACTS by means of PSO techniques. The hybrid character of the optimization problem (due to the duality of search spaces, that is, continuous for sizing and combinatorial for placement) is solved by combining two specific PSO techniques. The continuous aspect applies a conventional PSO approach, widely used in many applications. The discrete aspect of the problem is addressed by the "velocity likelihoods" type method.

A better exploration of the discrete search space set, capable of thus avoiding that algorithm becoming trapped too quickly in a "local" optimum, is obtained through an improvement of the *velocity likelihoods* methods. This improvement is based on the introduction of an additional random component in the update stage of the particles' velocity (and therefore of the definition of new positions).

In order to take into account the natural coupling (due to the topology of the network) between FACTS placement and sizing (that is to say of the hybrid character of the optimization problem), a first "hybridization" approach of both PSO techniques being used is proposed. The method thus implemented relies on a hierarchization between these two techniques, in the sense that placement is a priority compared to sizing.

The PSO algorithm has been applied and validated to the case of two benchmark IEEE networks: the 30-node network and the 57-node network. Due to its larger size, the 57-node network presents the first significant case study concerning the difficulty of the optimal search problem, in the sense that combinatorial and continuous search spaces are already quite extensive. The studies have been conducted for a fixed number and type of FACTS, namely two STATCOM to be placed and dimensioned in an optimal manner. The simulation results obtained from these two networks point out the performance of the proposed algorithm in terms of the search for an optimal solution and the consistency of the algorithm.

Changing the adjustment parameters of the algorithm shows that the obtained performance is significantly sensitive to these adjustments. Such sensitivity is not specific to the algorithm proposed here and is often recurs in the implementation of optimization techniques of the evolutionary type such as PSO or genetic algorithms. The problem of the optimal adjustment of these algorithms still remains an open problem that must be addressed later in the study.

In this chapter, an algorithm based on a population of agents (α-SLPSO) and a local search (α-SLLS) have been proposed. Very good and very encouraging results are presented in sections 4.4.3.4. As a matter of fact, a classification method (ELECTRE II) applied to a set of test functions highlights the performance of α-SLPSO compared to five other variants of PSO (PSO-2S, EPUS-PSO, CLPSO, CPSO-H and the standard SPO2007).

The α-SLPSO algorithm has been utilized within the context of the placement and sizing of FACTS of different types. The results obtained show that the α-SLPSO algorithm shows performances very close, to some extent even better, than those obtained with standard PSO2007. In addition, the α-SLPSO algorithm performs well in terms of convergence speed (gain of the order of 40%). This performance is correlated with the nature of the α-SLPSO algorithm that relies on the use of Lévy α-stable distributions, which enable a search strategy to introduce intermittency (alternation of local searches and significant ballistic "jumps").

Genetic Algorithm-based Wind Farm Topology Optimization

5.1. Introduction

A wind farm installation consists of using the wind to rotate a large-sized propeller. When the wind reaches the propeller, the particular shape of the blades allows it to easily be put into motion. At a height, the wind is stronger because it is free from the roughness of the ground. The propeller is therefore placed on top of a tower of several tens of meters. The addition of an automatic system enables the wind turbine to be placed facing the wind, which increases its efficiency. When the propeller starts to turn, it acquires the energy of the motion transmitted by the wind. The latter is then transformed into electric energy due to the dynamo effect and sent into the network.

Several wind turbines can be grouped on the same site to form a wind farm. In this case, maintenance is simpler and billing is easier. On the other hand, the operating strategy and the management of the complexity and risks incurred by such a farm become a sensitive matter. These difficulties include connecting wind turbines to the electric grid, which is not an easy task for operators. As a matter of fact, given the high cost of wires, the cost of feeders and their eventual unavailability, a bad interconnection in a wind farm can result in very significant safety and pecuniary losses.

In this chapter, the main objective of the work carried out was to satisfy a specific requirement, namely the implementation of a computational tool which makes it possible to "optimally" determine the interconnection of a wind farm. This study has been voluntarily achieved over a limited time period in order to validate, on the one hand, the contribution of optimization techniques, especially that of genetic algorithms, and, on the other hand, to develop a computational tool that can be directly exploited by the user.

5.2. Problem statement

Wind energy is one of the main components of renewable energy sources. Apart from the difficulty in designing wind farms (position facing the wind, wind turbine height, etc.), the connection to the electric network turns out to be a difficult task from an expert point of view.

5.2.1. *Context*

Wind power project developers can resort to tools for decision support during the design of their farm, in particular for the optimization of the internal electrical architecture. Their requirements mainly take into consideration the definition:

– of the internal network topology of the farm (20 kV or 33 kV);

– of the cable type of this internal network (section);

– of the location of the substation (MV/HV) in the case of an offshore wind farm with platform;

– of the substation configuration (MV/HV);

– of compensation requirements.

The first three points can be formulated in the form of an optimization problem and solved via a metaheuristic.

In this design phase of the farm, developers have knowledge:

– of the masts layout map (X, Y coordinates of wind turbines);

– of the location of the substation (MV/HV) for connection to the electric grid and thus of the connection voltage level (HV);

– of the turbine type (P, Q, U diagrams);

– of cables' parameters (section, impedance, cost, etc.).

The parameters of the cables (section, impedance, cost, etc.) are standardized. As an application of our decision-support tool, the values in Table 5.1 will be used for buried cables. However, this type of table is dedicated to a particular project.

Section (mm^2)	R (Ω/km)	L (mH/km)	C$(\mu F/km)$	Ampacity I (A)	Cost (e/m)
50	0.82	0.48	0.14	119.07	3.65
95	0.41	0.41	0.17	174.15	4.59
150	0.26	0.38	0.21	221.13	5.1
240	0.16	0.35	0.27	290.79	6.5
240 copper	0.10	0.35	0.27	372.6	15.4

Table 5.1. *Reference parameters by phase for buried cables 33 kV (onshore farm)*

The option of placing two cables in parallel can be considered, if the power to evacuate requires it. In this case, a declassifying factor is applied to the maximal current-carrying capacity in parallel lines (typically 0.83).

In this chapter, a group of wind turbines radially connected to a substation is called a "cluster". Figure 5.1 represents a four-clustered topology. The cost of an MV feeder is estimated at €20,000.

It should be noted that the present problem can be modeled in the form of a multiobjective problem. As a matter of fact, increasing the number of clusters:

– increases the number of feeders (cost deterioration);

– decreases cable section (cost reduction);

– increases the availability of the farm (the loss of a feeder is less critical) and makes maintenance easier.

In this case, the number of feeders (clusters) is no longer a decision variable but rather a criterion to be optimized, which will reduce, without any doubt, the number of possibilities for interconnections (Table 5.3). On the other hand, this will complicate the problem's solution. This is the reason why initially we focused on solving the problem in its single-objective form.

In the case of an offshore farm, it is possible for an MV/HV substation to be installed on a platform. The positioning of this platform is free (provided a safety distance of 100 m from the nearest wind turbine). The offshore platform

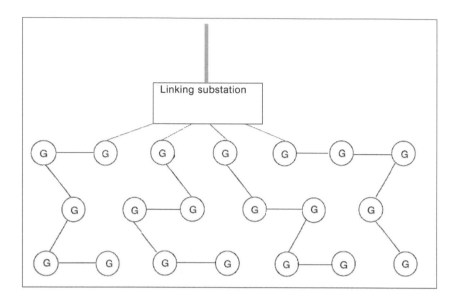

Figure 5.1. *Four-cluster solution*

substation is then connected in HV to the onshore substation of the electrical network (via an HV submarine cable).

The criterion to be minimized is a cost criterion consisting of four basic costs, namely:

– cable cost (depending on their length and their section);

– Joule losses cost (according to the resistance and current flowing in the cable);

– feeder cost (depending on the number of clusters);

– non-distributed energy cost (depending in particular on the number of clusters).

As in the majority of real optimization problems, the objectives to minimize are subject to a set of constraints, which complicates the problem's solution. In this case, the minimization of the "cost" must take into account the following constraints:

– it is necessary to ensure that the number of different sections used in cables remains below a certain value (typically no more than five types of sections);

– the types of cable used must be those in Table 5.1;

– the crossing of cables is to be avoided;

– the voltage drop in a cluster must be less than 2%;

– each wind turbine can have only one or two feeders (see Figure 5.2);

– all turbines must be connected (directly or via other turbines) to the connection substation;

– the positioning of masts is not reversible;

– the current-carrying capacity for each cable must be higher than the current flowing through the cable under consideration.

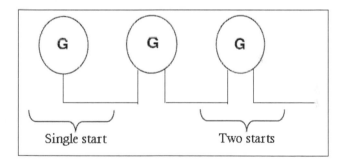

Figure 5.2. *Connection of a wind turbine (1/2 feeders)*

5.2.2. *Calculation of power flow in wind turbine connection cables*

For power flow calculations, we consider the most critical case in terms of losses, permanent maximum current and voltage drop, namely:

– each turbine is operating at P_{max}, Q_{max};

– a minimal voltage at the supply point (MV/HV substation).

Furthermore, it should be noted that cables are modeled by an electrical π model.

5.2.2.1. *Calculation of non-distributed energy*

The optimization algorithm requires, among other things, a cost criterion (or objective function). The latter is based on the cost of Joule losses in cables and on the cost of the initial investment related to the lengths and types of cable used. It is also important to recall that the voltages calculated at each of the nodes verify imposed constraints (the voltage drop along a cluster must be less than 2%).

Joule losses are determined by the calculation of the current in each cable (through an AC *Power Flow* based calculation.) This latter also provides the voltage in each node. Losses and resulting voltages will be used for the calculation of the objective function described hereafter.

The goal is to determine the cost of non-distributed energy updated over 20 years. In fact, if a failure occurs in circuit breakers or in transformers, the energy produced by wind turbines cannot be distributed. This represents a loss of profit that must be quantified.

Each feeder is associated with an average downtime μ per year (typically $\mu_c = 5$ h/year). The average downtime μ_f of the farm is therefore:

$$\mu_f = N_d \times \mu_c \tag{5.1}$$

From which, the non-distributed energy cost Σ_e is expressed as:

$$\Sigma_e = \sum_{i=1}^{20} \frac{P_{max} \times \kappa \times \mu_f}{(1+\tau)^i} \times \psi \tag{5.2}$$

In the end, the formula for the cost of non-distributed energy is:

$$\Sigma_e = P_{max} \times \kappa \times \mu_f \times \frac{\left(1 - \left(\frac{1}{1+\tau}\right)^{20}\right)}{\tau} \times \psi \tag{5.3}$$

and designated by:

- N_d, the number of feeders (clusters);

- P_{max}, the maximal power (nominal power) of the wind farm;

- κ, the load factor (that is the mean power actually produced from the nominal power);

- τ, the update rate;

- ψ, the redemption price of the KW/h.

The calculation of non-distributed energy is achieved on the basis of the data in Table 5.2.

Redemption price $MWh(e)$	180
Factor load	0.34246575
Update rate	2 %
Cluster downtime (μ_c in h/year)	5

Table 5.2. *Parameters to be used for the calculation of non-distributed energy*

5.2.2.2. *Computation of losses cost*

Joule losses are evaluated according to the formula $\varphi = RI^2$.

The purchase price ψ of the MWh allows the cost of losses to be quantified (Table 5.2). These losses must also be updated over 20 years; which amounts to stating that losses costs Σ_p are calculated as follows (equation [5.4]):

$$\Sigma_p = \varphi \times \kappa \times \frac{\left(1 - \left(\frac{1}{1+\tau}\right)^{20}\right)}{\tau} \times \psi \times N_h \qquad [5.4]$$

At this level of formalism, all the ingredients necessary to understanding, to the calculations of installation costs and to the modeling of the interconnection problem of a wind farm are drafted. In summary, the decision-support tool, which will be detailed in the following sections assumes as parameters and input variables:

– the layout of the masts plan in the form of (X, Y) coordinates;

– the location of the onshore substation in the form of (X, Y) coordinates;

– the wind turbine type (P_{max}, Q_{max});

– the parameters of cables to use (section, R, L, C, ampacity I, cost, $U_{nominal}$);

– the feeder cost;

– the MWh purchase price;

– the projected load factor of the farm;

– the cluster downtime;

– the update rate.

On output, the optimization program that will be implemented return, as output variables:

– the internal network topology of the farm;

– the cable types of this internal network (sections);

minimizing losses Σ in the internal network of the farm (equation [5.5]):

$$\Sigma = \Sigma_e + \Sigma_p \qquad\qquad [5.5]$$

where Σ_e and Σ_p, respectively, are the non-distributed energy cost and the losses cost, defined earlier.

Although the problem that is described in this section is purely combinatorial and non-hybrid, it, nevertheless, presents a complexity which increases very quickly with the number of wind turbines to be connected. As a matter of fact, the number of possibilities (for configurations) is of the order of:

$$(n-1) \times n! \times (Nb\_Type)^n$$

where n denotes the number of existing turbines in the farm and Nb_Type refers to the number of cable types available, namely $(n-1) \times (Nb\_Type)^n$ times more complex than the traveling salesman problem.

Table 5.3 shows the combinatorial explosion of the problem. It is assumed that one configuration is evaluated in $1\ \mu s$.

Number of wind turbines	Number of possibilities	Computational time
5	1,500,000	1.5 sec
10	3.1894e+014	10 years
15	5.5870e+023	17,716 billion years
20	4.4084e+033	1.3979e+020 billion years
30	7.1640e+054	2.2717e+041 billion years

Table 5.3. *Number of possibilities for five cable types based on the number of wind turbines*

5.3. Genetic algorithms and adaptation to our problem

5.3.1. *Solution encoding*

Coding individuals is a crucial phase in the design of a genetic algorithm. It must comprehensively cover the search space and satisfy, among other things, the maximum number of constraints. Crossover and mutation operators should be easily adaptable to the chosen type of encoding.

Within the context of our problem, an individual (chromosome) is represented as follows:

$$(E_1, E_2, ..., E_n | 1, l_1, l_2, ..., l_{n-1}) \qquad [5.6]$$

where $E_i \in \mathbb{N}$, $(E_1, E_2, ..., E_n)$ form a permutation, $l_i \in \{1, -i\}$:

– when l_i is equal to 1, this means that the element E_{i+1} of the permutation is connected to the connection substation;

– when l_i is equal to $-i$, this means that the element E_{i+1} of the permutation is connected to the element E_i of the same permutation.

Such coding ensures that all turbines be connected and that each turbine be connected at most to only two elements (turbine or connection substation).

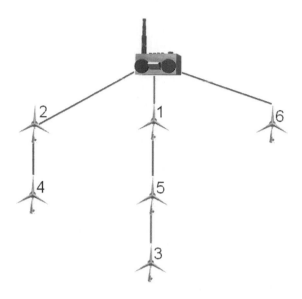

Figure 5.3. *Graph corresponding to the individual Example_Coding.*
For a color version of this figure, see
www.iste.co.uk/heliodore/metaheuristics.zip

EXAMPLE 5.1.– The graph corresponding to the next *Example_Coding*
individual is shown in Figure 5.3:

$$Example\_Coding = (2, 4, 1, 5, 3, 6|1, -1, 1, -3, -4, 1)$$

In this example, the permutation elements E_i, $i \in \{1, ..., 6\}$, respectively,
correspond to wind turbines 2, 4, 1, 5, 3 and 6 and the elements
l_j, $j \in \{1, ..., 6\}$ are, respectively, equal to 1, -1, 1, -3, -4 and 1. The
elements l_1, l_3 and l_6 are equal to 1, which means that turbines 2, 1 and 6 are
connected to the connection substation. Moreover, the element l_4 is equal to
-3, which means that the element E_4 of the permutation, that is turbine 5,
will be connected to the element E_3 of the permutation, that is turbine 1
(Figure 5.3).

It should be observed that the element E_1 in equation [5.6] is always equal
to 1, which means that the turbine corresponding to the first element E_1 of
the permutation is by default connected to the link substation. Furthermore, a
topology that respects the constraints predefined in section 5.2.1 must have at
least one turbine connected to the station.

5.3.2. *Selection operator*

Although this phase does not present any adjustment problems to any selection operator, it is part of the crucial phases of genetic algorithms. In fact, a bad selection of individuals systematically leads to the premature convergence of the algorithm or, if this is the case, to the divergence of the algorithm.

As a general rule, parents are selected for the reproduction phase (crossover) according to their performance (equation [5.7]), where $f(A_i)$ and $P[A_i]$ are, respectively, the performance and the probability with which chromosome A_i will be reintroduced in the new population:

$$aP[A_i] = \frac{f(A_i)}{\sum\limits_{j=1}^{N} f(A_j)} \qquad [5.7]$$

In our case, the selection operator implemented is that of the biased roulette wheel. For this purpose, the procedure is as follows:

– the individuals of the population are sorted according to performance order by means of equation [5.7];

– a surface section is attributed to each individual starting from the best to the worst;

– a random number between $[0, 1]$ is generated;

– a search is carried out to find out which interval the number generated belongs to and the corresponding individual is selected.

For instance, on four individuals, if the sum of performances equals 10 and if the performance of each individual is, respectively, 2.5, 2, 1 and 4.5, the state of the corresponding biased roulette wheel will be represented as shown in Figure 5.4.

The individual corresponding to the surface (a) has a 45% chance of being selected, whereas the individual corresponding to the white surface has only a 10% chance of being selected.

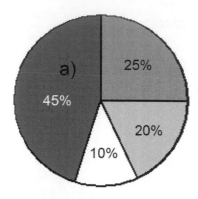

Figure 5.4. *Biased roulette wheel example*

To guarantee the elitism of our algorithm, the best individual will be kept at each generation. Furthermore, to avoid a premature convergence of the algorithm, a few bad individuals will be systematically kept (typically two).

5.3.3. *Crossover*

The crossover operator used in section 5.4 is the one described in [POO 95]. Its principle is the following:

– given two parents $P_1 = (v_1^1, ..., v_n^2)$ and $P_2 = (v_1^2, ..., v_n^2)$;

– randomly select two crossover positions. Let Pos_1 and Pos_2 denote these positions;

– copy the portion $[v_{Pos_1}^1, .., v_{Pos_2}^1]$ of the parent P_1 into the portion $[v_{Pos_1}^2, ..., v_{Pos_2}^2]$ of the parent P_2;

– remove the elements $v_{Pos_1}^1, .., v_{Pos_2}^1$.

The operator is then defined in two stages and one proceeds as follows.

Stage 1 (search for cycles):

– given two parents P_1 and P_2;

– consider the positions of the elements corresponding to the permutations of the two parents as being unmarked;

– let $i = 1$:

a) randomly generate an unmarked position (Pos_i denotes this position and Elt_i the corresponding element in the permutation of individual P_1). Mark the position Pos_i with i;

b) let y be the permutation element of the parent P_2 corresponding to position Pos_i:

– if $y = Elt_i$, let $i = i + 1$ and move to 1 (if there are unmarked positions remaining);

– otherwise let Pos_i be the position corresponding to the element y of the permutation of the parent P_1 and mark the position Pos_i with i and move to 2;

c) at the end of the previous steps, a sequence of numbers is obtained indicating which cycle each element of the two permutations of P_1 and P_2 belongs to. Denote by $Cycle$ this sequence of numbers.

Stage 2 (mix obtained cycles):

– randomly create a crossover mask M whose corresponding elements indicate which parent the child will inherit from in each cycle. There are as many elements in the mask as detected cycles (example: if there are three detected cycles, the mask will be, for instance, $M = P_1 P_2 P_1$);

– convert the sequence of numbers $Cycle$ into a permutation based on the mask in the following manner: $Cycle(i) \leftarrow M(i)$. For example, if the element i of the digit sequence $Cycle$ equals 2 and $M = P_1 P_2 P_1$, then $Cycle(i) \leftarrow P2$. This means that the element 2 of the permutation of the resulting child will inherit element 2 of the permutation of the parent P_2.

EXAMPLE 5.2.– The application of the geometric *crossover* to these two parents is performed in the following manner (Figure 5.5).

Given the two parents in Figure 5.5(a). Let $i = 1$ and generate a position between 1 and 6 (6 being the number of genes or elements in our coding), let $Pos_1 = 5$ be this position. The cycle $i = 1$ is then assigned to this position. The value of the element Elt_1 corresponding to the parent A equals 1 and that corresponding to the parent B equals 3. A search is performed for the gene that takes 3 as value in the parent A, this gene has position 4. The cycle $i = 1$ is then assigned to position 4. The element corresponding to position 4 of parent B is equal to 1, which also corresponds to the initial element Elt_1, a cycle is then obtained (Figure 5.5(b)). Let $i = 2$, in other words, a second cycle is searched for, and the same procedure is repeated until all cycles are obtained (all positions are marked).

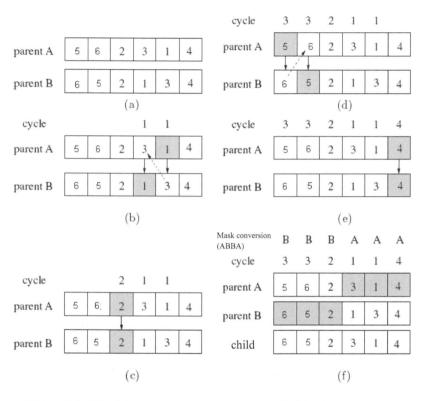

Figure 5.5. *Principle of geometric crossover applied to the two parents A and B. For a color version of this figure, see www.iste.co.uk/heliodore/metaheuristics.zip*

Now suppose that all cycles have been identified (Figure 5.5(e)). The sequence of identified cycles is then equal to, in order, $\{3, 3, 2, 1, 1, 4\}$. The number of cycles obtained is equal to 4, a four-value mask is then generated in $\{A, B\}$, namely *ABBA*, the mask thus generated. This means that the first cycle is attributed to the parent A, the second and third to the parent B and finally the fourth to parent A. To convert the sequence $\{3, 3, 2, 1, 1, 4\}$ in a permutation, the values $1, 2, 3$ and 4 therefore have to be replaced by A, B, B and A, respectively, which yields: $\{3, 3, 2, 1, 1, 4\} \implies \{B, B, B, A, A, A\}$.

Figure 5.6(c) represents the graph of the child obtained by crossing over the parents A and B in Figure 5.5. This figure shows that the resulting child has indeed inherited from both parents. In effect, wind turbines 1 and 4 of the child are only connected to the link substation, which is the signature of the parent A. Moreover, the connection of turbines 6, 5 and 3 has the same signature as parent B.

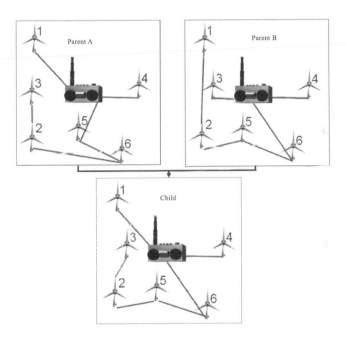

Figure 5.6. *Graphical representation of the example of the crossover in Figure 5.5: a) parent A, b) parent B, and c) the child obtained by crossing over parent A and B. For a color version of this figure, see www.iste.co.uk/heliodore/metaheuristics.zip*

REMARK 5.1.– In our application cases, the geometric *crossover* is applied to the permutations of individuals with high probability, whereas conventional *crossover* described in section 2.2 is applied to the second part (the links l_i) of individuals with low probability.

5.3.4. *Mutation*

Unlike crossover, standard mutation operators can, usually, be adapted to any type of coding. In our coding case, the mutation of individuals is achieved as follows:

– generate a position Pos_1 where the mutation can take place;

– if position Pos_1 corresponds to the "permutation" portion of the individual then (Figure 5.7(a)):

   - generate another position Pos_2, corresponding to the "permutation" part of the individual;

   - permute the two elements corresponding to both positions Pos_1 and Pos_2;

– otherwise, with fair probabilities:

   - increase, if possible, the number of turbines connected to the substation by 1, that is;

   - generate a position in the second part of the individual whose elements are negative;

   - mutate the corresponding element in 1 (Figure 5.7(b));

   - decrease, if possible, by 1 the number of wind turbines, connected to the substation, that is;

   - generate a position in the second part of the individual whose elements are equal to 1, namely position Pos_i;

   - mutate the corresponding element in $-i$ (Figure 5.7(c));

   - randomly change the position of one of the elements equal to 1 of the second portion of the individual (do not alter the first 1 because the first element of the permutation is always connected to the stepup substation) (Figure 5.7(d)).

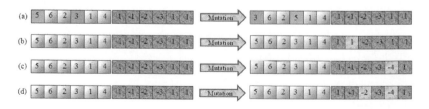

Figure 5.7. *Mutation examples of an individual. For a color version of this figure, see www.iste.co.uk/heliodore/metaheuristics.zip*

Therefore, the mutation operator defined as such allows any topology to be obtained, namely, the modification the turbines order within a cluster (Figure 5.8(b)), the addition of a cluster (Figure 5.8(c)), the removal of a cluster (Figure 5.8(d)) and finally, modification the number of turbines in each cluster (Figure 5.8(e)).

In addition, managing constraints in section 5.2.1 becomes simpler:

– the encoding thus defined in section 5.3.1 takes into account constraints 5 and 6, discussed in section 5.2.1;

– constraint 2 is an input variable; it is therefore considered *a priori* and cannot be breached, similarly for constraint 7;

– constraint 4 is taken into consideration by penalizing the objective function in the event of a breach;

– placing two cables in parallel, eventually several cables, makes it possible to satisfy constraint 8 in the event of overloading (that is to say, current too high);

– constraint 3 is not explicitly taken into account in the optimization process. However, due the high cost of cables, an optimal solution will necessarily involve few crossings, or even none (in a quadrilateral, the sum of the two diagonals is greater than the sum of both sides). In addition, the solutions which comprise cables that are too long will be penalized, which will favor the connection of turbines with their closest neighbors.

5.4. Application

Although on average a farm only comprises around 20 turbines, it is nonetheless considered as part of the world of electric networks. Consequently, similarly to all electric networks, it is governed by the equations and the constraints of the *Power Flow* model described in section 4.3.1. Thus, power flows circulating in a given topology are only valid if they satisfy equations in section 4.3.1. The nonlinear system of this model can easily be solved by descent methods and, in particular, Newton–Raphson-based methods.

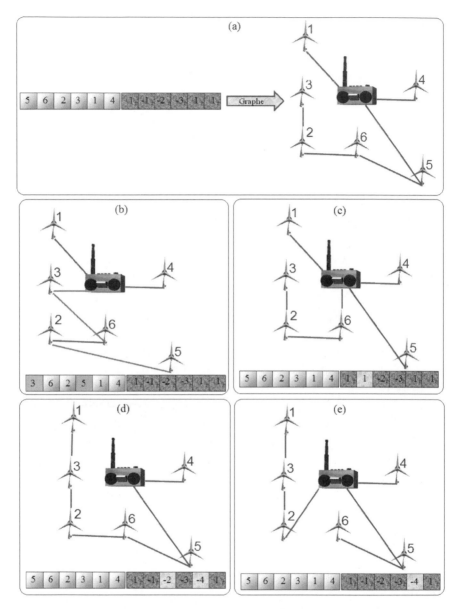

Figure 5.8. *Mutation examples: a) the graph in Figure 5.7, b) modification of the turbines order in a cluster, c) addition of a cluster, d) removal of a cluster and e) modification of the number of turbines in a cluster. For a color version of this figure, see www.iste.co.uk/heliodore/metaheuristics.zip*

The calculation of the current in each cable and of the voltage in each node is carried out by a function (NewtonPF) from the Pylon module, which is a translation in Python 2.6 of the Matlab Matpower program for *Power Flow* computations.

This function assumes the description (topology) of the network of cables interconnecting the turbines as input, that is:

— the definition of buses (bus type, active and reactive power demand, etc.);

– the definition of branches between buses (numbers of buses connected to each branch, resistance p.u., reactance p.u., susceptance p.u., etc.);

– the definition of generators (number of buses to which the generators are connected, active and reactive powers generated, etc.).

The NewtonPF function provides, as output, the voltage p.u. in each node (amplitude and phase) and the admittance matrix.

The currents p.u. in branches (amplitude and phase) are calculated by means of the admittance matrix determined by NewtonPF. A test is also carried out to know if currents in branches are compatible with the current-carrying capacity of the cable type of each branch. If necessary, and taking into account a declassification factor, the number of cables in parallel is corrected such as to comply with this constraint. In this case, if the number of cables in parallel has been changed in at least one branch, the *Power Flow* computation is relaunched.

Throughout applications that follow, the parameters of the algorithm will be fixed as follows:

– number of iterations: 1,000 (arbitrarily fixed, for a reasonable computation time);

– population size: 50;

– mutation probability: $P_m = 0.1$;

– crossover probability: $P_c = 0.8$;

– P_{max} : 1 MW;

– Q_{max} : 0.283 MW;

– number of regenerated individuals: 20% of the initial population;

– cable types: those in Table 5.1 of section 5.2.1;

– redemption price, load factor, update rate and downtime of a cluster: those in Table 5.2 of section 5.2.1;

– feeder cost; €20,000.

5.4.1. *Application to farms of 15–20 wind turbines*

Figure 5.9 shows the wiring proposed by the algorithm of a farm comprising 15 turbines. The *outputs* summary is presented in Table 5.4.

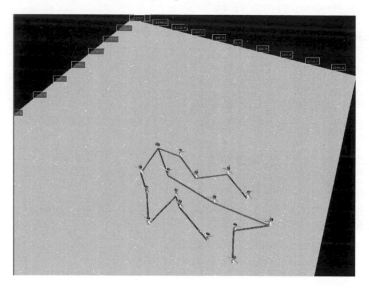

Figure 5.9. *Topology of a farm with 15 turbines obtained by the genetic algorithm. For a color version of this figure, see www.iste.co.uk/heliodore/metaheuristics.zip*

Figure 5.10 shows the wiring proposed by the algorithm of a farm comprising 20 turbines. The outputs summary is presented in Table 5.5.

5.4.2. *Application to a farm of 30 wind turbines*

Figure 5.11 shows the wiring proposed for a farm comprising 30 turbines. The *outputs* summary is presented in Table 5.6. The figure on the top-left represents the evolution of the three economic criteria (non-distributed energy cost, cables cost and joule losses cost) defined in section 5.2.1. The figure center-left represents the evolution of the objective function of the problem being addressed (the sum of the three economic costs defined in section 5.2.1). The bottom-left figure represents voltage drops at the edges of the turbines (as a percentage of the nominal voltage). Finally, the large figure to the right represents the topology of the wind farm proposed by the genetic algorithm.

$Energy\_cost\_nd$ (€)	Losses costs (€)	Cables costs (€)	Total costs (€)
226,792	132,911	106,425	466,128

Lost power (Joule)	Max voltage (p.u)	Min voltage (p.u)	Number of feeders	Iter
0.015	0.952	0.95	3	998

Table 5.4. *Outputs summary of a solution corresponding to a farm of fifteen turbines*

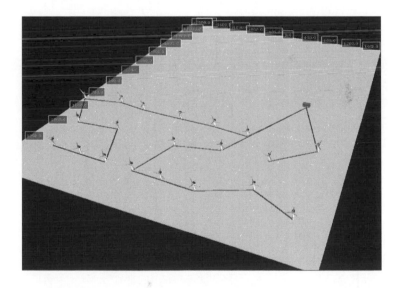

Figure 5.10. *Topology of a farm with 20 turbines obtained by the genetic algorithm. For a color version of this figure, see www.iste.co.uk/heliodore/metaheuristics.zip*

Table 5.7 represents the detail of the solution outputs corresponding to Figure 5.11.

$Energy\_cost\_nd$ (€)	Losses costs (€)	Cables costs (€)	Total costs (€)
302,389	534,951	316,303	1,213,644

Lost power (Joule losses) (MW)	Max voltage (p.u)	Min voltage (p.u)	Number of feeders	Iter
0.060	0.955	0.95	3	-

Table 5.5. *Outputs summary of a proposed solution corresponding to a farm of twenty turbines*

$Energie\_cost\_nd$ (€)	Losses costs (€)	Costs 3 clusters (€)	Cables costs (€)	Total costs (€)
453,584	494,474	60,000	294,366	1,302,425

Lost power (Joule losses) (MW)	Max voltage (p.u)	Min voltage (p.u)	Number of feeders	Iter
0.056	0.954	0.95	3	978

Table 5.6. *Outputs summary of a solution proposed by genetic algorithm, corresponding to a farm of thirty turbines*

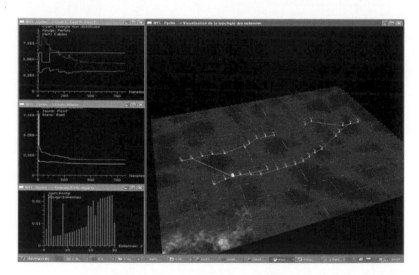

Figure 5.11. *Topology of a farm with 30 turbines obtained by the genetic algorithm. For a color version of this figure, see www.iste.co.uk/heliodore/metaheuristics.zip*

Cluster No.	Start turbine	End turbine	Distance m	Section mm^2
1	Cluster	1	385	240
	1	19	973	50
Totals	-	-	1,359	-
2	Cluster	2	159	240
	2	3	290	240 c
	3	4	198	240 c
	4	5	185	240 c
	5	6	187	240
	6	7	187	240
	7	8	187	240
	8	9	189	240
	9	10	186	240
	10	11	186	240
	11	12	187	150
	12	13	187	240 c
	13	14	577	240
	14	15	190	240
	15	16	282	240
	16	18	400	240
	18	17	200	150
	17	30	894	95
Totals	-	-	4,878	-
3	Cluster	21	893	240
	21	20	200	240
	20	22	400	240 c
	22	23	245	150
	23	24	437	240
	24	25	164	240
	25	26	227	240
	26	27	200	240
	27	28	192	95
	28	29	820	95
Totals	-	-	3,781	-

Table 5.7. *Outputs details of a solution proposed by genetic algorithm, corresponding to a farm of thirty wind turbines*

5.4.3. *Solution of a farm of 30 turbines proposed by human expertise*

Figure 5.12 shows the wiring proposed by human expertise for the same farm comprising 30 wind turbines. The summary of the outputs is presented in Table 5.8.

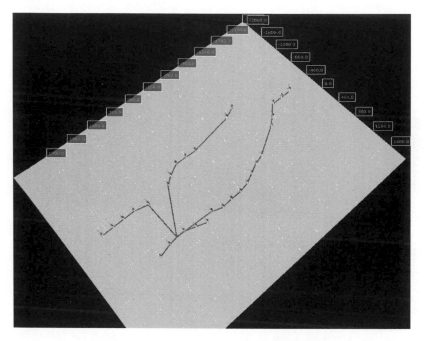

Figure 5.12. *Topology of a farm of 30 turbines proposed by human expertise. For a color version of this figure, see www.iste.co.uk/heliodore/metaheuristics.zip*

It should be observed from Tables 5.7 and 5.8 that the genetic algorithm reduces the costs by 22.5% compared to the solution proposed by human expertise.

Table 5.9 presents the details of outputs from the solution corresponding to Figure 5.12, which can then be compared to Table 5.7.

$Energy\_cost\_nd$ (€)	Cables costs (€)	Cost 5 clusters (€)	Cables costs (€)	Total costs (€)
755,973	651,615	100,000	173,150	**1,680,739**

Lost power (Joule losses) (MW)	Max voltage (p.u)	Max voltage (p.u)	Number of feeders	Iter
0.0737	0.955	0.95	5	-

Table 5.8. *Outputs summary of a solution proposed by human expertise, corresponding to a farm of thirty turbines*

5.4.4. *Validation*

The solutions obtained, on the one hand, by an expert and, on the other, numerically by means of a "genetic algorithm" are absolutely consistent. It has been found that the numerical solution exhibits an advantage that makes it possible to reduce costs by about 22%: this result is therefore significant.

The choice on genetic algorithms was conditioned by the discrete nature of the problem. Nevertheless, it seems natural to substitute them with population-based techniques (particle swarms, ant colonies, etc.).

5.5. **Conclusion**

In this chapter, a tool for decision making using genetic algorithms has been proposed. This tool can be utilized by electric network operators aiming to optimize the internal topology of their wind farms. Initially, an encoding model efficient for this kind of problem was proposed. We have seen through supported examples that this type of encoding gives significant flexibility regarding constraint management and the implementation of our genetic algorithm. Second, the implementation of a Python function performing an AC *Power Flow* computation was carried out. It is based only on Python code whose sources are accessible and free (Pylon module). We are therefore totally free from the MATLAB/MATPOWER environment whose usage implies costs that can be quite high. Although this is not mentioned in this chapter, a validation of this code by comparing the results given by a similar MATLAB/MATPOWER program has been successfully conducted.

Thus, entirely developed based on the Python platform, the executable available (version 1.0) allows for the determination of relevant solutions

Cluster no.	Start wind turbine	End wind turbine	Distance m	Section mm^2
1	Cluster	2	159	50
	2	1	226	50
Totals	-	-	385	-
2	Cluster	3	131	50
	3	4	198	50
	4	5	185	50
Totals	-	-	**514**	-
3	Cluster	6	658	240
	6	7	188	240
	7	8	188	150
	8	9	189	150
	9	10	187	150
	10	11	187	95
	11	12	187	95
	12	13	187	95
	13	14	577	95
	14	15	190	50
	15	16	282	50
	16	17	200	50
	17	18	200	50
Totals	-	-	**3 420**	-
4	Cluster	23	714	50
	23	22	245	50
	22	21	200	50
	21	20	200	50
	20	19	200	50
Totals	-	-	**1 559**	-
5	Cluster	24	873	95
	24	25	164	50
	25	26	227	50
	26	27	200	50
	27	28	192	50
	28	29	820	50
	29	30	215	50
Totals	-	-	**2 693**	-

Table 5.9. *Outputs details of a solution proposed by human expertise, corresponding to a farm of thirty wind turbines*

concerning the internal connection of a wind farm. A second version will enable the time necessary for the computation to obtain an "optimal" solution to be reduced.

The following elements are to be considered:

– based on the choices made, the number of iterations and the size of the population can be parametrized;

– the initialization of the genetic algorithm makes it possible to decrease the exploration domain in a meaningful way. The introduction of physical considerations should enable an acceleration of convergence;

– the graphical interface developed does not constitute a final version. It can be re-laid out at will, depending on the user's *desiderata*.

The design of the genetic algorithm (selection, crossover and mutation) may be the subject of further reflection. A preliminary study will then be required in order to identify sustainable avenues concerning the optimality of the solution.

Topological Study
of Electrical Networks

6.1. Introduction

In the face of large numbers of interconnections, electric energy transmission networks are experiencing increasing levels of complexity. For economic reasons, they are often operated close to their operational limit conditions. Most faults, such as cascade tripping or electrical faults, in these systems have serious consequences [TEA 06]. Although any power failure can be attributed to a particular cause (equipment failure, human error, etc.), the electric network should be considered as a complex system and special attention should be paid to its overall behavior, both static and dynamic. This is the main objective of the theory of complex networks [BOC 06]. In this sense, the study of electrical networks has had and is gaining considerable momentum [ALB 04, CAR 02, CRU 05, KIN 05].

Similarly to many systems, an electrical network must face faults which, given its great connectivity, can extend to entire regions: this is known as a *blackout* (a snow ball effect), that is to say one which has large-scale consequences. The size of electrical networks and their complexity can make it difficult to understand these phenomena which also can emerge locally. With regard to issues such as voltage collapse, network congestion or the *blackout* phenomenon, the topological complexity of the electrical network is one of the reasons why electrical networks operate within limiting operational conditions. There is a certain number of existing works that are based on the intensive use of statistical physics tools. The adaptation of percolation methods, characteristic degreeless networks and self-organized critical systems are the tools of choice to describe the statistical and topological properties of a network.

The main objective of this chapter is to determine the ability of electrical networks to overcome disruptions or failures (load variations, power lines outage, etc.) through the study of static robustness (namely without taking into account power flows transiting in the network). To this end, we first begin by a "non-comprehensive" study of phenomenological characteristics, or still of observables, which are extracted from the corpus of measures traditionally used for the description of complex networks. We will also study the vulnerability of the network through a study of robustness to attacks and failures. Second, in order to complete this static analysis, we will study the fractality of the network in question by applying three algorithms for the determination of the associated fractal dimension. In addition, we propose a model that may be representative of the dynamics of electrical networks in the last part of the chapter.

6.2. Topological study of networks

Complex systems are a major concern for engineers. For example, electrical networks can be considered as being complex systems with limiting operational conditions where steady increase in electricity demand associated with improving the quality of the network (dimensioning, maintenance, stability, etc.) can become an antagonistic force, leading then to sensitive perturbations. From the analysis of works issued in the scientific literature, different modeling avenues can be put forward, some focusing on the topological nature of the network, others following the direction provided by the dynamics of phenomena involved.

These works, essentially developed in the United States, emerge as the builders of the bridge bringing together the field of statistical physics and the electrical world. Rightly so, we can cite:

– *highly optimized tolerant* (HOT) models, introduced by Carlson and Doyle in 1999 [DOY 00, MAN 05, CAR 99], which are intended to model complex and robust systems within an uncertain environment;

– Dobson *et al.*'s models [DOB 01, CAR 01] based on stochastic processes whose authors have established close links between *self-organized critically* systems (SOC) and the electrical network;

– the structural approaches of the problem making use of graph theory.

In any case, the common denominator of these is the analysis of complexity to better serve it. The first order in this complexity is the existence of scale distributions, thus explaining a dynamic between these different levels of scales through, for instance, the appearance of low power distributions.

6.2.1. *Random graphs*

The concept of random graphs was introduced for the first time by Erdös and Rényi in 1959 [ERD 59]. Their first approach for the construction of a random graph consisted of establishing a number of links K to be connected and then in randomly selecting two nodes to be connected at each stage of the construction. This type of graph is denoted by $G_{N,K}^{ER}$. Another alternative to this approach involves the selection of two nodes and connecting them with probability $0 < p < 1$. This type of graph is denoted by $G_{N,p}^{ER}$.

In the case of small-sized random networks $G_{N,p}^{ER}$, the distribution of degrees $p(k)$ is a binomial distribution with parameter p unlike large-sized random networks $G_{N,p}^{ER}$, which have distribution degrees following the Poisson distribution with parameter $p(n-1)$.

In the following, the Erdös and Rényi graphs $G_{N,K}^{ER}$ and $G_{N,p}^{ER}$ are designated by ER.

6.2.2. *Generalized random graphs*

Despite ER graphs being the most studied models, they are still less representative of real networks. Therefore, it would be interesting to be able to reproduce the characteristics (degree distribution) of a certain type of network.

Random generalized networks allow us to build networks having a degree distribution   [BEN 78] $p(k)$ by   defining   a   sequence   of   integers $D = \{k_1, ..., k_N\}$ such that $\sum_{i}^{N} k_i = 2K$.

For the various construction methods of networks with a certain degree distribution $p(k)$, we will refer to Newman *et al.*'s works [NEW 02, NEW 03].

6.2.3. *Small-world networks*

One of the most surprising of Milgram's experiences was to deliver letters to a hundred people whose senders did not know the identity of the recipients and then to assess the number of steps necessary until targeted people received their package. The delivery of someone's letter to someone else is done in the following way: if the person holding the letter knows the recipient's identity, it is directly delivered to the latter; otherwise, it is given to another person who has a strong chance of knowing them. Milgram observed that only six steps (on average) are enough to ensure that recipients receive their parcel, hence, the "six degrees" theorem.

This impressive result can be explained by the "small-world" (small diameter) effect of a number of complex networks. Such networks are called "small world". They are usually characterized by:

– their small diameter that can be substituted by a small mean of geodesic paths;

– a large clustering coefficient C.

The *Watts and Strogatz* (WS) model [WAT 98] is one of the methods generating graphs denoted by $G_{N,K}^{WS}$ taking into account these two characteristics of small-world networks (small diameter and large clustering coefficient C).

6.2.4. *Scale-free networks*

Several real networks (Internet networks, protein interaction networks, etc.) have a degree distribution of power distribution of the form $P(k) \sim ck^{-\alpha}$. These networks are called *scale-free networks* and are characterized by the presence of a very small number of nodes of strong degrees. The concept of "scale-free" comes from power laws that are the only functionals $f(x)$ remaining unchanged (up to a multiplicative factor) after a change of scale.

Barabási-Albert (BA) models [ALB 02] are examples of models that produce scale-free networks. The basic principle for the construction of this kind of networks is that, starting from m_0 isolated nodes, we successively add $N - m_0$ nodes having degrees $m_k \leq m_0$, $k = 1...N - m_0$, and which are next connected to an already existing node proportionally to the degree of the latter. Thus, nodes with strong degrees will tend to become more easily connected to a new arriving node. In other words, arriving nodes connect to existing nodes in the graph in a *preferential* manner.

For more details on the definitions and models previously introduced, the reader can refer to [BOC 06, DOR 08, DOR 03, NEW 03].

6.2.5. *Some results inspired by the theory of percolation*

In [COH 00, COH 01], a general condition κ is defined, based on the theory of percolation, namely on the fraction of nodes to be removed before a complex network disintegrates (equation [6.1]). It is shown in particular that, in degree distribution networks of power $P(k) \sim ck^{-\alpha}$ ("scale-free" networks), the fraction p_c of nodes to be removed (faults) is expressed according to the connectivity k and quantity f_c (equation [6.2]).

This means that for $\alpha \leq 3$, the network almost never disintegrates, regardless of the fraction of nodes removed ($p_c \sim 0.99$ %). As a matter of fact, in this case, κ_0 in equation [6.2] converges, proportionally to K, to infinity. Consequently, the quantity $1 - p_c$ in equation [6.1] in turn converges to 0.

It should be recalled that the degree distribution of scale-free networks is given by $P(k) \sim ck^{-\alpha}$, designating by $k = m, m+1, ..., K$ node connectivity, and m, K, respectively, the minimal and maximal network connectivities. The quantity $< k^n >$ designates the n-order moment of variable k.

The general condition for the existence of a large connected component is:

$$\kappa \equiv \frac{< k^2 >}{< k >} = 2 \Rightarrow f_c = 1 - p_c = \frac{1}{\kappa_0 - 1} \qquad [6.1]$$

for "scale-free" networks:

$$\kappa_0 \rightarrow \left| \frac{2-\alpha}{3-\alpha} \right| \times \begin{cases} m, & \text{if } \alpha > 3 \\ m^{\alpha-2}K^{3-\alpha}, & \text{if } 2 < \alpha < 3 \\ K, & \text{if } 1 < \alpha < 2 \end{cases} \qquad [6.2]$$

In [COH 02], Cohen *et al.* expressed the percolation threshold by the probability P_∞ (equation [6.3]) that a node of connectivity k belongs to the largest connected component that depends of a criticality exponent β, which itself depends on α in the case of scale-free networks (equation [6.5]). On the one hand, results are found again for $\alpha \leq 3$ [COH 00] and on the other hand, it is shown that for $3 < \alpha < 4$, the criticality exponent β strongly depends on α. Moreover, they have been able to express the mean of connected components $< s >$ after removing a fraction p_c of nodes (governed by an exponent γ, equation [6.6]), by equation [6.4]:

$$P_\infty \sim (q - q_c)^{-\beta} \qquad [6.3]$$

$$< s >= (q - q_c)^{-\gamma} \qquad [6.4]$$

by designating $q = 1 - p$ (p being the fraction of nodes removed or faulty).

Thus, for "scale-free" networks, the exponents of equations [6.3] and [6.4] can be reduced to:

$$\beta = \begin{cases} \frac{1}{3-\alpha}, & 2 < \alpha < 3 \\ \frac{1}{\alpha-3}, & 3 < \alpha < 4 \\ 1, & \alpha > 4 \end{cases} \qquad [6.5]$$

$$\gamma = \begin{cases} 1, & \alpha > 3 \\ -1, & 2 < \alpha < 3 \end{cases} \qquad [6.6]$$

In [SCH 02], Schwartz *et al.* have performed the same work as in [COH 02] to express critical exponents β and γ on oriented graphs correlated to the power law (equation [6.8]). They defined a phase diagram that indicates the existence of three states (Figure 6.1) determined by the degree distribution exponent α^*:

$$\alpha^* = \alpha_{in} + \frac{\alpha_{in} - \alpha_{out}}{\alpha_{in} - 1} \qquad [6.7]$$

designating by α_{in}, α_{out}, respectively, the connectivity of the incoming and outgoing arcs.

They concluded that in this type of network, the critical exponent β is the same as in the case of correlated graphs, by substituting α by α^*:

$$\beta = \begin{cases} \frac{1}{\alpha_{out}-2}, & 2 < \alpha_{out} < 3 \\ 1, & \alpha_{out} > 3 \end{cases} \qquad [6.8]$$

The study of the diameter of a complex network is one of the most important. In fact, a network becomes effective for energy (or information) transportation when its diameter is small. The small diameter characterizes *small-world* networks .

In [COH 03], Cohen *et al.* studied the diameter of random "scale-free" networks and showed that the latter is very small compared to regular random networks:

– for ER random networks, small-world networks:

$$d \sim ln\, N$$

– for "scale-free" networks:

$$d \sim \begin{cases} ln\, ln\, N, & 2 < \alpha < 3 \\ ln\, n, & \alpha > 3 \end{cases}$$

and designating by:

– d: the network diameter;

– N: the number of nodes;

– α: the power law parameter.

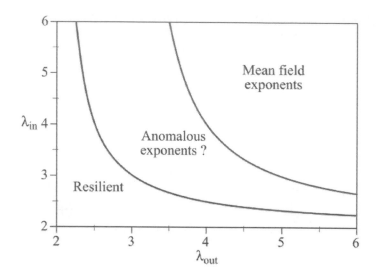

Figure 6.1. *Phase diagram of the various states in networks oriented and correlated to a power law*

In [BRA 03], the authors studied the average length of the optimal paths l_{opt} of ER and WS random networks as well as of small-world networks in the presence of heterogeneities (disorder):

– in the case of uncorrelated and disorderless networks, the average length of optimal paths is:

- for the three networks (ER, WS and small-world): $l_{opt} \sim ln\, N$,

- for "scale-free" networks: $l_{opt} \sim \begin{cases} ln\, ln\, N, & 2 < \alpha < 3 \\ ln\, n, & \alpha > 3 \end{cases}$

– in the case of uncorrelated and disorderless networks, the average length of optimal paths is:

- for ER and WS networks: $l_{opt} \sim N^{\frac{1}{3}}$;

- for "scale-free" networks: $(*)\, l_{opt} \sim \begin{cases} ln^{\alpha-1} N, & 2 < \alpha < 3 \\ N^{\frac{\alpha-3}{\alpha-1}}, & 3 < \alpha < 4 \\ N^{\frac{1}{3}}, & \alpha > 4 \end{cases}$

– in the case of correlated and disordered networks, the average optimal path length is:

- for "scale-free" networks: $l_{opt} \sim \begin{cases} N^{\frac{1}{3}}, & \lambda > 0 \, and \, \alpha > 2 \\ N^{\nu_{opt}}, & \lambda \leq 0 \end{cases} \nu_{opt}$

being the same exponent as in $(*)$.

In the presence of low heterogeneity, the length of the optimal path is the same as in disorderless networks. In contrast, in the presence of strong heterogeneity, the length of the optimal path l_{opt} is affected by disorder. The same authors [WU 06] have modeled correlations between distribution degrees in a network and have studied the average length of optimal paths of a scale-free network with correlations between distribution degrees. They have concluded that the length of the optimal path l_{opt} increases very significantly in strong heterogeneous networks.

Wang et al. [WAN 08a] have modeled the disorder of a weighted network with a blocking coefficient J:

$$ J = \text{"} \frac{\sum_{i=1}^{N} [\sum_{j \in \Omega(i)} \omega_{reu(j)}(i) - C_i]}{\sum_{i=1}^{N} C_i} > \nu >_{network} \quad [6.9] $$

designating by $\Omega(i)$ the set of neighbors of the node i:

$[x] = x$ if $x > 0$, 0 otherwise

$\omega_{reu(j)}(i)$ is the weight of the link (node i to node j), C_i the total weight coming out of node i, $< ... >_{\nu}$ is the average under the distribution ν, ν, $< ... >_{network}$ is the average under different network configurations.

They show, as in [BRA 03], that blocking (that is disintegration) in a network increases with its heterogeneity. Wang et al. [WAN 08b] studied the robustness of "scale-free" networks by attacking not the nodes of the network, but its links by partitioning the graph in two to find a minimum cut. They concluded that this kind of attack does not necessarily destroy the network and that the latter still remains a "scale-free" network with a very small diameter.

The heterogeneity can be measured by an entropy of the network [FER 03]. In [WAN 06], the authors have showed that maximizing robustness in a "scale-free" network is equivalent to maximizing the entropy of the network degree distribution (equation [6.11]). The entropy of a network is given by the quantity (equation [6.10]):

$$H = -\sum_{k=1}^{N-1} p(k)log(p(k)) \qquad [6.10]$$

$$max\ H(\alpha, m, N)\ sc :< k >= const \qquad [6.11]$$

designating by $p(k)$ the degree distribution of the network and m, the minimal network connectivity.

As a result, it has been shown that the entropy is maximal for exponential networks (the degree distribution of exponential networks is: $p(k) = (\frac{e^{-\frac{k}{\gamma}}}{\gamma})$.

Gallos *et al.* [GAL 05] have introduced a probability $w(k_i)$ (equation [6.12]) that a node with k_i links suffers a fault in order to consider the percolation threshold p_c when the degrees with highest significance are not known or, in other words, when the attackers do not know the positions of vulnerable nodes in the network:

$$w(k_i) = \frac{k_i^\alpha}{\sum_{i=1}^{N} k_i^\alpha}, -\infty < \alpha < +\infty \qquad [6.12]$$

This modeling provides a means to define a defense strategy against attacks when the costs necessary for the immunization of vulnerable nodes are too high. The authors conclude that a weak knowledge of the "scale-free" network quickly degrades the latter in the event of an attack ($\alpha > 0$). On the other hand, little knowledge (scale-free) of the network makes it possible to reduce the propagation of faults when defending ($\alpha <= 0$) against attacks (propagation of viruses in a social network, for example). Paul *et al.* [PAU 07] studied the percolation threshold p_c of regular random graphs by making use of the METIS graph partitioning algorithm [KAR 98], that is:

$$p_c = 1 - \frac{2}{k} \qquad\qquad [6.13]$$

where k is the network connectivity and p_c is the fraction of nodes removed.

At the percolation threshold p_c, the diameter and the size of the largest connected component are, respectively, $l \sim N^{0.25}$ and $S \sim N^{0.4}$.

They concluded that regular random graphs are difficult to attack, possibly to be immunized, because of their homogeneity.

It has been proven that bimodal degree distribution networks are optimal against attacks and failures separately [TAN 05].

Tanizawa et al. [TAN 05] studied the robustness of random "scale-free" and bimodal degree distribution networks, in particular, after a series of simultaneous attacks. They showed that n successive attacks weaken the network more than n simultaneous attacks because the attackers are informed of vulnerable nodes (degree distribution) after each attack. In addition, they concluded that as in [TAN 05], bimodal distribution networks were robust when facing attacks and successive faults.

Robust graphs are characterized by a fraction r of degree distribution nodes: $k_2 = (< k > -1 + r)/r$ and the other nodes of degree 1. Bimodal distribution networks are optimal for $0.03 <>< 0.9$ if $p_t/p_r \leq 1$, otherwise uniform distribution networks are more robust, designating by p_t and p_r the fractions of faulty and attacked nodes, respectively.

In [SHA 03], by means of algorithmics, Shargel et al. built a class of networks where "scale-free" and exponential networks are special cases and therefore inherit the benefits of both networks, namely, the robustness to attacks from exponential networks [SOL 08] and robustness to faults from "scale-free" networks [COH 00, COH 01].

The degree distribution of exponential networks is $p(k) = \frac{e^{-\frac{k}{\gamma}}}{\gamma}$. The critical threshold p_c is given by: $1 - (ln\, p_c - 1) = \frac{1}{2\gamma - 1}$.

In summary, due to their low global connectivity (mean degree) and their small diameter, so-called small-world networks and "scale-free" networks are effective for routing information (globally and locally). In other words, similarly to purely random networks, small-world graphs are statically robust (resistant to random failure). In contrast, they are more vulnerable to attacks (removal of elements of the highest degree or of more loaded nodes, for instance) [BOC 06, NEW 03, DOR 08]. Similarly, homogeneous networks, such as exponential networks, appear to be more resistant to attacks than heterogeneous networks [WU 08, MOT 02].

6.2.6. *Network dynamic robustness*

Several models can be found in the literature [CRU 04, KIN 05, CAR 02, WAT 02] destined to reproduce as faithfully as possible the life (or the dynamics) of a network and generally based on an iterative concept. Whether the network is weighted [WU 08, BOC 06, CRU 05, KIN 05] or not [BOC 06], the authors try to define laws for the redistribution of power flows by removing the faulty element (in most of the cases) or by penalizing power flows of faulty elements (for example according to their mean degree and their maximum capacity) [CRU 04, KIN 05]. This study allows, among other things, for the definition of a critical threshold cascade tripping. It is clear that the dynamics of a network strongly depends on its topology.

Rosas-Casas and Corominas-Murtra [ROS 12] in their study of the European electrical network have highlighted this relationship. They have identified three variables that affect the dynamics of a network:

– the mean degree $< k >$;

– the regularity of the distribution of optimal paths in the network;

– patterns in the graphs (or subgraphs).

In summary, the study of the robustness of a complex network consists of determining the ability of the system to survive disruptions (faults, attacks or load variations in the network). For this purpose, several vulnerability indices have been introduced, of which the most important are the degree distribution of the network (or its connectivity), the network homogeneity, the network diameter and the distribution of geodesic paths within the network, which can be expressed by centrality and betweenness coefficients of nodes or links and patterns (or the subgraphs of the network).

6.3. Topological analysis of the Colombian electrical network

In this section, an arsenal of topological and robustness indicators of electric networks is presented. First of all, we begin by drafting a few observables extracted from the lexicon of graph theory [BER 73] and complex systems [BOC 06, NEW 03] by applying them to the Colombian electrical network. Second, we focus on the study of the robustness and the fractality of the network and in particular, three algorithms will be presented.

6.3.1. *Phenomenological characteristics*

6.3.1.1. *Some topological indicators*

Before introducing some definitions (characteristics) of a graph, the latter is defined as follows.

A graph G, often denoted by $G = (V, E)$, is a pair of set (V, E) where $V = \{v_1, ..., v_N\}$ and $E = \{e_1, ..., e_K\}$, respectively, designates the sets of N nodes and K links $(i, j) \in V^2$ of the graph G.

The graph G can be described in the form of a matrix in two different manners:

– *adjacency matrix* A: this is a square matrix $N \times N$ of elements a_{ij} $(i, j = 1, ..., N)$ where $a_{ij} = 1$ if the node i is adjacent to the node j and 0 otherwise;

– *incidence matrix* B: this is a matrix of dimension $N \times K$ of elements b_{ik} $(i = 1, ..., N ; k = 1, ..., K)$, where $b_{ik} = 1$ if the node $i \in V$ is adjacent to the link $k \in E$ and 0 otherwise.

6.3.1.2. *Node degree, mean graph degree, homogeneity and correlations*

The degree, sometimes referred to as connectivity, of a node $i \in V$ denoted by k_i is the number of links $(i, j) \in V^2$ adjacent to the node i (that is the number of neighbors of i). More formally, $k_i = \sum_{i \in V} a_{ij}$ designating by a_{ij} the elements of the adjacency matrix A corresponding to the graph G. Thus, the mean degree of the graph G is the first-order moment (expectancy) $< k >$ of the degree distribution $P(k)$:

$$< k >= \sum_k kP(k) = \sum_{i \in V} \frac{k_i}{N} \qquad [6.14]$$

When the degree distribution $P(k)$ is not regular, it is said that the graph G is *heterogeneous*. Otherwise, the graph is known as *homogeneous* (regular).

The degree distribution $p(k)$ provides us with a representation of the connectivity of the nodes as they are actually connected in the graph. Nonetheless, correlations between node degrees can hide in the graph, that is to say, the probability that a node of degree k becomes connected to another node of degree k' depends on k. In other words, it is possible that there is a preferential linkage relationship between nodes. The correlations of the degrees of node i, $k_{nn,i}$, can be measured by introducing the *mean degree of nearest neighbors* of node i, defined as follows:

$$k_{nn,i} = \frac{1}{k_i} \sum_{j \in \eta_i} k_j = \frac{1}{k_i} \sum_{j=1}^{N} a_{ij} k_j$$

where η_i and k_i, respectively, designates the set of the neighbors of node i and its degree in the graph.

Therefrom, the *nearest neighbors mean degree*, $k_{nn}(k)$, of any node of degree k can be expressed by the quantity [PAS 01]:

$$k_{nn}(k) = \sum_{k'} k' P(k'|k) \qquad [6.15]$$

in which $P(k'|k)$ designates the conditional probability of a node of degree k' to become connected to another node of degree k.

When $k_{nn}(k)$ is increasing, the correlation is known as being *assortative*. It is referred to as *diassortative*, when $k_{nn}(k)$ is decreasing. In the absence of correlations, the quantity $k_{nn}(k)$ decreases to $\frac{<k^2>}{<k>}$, that is $k_{nn}(k)$ is independent of k.

In reality, formula [6.15] is hardly computable. To address this problem, the Pearson correlation coefficient r constitutes another alternative to calculate the quantity $k_{nn}(k)$. It is defined as follows [NEW 02]:

$$r = \frac{K^{-1} \sum_i j_i k_i - [K^{-1} \sum_i \frac{1}{2}(j_i + k_i)]^2}{K^{-1} \sum_i \frac{1}{2}(j_i^2 + k_i^2) - [K^{-1} \sum_i \frac{1}{2}(j_i + k_i)]^2} \qquad [6.16]$$

designating by j_i, k_i, respectively, the degrees of both nodes constituting the link i, with $i = 1, ..., K$.

6.3.1.3. Geodesic paths mean, diameter and efficiency

The *geodesic path* is one of the most important parameters of a graph. In fact, the transmission of information in a graph G necessarily involves the manipulation of the geodesic paths of the latter. Formally, the geodesic path between a node i and a node j, denoted by d_{ij}, is the quickest existing path in the graph between the two nodes. The maximal value of all the d_{ij} is called the *graph diameter* $(Diam(G))$. Therefrom, *the mean geodesic path L of a graph G* can be defined as follows:

$$L = \frac{1}{N(N-1)} \sum_{i,j \in V, i \neq j} d_{ij} \qquad [6.17]$$

In case the graph G is not connected (that is there are nodes unreachable from other nodes in the graph), *the mean geodesic path L and the diameter of the graph diverge*. Moreover, the latter are one of the efficiency measures of a network that can be used as network robustness indicators. In order to address this divergence problem, *the global efficiency E of the graph G* is defined as being the harmonic mean of geodesic paths, namely:

$$E = \frac{1}{N(N-1)} \sum_{i,,j \in V, i \neq j} \frac{1}{d_{ij}} \qquad [6.18]$$

6.3.1.4. Centrality and betweenness coefficient

The nodes *centrality and betweenness coefficient* (eventually of links) is one of the most widespread characteristics of a graph. In fact, this measure allows us to determine the role or importance of each node (possibly a link) of the graph. Originally, the centrality and betweenness coefficient had been introduced to measure the importance of an individual in social networks [WAS 94]. It is defined as the number of times that a node (link) has appeared in the construction of the geodesic paths of the graph. More specifically, the centrality and betweenness coefficient of a node i, which will be denoted by b_i, is defined by the relation [6.19]:

$$b_i = \sum_{j,k \in V, j \neq k} \frac{n_{jk}(i)}{n_{jk}} \qquad [6.19]$$

designating by n_{jk}, the number of geodesic paths between the node j and node k and $n_{jk}(i)$, the number of geodesic paths between nodes j and k, passing through node i.

As an illustration in graph G in Figure 6.2, we have:

$$\{b_1, ..., b_8\} = \{0.12, 0.12, 0.12, 0.13, 0.12, 0.13, 0.13, 0.12\}$$

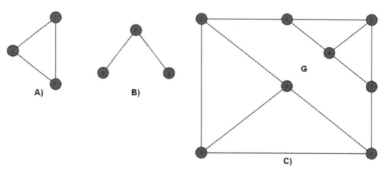

Figure 6.2. *a) Triangle, b) triplet and c) illustrative graph*

6.3.1.5. *Clustering coefficient*

People usually say "my friend's friend is my friend". This expression has nothing banal. As matter of fact, friends of an individual have a strong chance of knowing each other due to their similarity (interests, meeting places, proximity, etc.). This probability of relation between the friends of an individual can be measured by the *clustering coefficient* or *transitivity* of the latter. More formally, the clustering coefficient c_i of a node i is defined as follows:

$$c_i = \frac{2e_i}{k_i(k_i - 1)}$$ [6.20]

designating by e_i the maximum number of links in the subgraph of the neighbors of node i.

As an illustration in graph G of Figure 6.2(c), $c_1 = \frac{2 \times 2}{3 \times (3-1)} = \frac{2}{3}$ and $c_2 = \frac{2 \times 1}{3 \times (3-1)} = \frac{1}{3}$.

The quantity c_i is not a measure common to all nodes of the graph G. As a result, the overall behavior of the latter is difficult to define when using equation [6.20] only. Another quantity called "mean clustering coefficient" of a graph G can then be introduced, which is defined as the mean of all cluster coefficients of the nodes of G,

$$C = < c > = \frac{1}{N} \sum_{i \in V} c_i$$ [6.21]

The formula [6.21] measures the density of triangles that are present in the graph G (Figure 6.2) for the definition of a triangle and a triplet. Consequently, the measure c_i can be replaced by *transitivity* T defined as follows:

$$T = \frac{3 \times The\, number\, of\, triangles\, existing\, in\, G}{The\, number\, of\, triplets\, existing\, in\, G}$$ [6.22]

The examinations of equations [6.20]–[6.22] brings us to the following comments:

– $0 \leq c_i \leq 1, 0 \leq C \leq 1$;

– the cluster coefficient of the links can be similarly defined as for the nodes;

– the cluster coefficient $c(k)$ of a class of nodes of degree k can be defined.

As an illustration in graph G in Figure 6.2(c), we have:

$$-C = \frac{1}{8}\left(\frac{2}{3} + \frac{1}{3} + \frac{2}{3} + \frac{1}{3} + \frac{2}{3} + \frac{1}{3} + \frac{1}{3} + \frac{2}{3}\right) = \frac{1}{2};$$

$$-T = \frac{3 \times 4}{20} = \frac{3}{5}.$$

As stated at the beginning of the chapter, this list of indicators is far from being exhaustive. For other characteristics of a graph, we will refer to: [BOC 06, NEW 03, DOR 03, DOR 08].

6.3.1.6. *Results*

We have focused on the Colombian electrical network. The information available to us concerns the structure of the network, its workload and the history of incidents. In the data provided by the Colombian operator, we can find an *a priori* comprehensive map of its network and a database of incidents that occurred in the network since 1996. The map comes in the form of a backup file of a case study from the software program DigSilent. This software is a complete environment for the study of *Power Flow* published by a German company. Moreover, the GPS coordinates of the Colombian network have been provided in the form of a *Keyhole Markup Language* (KML) file.

To make these raw data usable by our algorithms, it has been necessary to extract them from their software environment (DigSilent). The procedure has consisted of exporting in a proprietary DigSilent format (.dgs ASCII format) the database of the operator and writing Python scripts to read the text file to extract the relevant data. Those of interest to us in this section of the chapter concern the topology (lines, stations and substations) of the network. It has thus been possible to perform the manipulation and the interaction of the results in the form of the KML language (*Google Earth*) by means of programs developed in Python. An example of a KML file of the resulting Colombian network is presented in Figure 6.3. Despite this Google Earth presentation being more elegant and practical, in the following we will make use of a module in the graph processing library in Python for visualization purposes: NetworkX.

Once a workable version of the Colombian network has been obtained, we have compiled the set of codes related with the characterization of graphs to make a coherent and comprehensive application, capable of executing all the processes in a target graph. This program has been named *BTGT*. It comprises a main kernel, including processing unit modules and a graph manager.

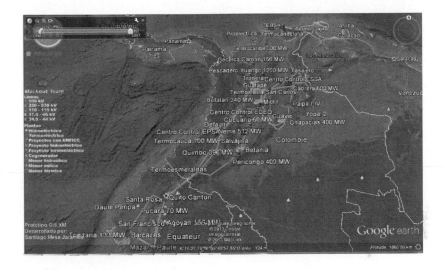

Figure 6.3. *Colombian network (500 kV and 220 kV lines)*
in KML file format (Google Earth). For a color version of this figure,
see www.iste.co.uk/heliodore/metaheuristics.zip

It has been designed in a modular to allow, via the Python legacy, the addition of future modules. The integrated modules are the modules for the computation of *betweennesses*, *clustering* indices and degree distributions. Subsequently, attack and fault vulnerability tests as well as a module for the computation of the fractal dimension of graphs have been added. Moreover, the Python program *BTGT* implemented generates a text file containing the main phenomenological characteristics of a network.

An example of a file obtained using the program applied to the Colombian network is outlined as follows:

Mean geodetic path:	L = 9.935340	Mean geodetic path:	L = 8.251822
Global efficiency:	E = 0.133844	Global efficiency:	E = 0.148346
Diameter:	D = 24	Diameter:	D = 21
Radius:	R = 13	Radius:	R = 11
Assortativity:	−0.2206276	Assortativity:	−0.141073
Pearson coefficient:	r = −0.220627	Pearson coefficient:	r = −0.141073
Transitivity:	T = 0.096045	Transitivity:	T = 0.107775
Mean clustering coefficient:	C = 0.085632	Mean clustering coefficient:	C = 0.112945
Density:	Dens = 0.009119	Density:	Dens = 0.006172
300-node network		Colombian Network	

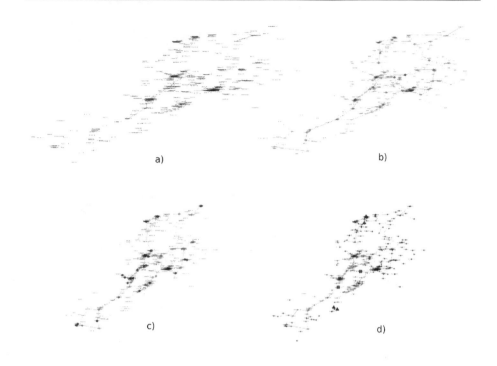

Figure 6.4. *Results with the Colombian network: a) link centrality coefficient (betweennesses); b) knot centrality coefficient; c) clustering coefficient (clustering); d) center and periphery*

The results obtained with the Colombian network are represented in Figures 6.4 and 6.5. Figures 6.4(a)–(c), (e) and (f), respectively, represent the links and the nodes centrality coefficients, the nodes clustering coefficients, the degree distribution in linear evolution and in loglog diagram of the Colombian electrical network.

The attenuated colors of the nodes or links in Figures 6.4(a)–(c), respectively, indicate that they are small centrality or clustering coefficients. In contrast, the nodes or links of larger coefficients are represented with darker colors.

In Figure 6.4(d), nodes having a square scheme represent the center of the network, those with a triangular scheme represent its periphery and darker colors indicate distance from the center network nodes. Conversely, nodes close to the center are represented by faded colors.

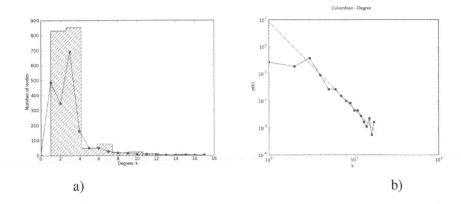

Figure 6.5. *Results with the Colombian network: a) degree distribution;
b) degree distribution in a loglog diagram*

After examination of these curves, the following comments can be made:

– the Colombian network is not locally efficient. In fact, clustering indices indicate the local efficiency of the network. In other words, if a node with a high clustering index (dark color) suffers a fault, its strong connectivity makes it possible to bring the energy through its nearest neighbors. Figure 6.4(d) clearly shows that there are few regions with a high clustering coefficient;

– the Colombian network can be considered as scale free, with as exponent: $\gamma = 3.26$. Furthermore, Figure 6.4(f) shows a linear behavior in the loglog diagram of the degree distribution of the Colombian network. Moreover, the network cannot be considered as being small world. As a matter of fact, the diameter and the mean geodesic path of the network are too large to be considered as such;

– the negative value of the Pearson correlation coefficient r suggests that the Colombian network is disassortative. In other words, preferential linkages are possible in the network.

6.3.2. *Fractal dimension*

The fractal dimension, denoted by D, is a quantity that gives an indication of how a fractal set fills the space. There are many definitions of the fractal dimension [THE 90]. The most important fractal dimensions encountered in the literature and formally defined are the Rényi dimension and the Hausdorff dimension.

Fractal dimensions are used in many research areas such as physics [ZHA 10], image processing [SOI 96, TOL 03], acoustics [EFT 04] and chemistry [EFT 04]. In addition to formal and theoretical aspects, many organizations and phenomena of the real world exhibit fractal properties (vegetation, cellular organisms, seismicity, etc.), namely self-similarity properties (deterministic or stochastic).

For this chapter, the need to be able to dispose of the estimation of the fractal dimension is what we will recall from this chapter because phenomena involved in the dynamics of electric networks suggest scale properties:

– scale properties at the level of the electrical network graph, knowing that the definition of the fractal dimension of graphs is carried out by extension, the concept of metric is hardly apprehensible [TAN 05, THE 90, SON 07];

– scale properties in the dynamics itself of these networks, from the moment the self-organized criticality model becomes relevant to them [CAR 02]. The object in question is a time series or a set of sampled data.

Concerning the estimation of graphs fractal dimensions, we present three of the most used algorithms namely:

– the graph coloring (GC) algorithm;

– the *Compact–Box–Burning* (CBB) algorithm;

– the *Maximum-Excluded-Mass-Burning* (MEMB) algorithm.

The benefit of the description of these algorithms is directly connected to the study of random walks in a graph, the emergence of faults in a node, eventually a link, and the topology of the graph. In other words, it would be interesting to detect self-similarity properties governing the graph (failure, random walk in the graph, topology of the graph, etc.).

Before presenting these methods, it is necessary to formally define what is a "box" and what is a "fractal" dimension:

DEFINITION 6.1.– *In a graph* $G = (V, E)$, *we call a box of size* l_B *(respectively, of radios* r_B*), a subgraph* $H = (V', E')$ *of* G *such that* $\nabla (i, j) \in V'^2$, $l_{ij} < l_B$ *(respectively,* $l_{ij} \leq 2 * r_B$*).*

DEFINITION 6.2.– *Let K be a compact subset of $\mathbb{R}^n$, $N_\varepsilon(K)$ designates the minimum number of closed balls of radius ε necessary to cover K. The fractal dimension is then defined (if it exists), denoted D_f, by:*

$$D_f = \lim \varepsilon \to 0 \ \frac{\log N_\varepsilon(K)}{\log \frac{1}{\varepsilon}} \qquad [6.23]$$

Referring to definition 6.2, the fractal dimension of the compact subset K then corresponds to the slope in the loglog diagram of $N_\varepsilon(K)$ and $\frac{1}{\varepsilon}$.

Despite the fact that in the field of mathematics the notion of fractal dimension is very specific, it remains, however, less obvious regarding its definition in a graph. In effect, we can define as many metrics as we wish in a graph. In the following and referring to definitions 6.1 and 6.2, we define a fractal dimension of graph $G = (V, E)$ in two ways [COS 07]:

– the first, originating from the box method, covers the network with N_B boxes with a side (diameter) ℓ_B, that is the distance between two nodes in a box is less or equal to ℓ_B. By denoting the fractal dimension by d_B, a fractal graph will then follow the law [6.24]:

$$N_B \sim \ell_B^{-d_B} \qquad [6.24]$$

– the second, issued from the *Cluster Growing* method, randomly chooses a seed node and forms a cluster from this node, that it to say, it takes all available nodes within a distance less than or equal to ℓ, then resumes operation until exhaustion of available nodes. Denoting by M_c the mean mass of the set of resulting clusters and the fractal dimension of the associated graph d_C, a fractal graph will then follow the law [6.25]:

$$M_C \sim \ell^{d_C} \qquad [6.25]$$

Despite the fact that these two definitions are exclusive in some cases, that is, there are situations where a graph is fractal following only one of these two definitions, these cases are, nonetheless, still rare. Subsequently, the first definition will be preferred because it is more consensual in the literature.

6.3.2.1. *The GC algorithm*

In [SON 07], it has been found that the problem of the optimal coverage of a graph G employing boxes with maximal size l_B is tantamount to solving the coloring problem of the associated dual graph G'. Starting from the initial graph G and by setting the boxes maximal size to l_B, two nodes i and j of the graph G' are connected if they are separated by a geodesic distance, in the original graph G, $l_{ij} \geq l_B$. In Figure 6.6(a), nodes 2, 3 and 8 are, relatively to node 1, at a distance less than or equal to 3. Therefore, they cannot be connected to node 1 in the dual graph G' (Figure 6.6(b)).

Algorithm 6.1: *Greedy coloring*, GC

---

1 Without assigning any color, **give** a unique identifier
  $Id(i) \in \{1, 2, ..., N\}$ for each node
2 For every value of l_B, **assign** the color 0 to the node with identifier
  $1 = Id$
3 **Let** $i = 2$
4 **While** $i \leq N$ **Do**
5 | **For each** *node of identifier* $Id(j) < Id(i)$ **Do**
6 | | **Compute** distance l_{ij}
7 | **End**
8 | **Let** $l_B = 1$
9 | **Assign** to the node of identifier $Id(i)$ a color C_{il_B} that is not taken
      by the other nodes of identifiers $Id(j) < Id(i)$ such that: $l_{ij} \geq l_B$
10 | **Let** $l_B = l_B + 1$ and repeat 9 as long as $l_B \leq l_B^{max}$
11 | **Let** $i = i + 1$
12 **End**

The algorithm proposed in [SON 07] utilizes a conventional constructive coloring method called (*Greedy*) and at the same time builds the dual graph G'. The general operating principle of the approach is described in algorithm [6.1].

It first starts by the indexation of the nodes, next the color 0 is assigned to the node of identifier $Id = 1$ and continues for all the values of l_B. In effect, each node of the graph will have as many colors as the number of variations of l_B. As an example, if l_B takes its values within $\{1,2,...,M\}$, each node will consequently have M colors. At each iteration i, the calculation of distances

l_{ij} are only performed for nodes j of identifier $Id(j) < Id(i)$. At the end of the algorithm, the fractal dimension of the graph is identified as the slope in the $loglog$ diagram of the number of boxes needed to cover the whole of the graph according to the maximal size of the latter (that is l_B).

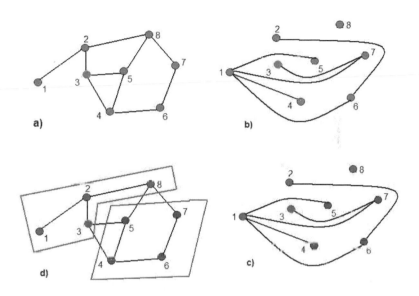

Figure 6.6. *Example of the application of the coloring algorithm, $l_B = 3$: a) the initial graph G; b) the dual graph G'; c) solution of the coloring problem of the dual graph G'; d) the final result (number of boxes $N_B = 2$). For a color version of this figure, see www.iste.co.uk/heliodore/metaheuristics.zip*

6.3.2.2. *The CBB algorithm*

The general operating principle of the CBB algorithm is outlined as follows:

– first, all nodes are likely to be selected to belong to the current box. A node p is randomly selected in the graph (Figure 6.7(a)), this node represents the center of the box under consideration (the nodes in black in Figure 6.7);

– next, all nodes i of the graph (nodes in red in Figure 6.7) that are at a geodesic distance $l_{ip} \geq l_B$ are set aside;

– the selection process is reiterated for a new center of the box in the subgraph resulting from every selection stage until none of the node is likely to belong to the box (Figures 6.7(b) and (c));

– at the end of these steps, a box is built containing nodes at geodesic distance at most $l_B - 1$ (Figure 6.7(c));

– lastly, the procedure for the construction of the boxes is repeated until all nodes are assigned to a box (Figures 6.7(d)–(f) for iteration 2, Figure 6.7(g)–(i) for iteration 3, Figure 6.7(j) for iteration 4).

The summary of the CBB technique is presented in algorithm 6.2.

Algorithm 6.2: *Compact–Box–Burning*, CBB

---

1 **Let** $C = \{$the set of nodes non-assigned to a box$\}$
2 Randomly **choose** a node $p \in C$ and let $C = C \backslash \{p\}$
3 **Let** $C = C \backslash \{i$ such that $l_{pi} \geq l_b\}$
4 **Repeat** steps 2 and 3 as long as $C \neq \varnothing$

6.3.2.3. *The MEMB algorithm*

The MEMB algorithm aims to improve the randomness aspect in the selection of the central nodes of the boxes of the CBB algorithm. The concept of the algorithm is based on the choice of hubs (nodes with stronger degree) as boxes centers, which *a priori* brings us closer to the optimal solution.

To this end, we first define the notion of "excluded mass" as follows:

– for a given covering radius r_B, the "excluded mass" of a node i is equal to the number of nodes j (including the node i in question) that are at geodesic distance $l_{ij} \leq r_B$ and which are not yet assigned to a box (visited). In Figure 6.8(a), node 3 includes three nodes that are at geodesic less than $r_B = 1$, its "excluded mass" is thus equal to 4;

– it then simply suffices to calculate the "excluded masses" of all the non-central nodes at every stage of the algorithm and choose the node p of the most significant "excluded mass" as the new center of the new box and then mark all the nodes i at geodesic distance $l_{jp} \leq r_B$ as being "marked".

The summary of the MEMB technique is presented in algorithm 6.3 and Figure 6.8 illustrates the application of the MEMB algorithm when $r_B = 1$.

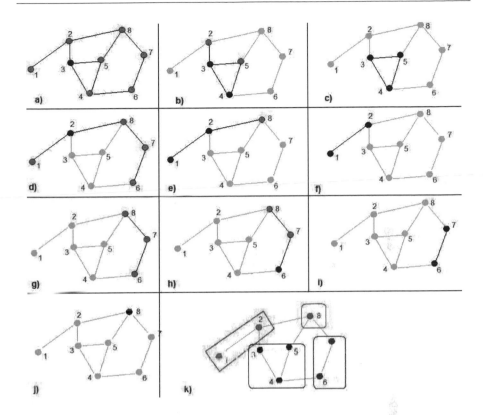

Figure 6.7. *Application example of the CBB algorithm, $l_B = 2$: nodes in red correspond to nodes "set aside" (geodesic distance $\geq l_B$), in black to "central" nodes, in green to nodes that are at geodesic $< l_B$. a) Random selection of node 3 and removal of nodes at a distance $\geq l_B$ from node 3. b) Random selection of node 4 and removal of nodes at distance $\geq l_B$ from node 2. c) Selection of the remaining node 5. Iteration 1: (a)–(c). Iteration 2: d)–f). Iteration 3: g)–i). Iteration 4: j). (d) The final result (number of boxes $N_B = 4$). For a color version of this figure, see www.iste.co.uk/heliodore/metaheuristics.zip*

Algorithm 6.3: *Maximum–Excluded–Mass–Burning*, MEMB

1 **Initialize** all nodes to "unmarked"
2 **Compute** the "excluded mass" for all "non-centered" and "unmarked" nodes, and select node p of "maximal excluded" mass as center and set node p as "marked"
3 **Let** all nodes i that verify the relation $l_{ip} \leq r_b$ as being "marked"
4 **Repeat** steps 2 and 3 as long as there are "unmarked" nodes

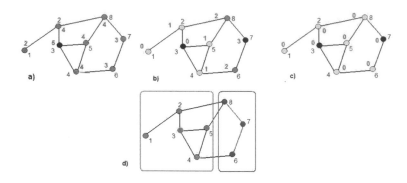

Figure 6.8. *Application example of the MEMB algorithm, $r_B = 1$: nodes in green correspond to "unmarked" nodes, in yellow to "marked nodes" and black nodes to "central nodes". The gray nodes are nodes that already belong to a box. (a)–(c) Intermediate results of the MEMB algorithm; (d) final result (number of boxes $N_B = 2$ = number of hubs). For a color version of this figure, see www.iste.co.uk/heliodore/metaheuristics.zip*

6.3.2.4. *Results*

Figures 6.9(a)–(c), respectively, represent the results obtained when applying algorithms GC, CBB and MEMB to the IEEE 57-node, 118-node and 300-node networks benchmarks.

On the other hand, Figures 6.10(a) and (b) represent the comparison of fractal dimensions obtained by the application of the three algorithms to the IEEE 57-node network (the number of executions of each algorithm is 10^2).

Finally, Figure 6.11 represents the results obtained by the application of CBB and MEMB algorithms to the Colombian network.

The measurements performed on electrical networks considered as benchmarks (IEEE 57-, 118- and 300-node) reveal that the notion of fractal dimension may have a meaning. In effect, we find a linear behavior over approximately two decades and this occurs in all cases. Although the three algorithms (GC, CBB and MEMB) give almost similar results on the estimation of the fractal dimension with the various benchmarks (Figure 6.10(a)), it can, however, be observed that the fractal dimension of the IEEE 57-node network (which is approximately 1.6) is not the same as those of IEEE 118- and 300-node networks (which are approximately 1.8). Nonetheless, taking into consideration that the three benchmark networks originate from the same main network (the northeast American network), Figure 6.9 appears to suggest that their fractal dimension is approximately equal to 1.8. On the other hand, the examination of Figure 6.11 reveals that the determination of the fractal dimension of the Colombian network, regardless of the method being used, leads to a value of $d = 2.1$.

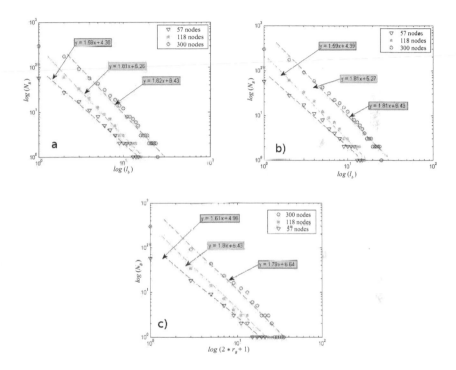

Figure 6.9. *Results of the three algorithms applied to the IEEE 57-node, 118-node and 300-node networks: a) coloring algorithm (Greedy algorithm), b) CBB algorithm and c) MEMB algorithm. For a color version of this figure, see www.iste.co.uk/heliodore/metaheuristics.zip*

Moreover, Figure 6.10(b) shows that the MEMB algorithm is slightly less sensitive to the realizations of the latter. As a matter of fact, the results obtained after 1,000 realizations of the MEMB algorithm are closer to the mean than the other two algorithms. This means that the MEMB algorithm needs less realizations to provide us with a "good" solution close to the optimum, in addition, the complexity in terms of computational time of the MEMB algorithm is better than those of the other two algorithms.

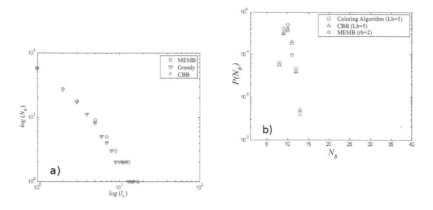

Figure 6.10. *a) Comparison of the fractal dimensions obtained by the application of the three algorithms to the IEEE 57-node network (the number of executions of each algorithm is 10^2). b) Comparison of the distributions of the number of boxes N_B necessary to cover the IEEE 57-node network (the number of realizations of each algorithm is 10^3). For a color version of this figure, see www.iste.co.uk/heliodore/ metaheuristics.zip*

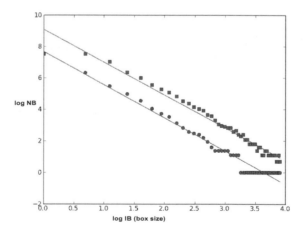

Figure 6.11. *Fractal dimension of the Colombian network (in red, the CBB algorithm and in blue the MEMB algorithm). Case of the Colombian network (1,873 nodes)*

In conclusion, it appears that the notion of graph fractal dimension of electrical networks can have a legitimate existence. We will not go further with the interpretation because additional tests must be established to strengthen the physical meaning. In particular, one of the avenues that we are conceiving is to consider the perspective of scale relativity developed by Nottale [NOT 11] in which the notion of fractal dimension becomes relative and consequently is no longer a constant.

6.3.3. *Network robustness*

In the previous sections, a few indicators of the topology of electric networks have been outlined. Therefore, the determination of the general characteristics of a network, namely the degree distribution, the clustering coefficient, the diameter, etc., have allowed us to gain an overall perspective (in statics) about the robustness of a network by comparing it to already existing models (small-world, "scale-free", random graphs, etc.). In this section, we are going to look at the robustness of electrical networks by simulating faults therein.

The safety of a network breaks down into two subproblems, static and dynamic:

– a static robustness study refers to the fact that no consideration of the power flow, and possibly of information flow, are taken into account;

– a dynamic study of robustness needs to take into consideration power flows circulating in the electric network. In other words, when a fault occurs in a node or a link of the electrical network, a redistribution of power flows is performed in order to determine the state $t + 1$ of the network.

In the following, we will mainly focus on the static robustness of complex networks.

Several efficiency measures can be used as network robustness indicators [NEW 03, DOR 08, BOC 06]. For instance, it is possible to study a network by quantifying the largest connected component (or subnetwork) after voluntary and random removal of a fraction of the system components, *commonly known as fault*, or after removing a fraction of components of the utmost importance (more precisely, the nodes with a strong degree, high load, etc.), *commonly known as attack*. The larger the size of the largest connected component is, the more reliable the network remains. Moreover, the mean of geodesic paths L (equation [6.17]), which can be replaced by E the overall or E_{loc} the local efficiency (which are the harmonic means of the geodesic paths between each node, equation [6.18]), is another network indicator of the robustness [CRU 05, MOT 02]. A highly robust network has thus an overall efficiency close to 1.

Another approach to measure the network robustness consists very simply of counting the number of defective elements in the system [CAR 09]. Other robustness indicators can be defined depending on the type of network, such as the loss of connectivity C_L utilized in [ALB 04]:

$$C_L = 1- < \frac{N_g^i}{N_g} > \qquad\qquad [6.26]$$

where N_G is the total number of generators and N_g^i is the number of generators connected to the node i.

The study of the robustness of a network by means of removing an element of the system is called "N-1 study" (or N-1 contingency) [BOC 06, ROZ 09].

Faults (Figure 6.12(a)) and attacks simulations (Figure 6.12(b)) have been made with our real test network, the Colombian electrical network. Indicators such as the overall efficiency, the mean geodesic path, the diameter and the size of the giant component indicate that the Colombian network is vulnerable to attacks and moderately robust to faults. Indeed, it can be observed that removing a ratio of 10% of the most important nodes (attack case) is enough for the network to break down. However, in the event of faults, a ratio of 50% of the nodes is necessary for the network to collapse.

However, although the network is scale-free, it is, nevertheless, slightly more robust to attacks than a scale-free graph model of the Barabási type. In fact, simply removing 2% of highest degree nodes in the Barabási network is enough for it to sag.

This slight difference can be explained by the fractal character of the Colombian network, which we have developed in section 6.3.2. The latter can increase robustness to intentional attacks if compared to the robustness of scale-free networks having the same exponent $\gamma = 3.26$. In effect, the fractal property provides better protection when "hubs" are removed from the system due to dispersion effect (isolation of "hubs" between them).

Columbian network attack simulation

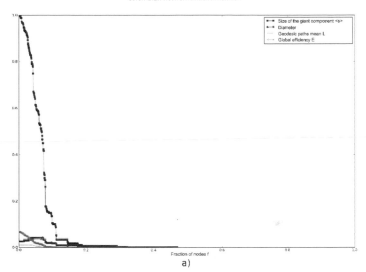

a)

Columbian network failure simulation

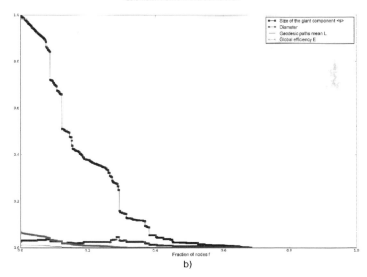

b)

Figure 6.12. *Robustness of the Colombian network:*
a) to faults and b) attacks

6.4. Conclusion

This chapter is dedicated to the topological study of electrical networks, including the Colombian network. First, a few indicators and observables, which have been helpful in guiding us in the description of electric networks, have been presented and then applied to the Colombian electrical network.

After examination of the different results obtained, four key findings can be outlined concerning the Colombian network:

– the Colombian network proves to be particularly vulnerable to attacks (intentional faults) and moderately robust to random failures. Therefore, it suffices that 10% of the nodes of stronger degree do break down for the whole network to become inoperative;

– the Colombian network exhibits "scale-free" properties, which would explain its vulnerability with regard to intentional attacks;

– nevertheless, the Colombian network, which is also the case of the Northeastern American network, *a priori* presents fractal properties, which would enable it to be a little more robust to attacks than "scale-free" networks;

– because of its low consolidation coefficient, the Colombian network is not "locally" efficient, inasmuch as it does not belong to the family of small-word networks.

7

Parameter Estimation of α-Stable Distributions

7.1. Introduction

The advantages and the potential benefits of α-stable probability distributions are now widely recognized by researchers and the reverse engineering community. For the sake of the argument, Lévy-Véhel and Walter [LEV 02] have already brought forward the advantages of α-stable distributions in the modeling of financial markets. As a result, the non-normality of probability distributions is now an accepted fact. Mandelbrot [MAN 63] and Fama in the 1960s [FAM 65] suggested a possible alternative consisting of introducing α-stable distributions. The second most striking example is the proof of asymmetry in stock markets returns. In effect, Fieletz and Smith [FIE 72], on the one hand, and Leitch and Paulson [LEI 75], on the other, have defended the requirement for the relaxation of the Fama/Rolls symmetry hypothesis [FAM 65, FAM 71]. Due to its symmetry and its excessively blurred tail, Gaussian probability distributions fail in modeling most physical phenomena having a scale-invariant nature. α-stable distributions then generalize the analytical framework.

The current challenge is then to obtain an adequate estimate of these probability distributions. Most of these methods aiming to estimate the parameters of α-stable distributions (equation [7.2]) are time-intensive and/or often centered on only two parameters (α, γ) or with restrictions on parameters. Examples include estimators based on distribution quantiles [FAM 71, MCC 86, FEU 81], the estimator based on a transformation of the characteristic function [PRE 72], the technique developed by Kogon and Williams [KOG 98] using an empirical estimate of the characteristic function, the regression method developed by Koutrouvelisv [KOU 80] and still maximum likelihood-based methods [BRO 83, HOL 73, PAN 92, WOR 75]. In the literature, there are several comparative studies on methods for estimating the parameters of the α-stable distribution. Most of them are concentrated on certain classes of the most cited estimators [MIT 01, KOG 98, WER 95].

In this chapter, we propose a new approach to address the parameter estimation problem of an α-stable probability distribution. As a first step, we outline the notions and the fundamental properties of α-stable distributions. In particular, we give two of their main characterizations and we insist on their self-similar character (scale invariant or even indefinitely divisible). Then, we will very briefly describe the tools employed to achieve our α-stable distribution non-parametric estimator, emphasizing the Kolmogorov–Smirnov statistical test and the α-stable distribution generator. Second, we will transform the problem of the parameters' estimation of an α-stable distribution (equation [7.1]) using metaheuristics and more particularly optimization by particle swarm (OEP) [KEN 95, EBE 01, DRE 03]:

$$Prob^1 \begin{cases} \min_{\alpha,\beta,\gamma,\delta} f(\alpha,\beta,\gamma,\delta) \\ g_i : g_i(\alpha,\beta,\gamma,\delta) \in Support_i \end{cases} \qquad [7.1]$$

The estimator has the advantage of being inherently parallelizable. In the third section of this chapter, we propose a set of functions that can be used with GP/GPUs in order to improve the execution time of our estimator.

7.2. Lévy probability distribution

7.2.1. Definitions

When a linear combination of copies of independent and identically distributed (iid) random variables is a random variable of the same probability distribution up to a scale and positioning parameter, the variable in question is said to be "stable". In other words, the random variable X is said to be stable if and only if for any positive constant a_i and for every n independent random variable $X_{i,\dots,n}$ identically distributed and with the same probability distribution as X, the random variable $Y_n = \sum_{i=1}^{n} a_i X_i$ has the same probability distribution as Y, for some constant $c_n \in \mathbb{R}^+$ and $d_n \in \mathbb{R}$, such that $Y = c_n X + d_n$.

For a certain $\alpha \in [0, 2]$, the constant c_n is necessarily of the $n^{1/\alpha}$ form, hence the name "α-stability". This family of probability distributions is called "Lévy α-stable probability distributions".

More formally, a random variable X of an α-stable probability distribution has the characteristic function $\varphi(t)$ (equation [7.2]).

DEFINITION 7.1.– *The characteristic function $\varphi(t)$ of α-stable distributions is given by:*

$$\begin{cases} \varphi(t, \alpha, \beta, \gamma, \mu) & = e^{it\mu - |\gamma t|^\alpha (1 - i\beta Sign(t)\Phi)} \\ \Phi = -(\frac{2}{\pi}) \log |t| & if\ \alpha = 1 \\ \Phi = \tan(\frac{\pi \alpha}{2}) & otherwise \end{cases} \qquad [7.2]$$

and the probability distribution $f(x)$, which has no analytical form, is implicitly defined by equation [7.3]:

$$f(x) = \frac{1}{2\pi} \int_{-\infty}^{+\infty} \varphi(t) e^{-ixt} dt \qquad [7.3]$$

The characterization of α-stable distributions in equation [7.2] has the disadvantage of being non-continuous for all parameters α, β, γ and μ, especially when $\alpha = 1$. To address this problem, Zolotarev [ZOL 66] has proposed the following characterization.

DEFINITION 7.2.– *A random variable X follows an α-stable distribution if and only if its characteristic function is expressed in the form:*

$$\log(\varphi(t)) = \begin{cases} -\gamma_2^\alpha |t|^\alpha \exp\{-i\beta_2 sign(t)\frac{\pi}{2}K(\alpha)\} + i\mu t, & if\ \alpha \neq 1 \\ -\gamma_2 |t| \exp\{\frac{\pi}{2} + i\beta_2 sign(t) \log |t|\} + i\mu t, & if\ \alpha = 1 \end{cases} \qquad [7.4]$$

with:

$$K(\alpha) = \alpha - 1 + sign(1 - \alpha) = \begin{cases} \alpha, & if\ \alpha < 1 \\ \alpha - 2, & if\ \alpha > 1 \end{cases} \quad [7.5]$$

Parameters β and γ, defined in equation [7.2], are related to β_2 and γ_2 by equations [7.6] and [7.7]:

$$\alpha \neq 1 \Rightarrow \begin{cases} \tan\left(\beta_2 \frac{\pi K(\alpha)}{2}\right) = \beta \tan(\frac{\pi\alpha}{2}) \\ \gamma_2 = \gamma(1 + \beta^2 \tan^2 \frac{\pi\alpha}{2})^{\frac{1}{2\alpha}} \end{cases} \quad [7.6]$$

$$\alpha = 1 \Rightarrow \begin{cases} \beta_2 = \beta \\ \gamma_2 = \frac{2}{\pi}\gamma \end{cases} \quad [7.7]$$

The characteristic function $\varphi(t)$ is then continuous at every point. A random variable X of α-stable distribution and stability index α, asymmetry parameter β, scale parameter γ and positioning parameter μ is usually denoted by $S_\alpha(\gamma, \beta, \mu)$.

To simulate non-uniform random variables, the probability distribution or the cumulative distribution function F is used and not the characteristic function. It is therefore important to have a characterization of this probability distribution which is as accurate as possible. Zolotarev [ZOL 66] gives a complete form of the distribution function $F(x, \alpha, \beta_2)$ valid for all parameters α, β, γ and μ. This characterization of α-stable distributions is summarized in proposition 7.1.

PROPOSITION 7.1.– Given:

$$\epsilon(\alpha) = sign(1 - \alpha)$$

$$\gamma_0 = -\frac{\pi}{2}\beta_2 \frac{K(\alpha)}{\alpha}$$

$$C(\alpha, \beta_2) = 1 - \frac{1}{4}\left(1 + \beta_2 \frac{K(\alpha)}{\alpha}\right)(1 + \epsilon(\alpha))$$

$$U_\alpha(\gamma, \gamma_0) = \left(\frac{\sin \alpha(\gamma - \gamma_0)}{\cos(\gamma)} \right) \qquad\qquad [7.8]$$

$$U_1(\gamma, \beta_2) = \frac{\frac{\pi}{2} + \beta_2 \gamma}{\cos(\gamma)} \exp\left(\frac{1}{\beta_2}(\frac{\pi}{2} + \beta_2 \gamma) \tan(\gamma) \right) \qquad\qquad [7.9]$$

the distribution function $F(x, \alpha, \beta_2)$ of an α-stable random variable, having as its characteristic function equation [7.4], is then given by:

$$
\begin{cases}
F(x, \alpha, \beta_2) = C(\alpha, \beta_2) \\[2mm]
\quad + \frac{\epsilon(\alpha)}{\pi} \displaystyle\int_{\gamma_0}^{\frac{\pi}{2}} \exp\left(-x^{\alpha/(\alpha-1)} U_\alpha(\gamma, \gamma_0) \right) d\gamma & if\ x > 0\ and\ \alpha \neq 1 \\[2mm]
& \qquad\qquad\qquad [7.10] \\[2mm]
F(x, 1, \beta_2) = \frac{1}{\pi} \displaystyle\int_{-\frac{\pi}{2}}^{\frac{\pi}{2}} \exp\left(-e^{-x/\beta_2} U_1(\gamma, \beta_2) \right) d\gamma & if\ x > 0\ and\ \alpha = 1
\end{cases}
$$

Referring to equations [7.2] and [7.3], the shape of α-stable probability distributions (Figure 7.1) is completely determined by four main parameters:

– the stability index $\alpha \in [0, 2]$, which determines the speed with which the tail of the distribution tails off. For $\alpha < 2$, the stability index α characterizes the asymptotic behavior of the distribution under consideration;

– the asymmetry parameter $\beta \in [-1, 1]$, which controls the symmetry of the distribution. However, the usual asymmetry parameter is undefined because moments of order k for $k > 1$ do not exist. Consequently, the estimate of the asymmetry parameter β is not simple in this context;

– the scale parameter $\gamma > 0$, which concentrates or scatters the observations around the mean. In other words, it controls the thickness of the distribution;

– the location or positioning parameter $\delta \in \mathbb{R}$ that controls the position of the distribution.

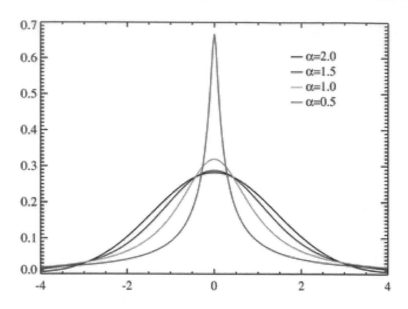

Figure 7.1. *Influence of the parameter α on α-stable probability distributions. For a color version of this figure, see www.iste.co.uk/heliodore/metaheuristics.zip*

This type of probability distribution has interesting properties, namely:

1) $X_1 \rightsquigarrow S_{\alpha_1}(\gamma_1, \beta_1, \mu_1)$ and $X_2 \rightsquigarrow S_{\alpha_2}(\gamma_2, \beta_2, \mu_2)$ (iid), then $X_1 + X_2 \rightsquigarrow S_\alpha(\gamma, \beta, \mu)$ with:

$$\beta = \frac{\beta_1 \gamma_1^\alpha + \beta_2 \gamma_2^\alpha}{\gamma_1^\alpha + \gamma_2^\alpha} \qquad [7.11]$$

$$\gamma = (\gamma_1^\alpha + \gamma_2^\alpha)^{\frac{1}{\alpha}} \qquad [7.12]$$

$$\mu = \mu_1 + \mu_2 \qquad [7.13]$$

2) $X \rightsquigarrow S_\alpha(\gamma, \beta, \mu)$ and $a \in \mathbb{R}$ then:

$$aX \rightsquigarrow \begin{cases} S_\alpha(|a|\gamma, sgn(a)\beta, a\mu) & \text{if } \alpha \neq 1 \\ S_\alpha(|a|\gamma, sgn(a)\beta, a\mu - \frac{2}{\pi}a(log|a|)\gamma\beta) & \text{if } \alpha = 1 \end{cases} \qquad [7.14]$$

$$X + a \rightsquigarrow S_\alpha(\gamma, \beta, \mu + a) \qquad\qquad [7.15]$$

3) $X \rightsquigarrow S_\alpha(\gamma, \beta, 0)$ then:

$$\lim_{x \to \infty} x^\alpha P(X > x) \rightsquigarrow C_\alpha(1 + \beta)\gamma^\alpha, \, with \, C_\alpha \, a \, constant \, according \, to \, \alpha$$

$$-X \rightsquigarrow S_\alpha(\gamma, -\beta, 0)) \qquad\qquad [7.16]$$

4) $X \rightsquigarrow S_\alpha(\gamma, \beta, \mu)$ then:

$$\begin{cases} E|X|^p < \infty & if \, 0 < p \leq 2 \\ E|X|^p \, does \, not \, exist & if \, p > 2 \end{cases} \qquad\qquad [7.17]$$

5) $X \rightsquigarrow S_\alpha(\gamma, \beta, \mu)$ then the process described by the v.a. X is self-similar in distribution;

6) $X \rightsquigarrow S_\alpha(\gamma, \beta, \mu)$ then as a particular case we have:

    $- \alpha = 2$, the distribution is reduced to a Gaussian probability distribution $\aleph$ $(\mu = \delta, \sigma = 2\gamma^2)$;

    $- \alpha = 1$ and $\beta = 0$, the distribution is reduced to a Cauchy probability distribution with γ the scale and δ as positioning parameter;

    $- \alpha = 1/2$ and $\beta = 1$, the probability distribution is a Lévy probability distribution having γ the scale and μ the positioning parameter.

This chapter does not seek to provide a thorough study of α-stable distributions. For more details on this family of probability distributions, we will refer to [FEL 66, NIK 95].

7.2.2. McCulloch α-stable distribution generator

As we have mentioned in the introduction, our algorithm needs an α-stable distribution generator. This will generate realizations of an α-stable distribution $S_\alpha(\gamma, \beta, \mu)$ and will make a comparison of them possible in the data sequence that we want to adjust. The design of such a tool is far from being an easy task from the probability experts' point of view. As a matter of fact, because of the non-existence of the analytical function F^{-1} corresponding to the α-stable probability distribution (except in special cases), the inverse transform method [DEV 86] cannot be used.

One of the first α-stable distribution simulators consisted of generating uniform and independent pseudo-numbers between [0,1] then to approximate the inverse function F^{-1} (equation [7.3]) for each support point. We then obtain realizations of random pseudo-variables (iid) of α-stable distributions [FAM 68, PAU 75]. Several variants destined for large samples have been proposed by DuMouchel [DUV 71]. Mantegna has proposed [MAN 94] a method consisting of generating a series of nonlinear transformations of two Gaussian variables to obtain random α-stable variables by means of the central limit theorem. Finally, another method involves approximating the integral in equation [7.3] by another system of mutually exclusive functions [PRE 92].

In our α-stable distribution estimator, we have opted for the generator coded by McCulloch and Ohio, themselves inspired by Chambers *et al.*'s works [CHA 76]. This generator has the advantage of being faster, as indicated in Table 7.1.

This generator developed by Chambers *et al.*, also inspired by Kanter's works [KAN 75] (positive α-stable distribution generation, $\beta = 1$), is built by achieving a series of nonlinear transformations of uniform variables into an α-stable variable. Two fundamental results (Lemma 7.1 and Theorem 7.1) have been demonstrated and will be subsequently used to generate any α-stable distribution.

	McCulloch		Mantegna		Rejection	
α	1,000	100,000	1,000	100,000	1,000	100,000
0,3	0,01	0,11	0,11	9,20	28,28	31,33
0,6	0,00	0,20	0,10	9,25	3,93	4,71
1	0,00	0,05	0,00	0,44	1,28	1,79
1,3	0,01	0,20	0,02	0,90	1,14	1,58
1,7	0,01	0,22	0,02	0,90	0,90	1,32

Table 7.1. *McCulloch, Mantegna and rejection algorithms execution time*

LEMMA 7.1.– *Given γ_0 and $U_\alpha(\gamma, \gamma_0)$ as defined in proposition 7.1, for $\alpha \neq 1$ and $\gamma_0 < \gamma < \frac{\pi}{2}$, X is an α-stable distribution $S_\alpha(1, \beta_2, 0)$ if and only if for $x > 0$:*

$$\frac{1}{\pi} \int_{\gamma_0}^{\frac{\pi}{2}} \exp\left[-x^{\frac{\alpha}{(\alpha-1)}} U_\alpha(\gamma, \gamma_0)\right] d\gamma = \begin{cases} P(0 < X < x), & if\ \alpha < 1 \\ P(X \geq x), & if\ \alpha > 1 \end{cases} \qquad [7.18]$$

THEOREM 7.1.– *Given γ_0 as defined in proposition 7.1, let γ and W be two random variables (iid) evenly distributed on $[-\frac{\pi}{2}, \frac{\pi}{2}]$ and exponential, respectively. Then:*

$$\begin{cases} X = \frac{\sin \alpha(\gamma - \gamma_0)}{(\cos \gamma)1/\alpha} \left(\frac{\cos(\gamma - \alpha(\gamma - \gamma_0))}{W}\right)(1-\alpha)/\alpha \rightsquigarrow S\alpha(1, \beta2, 0), & if\ \alpha \neq 1 \\ X = (\frac{\pi}{2} + \beta2\gamma) \tan \gamma - \beta2 \log\left(\frac{W \cos \gamma}{\frac{\pi}{2} + \beta2\gamma}\right) \rightsquigarrow S\alpha(1, \beta2, 0), & if\ \alpha = 1 \end{cases} \qquad [7.19]$$

Based on this theorem, it is now possible to easily build an α-stable distribution simulator (Algorithm 7.1). However, the results outlined in these formulas only allow for the standard case of an α-stable distribution $S_\alpha(1, \beta, 0)$ to be addressed. Nonetheless, by making use of Properties [7.14] and [7.15] of α-stable distributions, the other cases can easily be covered. The algorithm summarizes the simulator that will be used subsequently in this study.

7.3. Elaboration of our non-parametric α-stable distribution estimator

In this section, we provide the basic tools necessary for the construction of the proposed algorithm. However, it should be noted that this list of tools is not absolute and not exhaustive. It is possible to use a different method to build an algorithm that coincides with the skeleton of our approach by using metaheuristics among other methods. Here we wish to highlight the originality of our approach and therefore we are not interested in building the best possible algorithm using the concepts presented in this chapter; the use of a few properties of α-stable distributions, the choice of the OEP utilized or the adjustment of its parameters could be the subject of an in-depth study in order to make the algorithm more efficient.

Algorithm 7.1: McCulloch α-stable distribution simulator

/* The aim is to simulate N realizations of a $S_\alpha(\gamma, \beta, \mu)$
   distribution   */

1 **For** i *ranging from* 1 *to* N **Do**

2   **Generate** a uniform random variable $V \in [-\frac{\pi}{2}, \frac{\pi}{2}]$

3   **Generate** an exponential random variable W of mean 1

4   **If** $\alpha \neq 1$ **Then**

5   **Compute** $B_{\alpha,\beta} = \dfrac{\arctan(\beta \tan \frac{\pi\alpha}{2})}{\alpha}$

6   **Compute** $S_{\alpha,\beta} = \left[1 + \beta^2 \tan^2 \frac{\pi\alpha}{2}\right]^{1/(2\alpha)}$

7   **Compute**

$$X(i) = S_{\alpha,\beta} \times \frac{\sin(\alpha(V+B_{\alpha,\beta}))}{(\cos(V))^{1/\alpha}} \times \left(\frac{\cos(V - \alpha(V+B_{\alpha,\beta}))}{W}\right)^{(1-\alpha)/\alpha}$$

8   **Compute** $X(i) = \gamma X(i) + \mu$

9   **Else**

10   **Compute** $X(i) = \frac{2}{\pi}\left[\left(\frac{\pi}{2} + \beta V\right)\tan V - \beta \log\left(\frac{W \cos V}{\frac{\pi}{2} + \beta V}\right)\right]$

11   **Compute** $X(i) = \gamma X(i) + \frac{2}{\pi}\beta\gamma \log \gamma + \mu$

12   **End**

13 **End**

7.3.1. *Statistical tests*

One of the most powerful and most utilized tools in statistics is the hypothesis test. This test is based on an "inferential statistic" calculated based on a reference sample in order to *reject* or *not to reject* a statistical hypothesis by associating an error risk to the conclusion. In other words, statistical tests deal with methods that make it possible to decide, in the light of a sample, the choice between two opposite hypotheses made in regards to the population or the parameters. A statistical test is based on experimental data and the essence of a test is a rule indicating to decision makers whether the data collected will drive them to reject or accept their initial hypothesis. Solving a test problem therefore consists of finding the rejection region also called the critical region of the hypothesis. The decision (to reject or not to reject the hypothesis) is related to the structure of the sample which is random. The decision made is thus random (Table 7.2).

Hypothesis H_0	Accept H_0	Reject H_0
True	no error	1st kind error
False	2nd kind error	no error

Table 7.2. *Error kinds in statistical tests*

Depending on their purpose, statistical tests are divided into four main classes:

– the compliance test that validates statistical quantities, mean and variance for instance;

– the test for goodness of fit that fits a probability distribution to another distribution selected *a priori*;

– the test for homogeneity (or comparison) that compares two samples that originate from the same population;

– the test for association (or independence) that tests the independence of two variables.

In our estimation problem, a reference sample and a stable law generator are available (section 7.2.2). The problem is therefore tantamount to comparing this reference sample to another generated sample. We are therefore in the presence of a homogeneity test. One of the most widely used tests is the "Kolmogorov–Smirnov" test [MAS 51, STE 70].

The Kolmogorov–Smirnov test is a non-parametric test used to compare a sample to a probability distribution chosen *a priori* (in this case, this is referred to as a test for goodness of fit) or to compare two distinct samples (in this case, this is referred to as a test for homogeneity). This non-parametric test is based on the empirical properties of the probability distribution of the reference sample.

Given $S_n = (x_1, ..., x_n)$ for n realizations of a random variable of probability distribution f, the empirical distribution function of the n-sample S is given by equation [7.20]:

$$F_n(x) = \frac{1}{n} \sum_{i=1}^{n} \delta_{x_i \leq x} \qquad [7.20]$$

with:

$$\begin{cases} \delta_{x_i \leq x} = 1, & \text{if } x_i \leq x \\ \delta_{x_i \leq x} = 0, & \text{otherwise} \end{cases} \qquad [7.21]$$

Referring to equation [7.20], the empirical distribution function $F_n(x)$ describes a process that takes its values from the set of increasing functions in $[0, 1]$. As a result of this characteristic, we get the following convergence (equation [7.22]):

$$\mathbb{P}\left[\sup_x |F_n(x) - F(x)| > \frac{c}{\sqrt{n}}\right] \xrightarrow{n \to \infty} \alpha(c) = 2\sum_{r=1}^{+\infty}(-1)^{r-1}e^{-2r^2c^2} \quad [7.22]$$

designating by $\alpha(c) \in [0, 1]$ the P-value (or the quantile) of the statistical test.

At first sight, the main concept behind how the test operates consists of calculating:

– a statistic, called the Kolmogorov–Smirnov statistic D_n (formula [7.23]), which is the distance between the empirical distribution function $F_n(x)$ of the n-sample S_n that is to be fitted and the theoretical distribution function $F(x)$ fixed *a priori* (in the case of a test for goodness of fit, Figure 7.2);

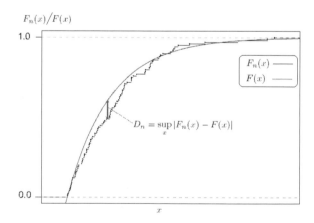

Figure 7.2. *The basic concept of the Kolmogorov–Smirnov test. For a color version of this figure, see www.iste.co.uk/ heliodore/metaheuristics.zip*

– or $D_{n,n'}$ (equation [7.24]), which represents the distance between the two empirical distribution functions $F_n(x)$ and $F_{n'}(x)$ corresponding to the two samples S_n and $S_{n'}$ respectively (in the case of a test for homogeneity):

$$D_n = \sup_x |F_n(x) - F(x)| \qquad\qquad [7.23]$$

$$D_{n,n'} = \sup_x |F_n(x) - F_{n'}(x)| \qquad\qquad [7.24]$$

In general, statistics D_n and $D_{n,n'}$ are calculated under the null hypothesis H_0:

– H_0: The two samples S_n and $S_{n'}$ are drawn from the same probability distribution (in the case of a test for homogeneity);

– H_0: The sample S_n is taken from the probability distribution $F(x)$ fixed *a priori* (in the case of a test for goodness of fit).

In addition, the null hypothesis H_0 is rejected if:

– the statistics $\sqrt{n}\,D_n > c$ (in the case of a test for goodness of fit);

– $\sqrt{\frac{nn'}{n+n'}}\,D_{n,n'} > c$ (in the case of a test of homogeneity);

where $c > 0$ is the quantile defined in [MIL 56] read in the Kolmogorov–Smirnov table.

In both cases, the probability distributions considered in the null hypothesis H_0 are supposed to be continuous. Moreover, no restrictions are imposed.

7.3.2. *Identification of the optimization problem and design of the non-parametric estimator*

Given $S_n = (x_1, ..., x_n)$, n independent realizations of a random variable X with α-stable distribution having stability index α, positioning parameter μ, asymmetry parameter β and scale parameter γ. From now on, we will denote $S(\alpha, \beta, \gamma, \mu)$ instead of $S_\alpha(\gamma, \beta, \mu)$. It is assumed that these parameters are unknown and that we have an α-stable distribution generator (the McCulloch generator in section 7.2.2 is a good initial generator). Therefore, the aim is to build a good estimator for the parameters of the random variable X of α-stable distribution $S(\alpha, \beta, \gamma, \mu)$.

As a result, the decision variables of the optimization process are the parameters α, β, γ and μ. Each particle is represented by a vector of dimension 4.

Let $\alpha^j(t)$, $\beta^j(t)$, $\gamma^j(t)$ and $\mu^j(t)$ be, respectively, the stability index α, the asymmetry parameter β, the scale parameter γ and the positioning parameter μ of the particle j at iteration t.

The main idea of our approach involves testing, at each iteration t of the optimization process and for each particle j (that is $\alpha^j(t)$, $\beta^j(t)$, $\gamma^j(t)$ and $\mu^j(t)$ determined by the optimization algorithm), the homogeneity of the two samples S_n and $S_n^j(t)$ corresponding respectively to the reference sample whose parameters are to be estimated and to the sample drawn from an α-stable distribution of parameters $(\alpha^j(t)$, $\beta^j(t)$, $\gamma^j(t)$ and $\mu^j(t))$ by means of the McCulloch generator.

In other words, the problem $Prob^1$ defined in equation [7.1] becomes:

$$Prob^2 \begin{cases} \min\limits_{\alpha,\beta,\gamma,\delta} f(\alpha, \beta, \gamma, \delta) = MinD_{n,n'} \\ \quad = Min(\sup_x |F_n(x) - F_{n'}(x)|) \\ g_1 : \alpha \in]0,2], \\ g_2 : \beta \in [-1,1], \\ g_3 : \gamma > 0, \\ g_4 : \delta \in \mathbb{R} \end{cases} \qquad [7.25]$$

and designating by:

– $D_{n,n'}$ the Kolmogorov–Smirnov objective function to be minimized (fitness of particles);

– $F_n(x)$ and $F_{n'}(x)$ respectively the distribution functions of the reference sample S_n that is to be adjusted and $S_n^j(t)$ returned by the optimization process (using the McCulloch generator).

At each iteration t, the positions of the jth particle are updated using equations [7.27] and [7.26] to evaluate the new performance (or fitness) of the

jth particle by calculating again the Kolmogorov–Smirnov statistic $D_{n,n'}$ (for more information about the optimization technique employed in this chapter, in particular the PSO, the reader should refer to Chapters 2 and 4):

$$\vec{x_i}(t+1) = \vec{x_i}(t) + \vec{v_i}(t+1) \tag{7.26}$$

designating by $\vec{v_i}(t)$ the velocity of the ith particle at iteration t (equation [7.27]) and k, $\varphi_1 = rand(0,1) * k$ and $\varphi_2 = rand(0,1) * k$, the inertia and the degree of confidence of the particles respectively:

$$\vec{v_i}(t+1) = k[\vec{v_i}(t) + rand(0,1) * (\vec{p_i} - \vec{x_i}(t)) \tag{7.27}$$
$$+ rand(0,1) * (\vec{p_{best_i}} - \vec{x_i}(t))]$$

with:

$$k = \frac{2}{|2 - (c_1 + c_2) - \sqrt{(c_1 + c_2)^2 - 4(c_1 + c_2)}|} \tag{7.28}$$

and: $c_1 + c_2 > 4$.

In the end, the synoptic of the approach proposed in this chapter is summarized in algorithm 7.2 whilst Figure 7.3 shows the flow chart (block diagram) of the proposed algorithm.

7.4. Results and comparison with benchmarks

7.4.1. *Validation with benchmarks*

To test the estimator, we have considered α-stable distribution benchmarks, in particular employing the McCulloch α-stable distribution generator described in section 7.2.2.

In order to observe the behavior of the algorithm, we have tested it on the set of different parameters $\alpha \in \{0.2, 0.5, 0.7, 1.3, 1.5, 1.8\}$ $\beta \in \{-0.5, 0. 0.5\}$, $\gamma \in \{1, 5\}$, $\mu \in 0$ and on the set of different sample sizes $n \in \{250, 500, 5,000, 10,000\}$. The results will be compared to the McCulloch estimator [MCC 86]; this estimator is considered to be the most relevant.

Algorithm 7.2: α-Stable distribution estimator using OEP

/* $\alpha^j(t)$, $\beta^j(t)$, $\gamma^j(t)$, and $\mu^j(t)$ are the stability indices, the asymmetry parameter, the scale parameter and the positioning parameter of particle j at iteration t.   */

/* $\hat{\alpha}$, $\hat{\beta}$, $\hat{\gamma}$, and $\hat{\mu}$ are the best parameters estimated, $\overrightarrow{p_j}$ is the best position found by the jth particle, $\overrightarrow{p_{best_j}}$ is the position of the neighbors of the jth particle.   */

/* $\overrightarrow{v_j}(t)$ is the velocity of the jth particle at iteration t, t_{max} is the maximal number of iterations.   */

/* $S_{n'}^j$ contains n' independent realizations of an α-stable distribution S $(\alpha^j(t)$, $\beta^j(t)$, $\gamma^j(t)$, $\mu^j(t))$.   */

1 **Let** $t \leftarrow 0$
2 **For each** *particle* j **Do**
3   **Initialize** $\alpha^j(t)$, $\beta^j(t)$, $\gamma^j(t)$, $\mu^j(t)$ and $\overrightarrow{v_j}(t)$
4   **Generate** a sample e $S_{n'}^j$, using the McCulloch generator (algorithm 7.1) with parameters $(\alpha^j(t)$, $\beta^j(t)$, $\gamma^j(t)$, $\mu^j(t))$
5   **Evaluate** the j-th particle by calculating $D_{n,n'}$ (Formula [7.24])
6   **Let** $\overrightarrow{p_j}$ be the best position of particle j encountered until then
7 **End**
8 **For each** *particle* j **Do**
9   **Let** $\overrightarrow{p_{best_j}}$ as the best position of the neighbors of the particle j
10 **End**
11 **Let** $\hat{\alpha}$, $\hat{\beta}$, $\hat{\gamma}$, and $\hat{\mu}$ as the best position (solution) of all particles
12 **For** t *ranging from* 1 *to* t_{max} **Do**
13   **For each** *particle* j **Do**
14   **Update** $\overrightarrow{v_j}(t)$ using [7.27]
15   **Update** $\alpha^j(t)$, $\beta^j(t)$, $\gamma^j(t)$, $\mu^j(t)$ using [7.26]
16   **Update** $\overrightarrow{p_j}$
17   **End**
18   **Update** $\overrightarrow{p_{best_j}}$ for all particles
19   **Update** the best estimate of parameters $\hat{\alpha}$, $\hat{\beta}$, $\hat{\gamma}$, and $\hat{\mu}$ of the original signal S_n
20 **End**
21 **Return** $\hat{\alpha}, \hat{\beta}, \hat{\gamma},$ and$\hat{\mu}$

As a first step, for each set of parameters $(\alpha_i$, β_i, γ_i, $\mu_i) - i$ being the ith benchmark – we simulate 1,000 samples of the same size n_j and independent of each other (iid) where each sample contains the realizations of the random α-stable variable $B_i(\alpha_i, \beta_i, \gamma_i, \mu_i)$. Second, for each sample i, the parameters of the random variable B_i are estimated using two estimators: ours and McCulloch's. Next, we calculate for each benchmark i – that is to say for each 1,000 achievements – the mean and the standard deviation of

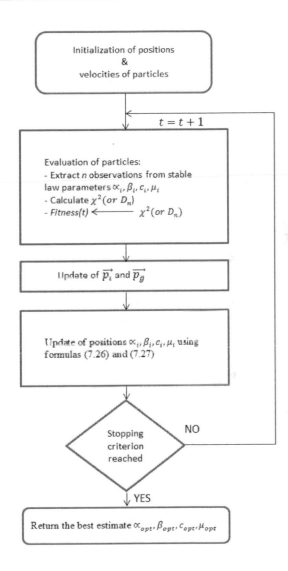

Figure 7.3. *Block diagram of the estimator of α-stable distribution parameters using OEP*

estimates. Knowing that the parameters to be estimated are known in advance, i.e. α_i, β_i, γ_i and μ_i, we are able to calculate the error estimates and therefore to compare our estimator with McCulloch's.

The results of the estimates for each set of parameters $(\alpha_i, \beta_i, \gamma_i, \mu_i)$ and each sample size n_j are summarized in Tables 7.3–7.18. These are, by convention, organized into:

– three main groups with small-sized ($n = 250$ and $n = 500$), medium-sized (n=5,000) and large-sized benchmarks (n=10,000);

  – two subgroups, in particular $\alpha < 1$ and $\alpha > 1$.

In all cases, the algorithm parameters are set as follows:

– the construction coefficient K defined in equation [7.28] is set to 0.7298;

– the swarm size is set to 24;

– the number of neighbors is set to 3;

– the number of iterations is set to 400;

– the search space is $\alpha \in [0.1, 2], \beta \in [-1, 1]; \gamma \in [0, 50], \mu \in [-50, 50]$.

Tables 7.3, 7.4, 7.5 and 7.6 bring forward the relevance of our estimator when $\alpha \prec 2$ and in particular when $\alpha < 1$ for the various values of $\alpha, \beta, \gamma, \mu$ and for all the sample sizes n. As a matter of fact, although the sample sizes n are small, the estimates given in Tables 7.3 and 7.4 are very close to the actual values of the parameters.

The estimates obtained using the McCulloch algorithm for values of $\alpha < 1$ (Tables 7.7, 7.8, 7.9 and 7.10) are very bad, in particular for values of $\alpha < 0.5$. The McCulloch method is designed for values of $\alpha > 0.6$. For values of $\alpha > 0.6$, the McCulloch method gives interesting results but still remains of lower quality compared to our estimates. Only the case involving symmetrical samples ($\beta = 0$) gives more or less similar results.

α	β	γ	$\hat{\alpha}$	$\hat{\beta}$	$\hat{\gamma}$	$\hat{\mu}$
0.2	-0.5	1	0.20 (0.0150)	-0.49 (0.0659)	1.26 (0.9177)	0.00 (0.0048)
		5	0.20 (0.0145)	-0.49 (0.0628)	5.78 (1.9554)	0.00 (0.0127)
	0.0	1	0.20 (0.0148)	-0.00 (0.0724)	1.20 (0.8452)	0.00 (0.0039)
		5	0.20 (0.0149)	-0.00 (0.0757)	5.71 (2.0174)	0.00 (0.0154)
	0.5	1	0.20 (0.0138)	0.47 (0.0670)	1.21 (0.8178)	0.00 (0.0039)
		5	0.20 (0.0147)	0.48 (0.0653)	5.76 (1.9799)	0.00 (0.0157)
0.5	-0.5	1	0.51 (0.0947)	-0.50 (0.0850)	1.04 (0.1894)	-0.08 (0.8496)
		5	0.50 (0.0384)	-0.50 (0.0728)	5.17 (0.8849)	0.03 (0.4231)
	0.0	1	0.50 (0.0567)	-0.00 (0.0828)	1.02 (0.1667)	0.00 (0.1172)
		5	0.50 (0.0522)	-0.00 (0.0835)	5.10 (0.8470)	0.00 (0.6470)
	0.5	1	0.51 (0.0859)	0.49 (0.0893)	1.04 (0.1907)	0.04 (0.6642)
		5	0.50 (0.0374)	0.48 (0.0752)	5.18 (0.8672)	0.03 (0.4159)
0.7	-0.5	1	0.70 (0.0570)	-0.50 (0.0882)	1.00 (0.1212)	0.05 (0.3656)
		5	0.70 (0.0645)	-0.50 (0.0900)	5.02 (0.6027)	0.21 (1.7238)
	0.0	1	0.70 (0.0585)	0.00 (0.0893)	1.01 (0.1261)	0.01 (0.2065)
		5	0.70 (0.0590)	-0.016 (0.0932)	5.07 (0.6219)	0.13 (1.0966)
	0.5	1	0.70 (0.0591)	0.48 (0.0876)	1.01 (0.1214)	-0.06 (0.4738)
		5	0.70 (0.0596)	0.48 (0.0885)	5.08 (0.6052)	-0.30 (1.8679)

α	β	γ	$\hat{\alpha}$	$\hat{\beta}$	$\hat{\gamma}$	$\hat{\mu}$
0.2	-0.5	1	0.20 (0.0100)	-0.49 (0.0458)	1.08 (0.3176)	0.00 (0.0012)
		5	0.20 (0.0107)	-0.49 (0.0451)	5.45 (1.5223)	0.00 (0.0059)
	0.0	1	0.20 (0.0104)	-0.00 (0.0494)	1.09 (0.4644)	0.00 (0.0015)
		5	0.20 (0.0102)	-0.00 (0.0502)	5.44 (1.5519)	0.00 (0.0067)
	0.5	1	0.20 (0.0104)	0.48 (0.0472)	1.08 (0.3033)	0.00 (0.0017)
		5	0.20 (0.0103)	0.48 (0.0444)	5.50 (1.5389)	0.00 (0.0064)
0.5	-0.5	1	0.50 (0.0360)	-0.50 (0.0547)	1.01 (0.1246)	0.01 (0.0949)
		5	0.50 (0.0270)	-0.49 (0.0516)	5.07 (0.6108)	0.00 (0.2897)
	0.0	1	0.50 (0.0272)	-0.00 (0.0569)	1.01 (0.1185)	0.00 (0.0505)
		5	0.50 (0.0270)	-0.00 (0.0547)	5.02 (0.5678)	0.02 (0.2421)
	0.5	1	0.50 (0.0306)	0.48 (0.0575)	1.01 (0.1175)	0.00 (0.0812)
		5	0.50 (0.0266)	0.49 (0.0519)	5.11 (0.6745)	0.00 (0.2922)
0.7	-0.5	1	0.70 (0.0546)	-0.50 (0.0625)	1.00 (0.0898)	0.02 (0.2943)
		5	0.70 (0.0478)	-0.50 (0.0609)	5.01 (0.4433)	0.09 (1.2013)
	0.0	1	0.70 (0.0449)	-0.00 (0.0662)	1.00 (0.0846)	0.02 (0.4887)
		5	0.70 (0.0415)	-0.00 (0.0631)	5.03 (0.4520)	0.05 (0.6811)
	0.5	1	0.70 (0.0474)	0.49 (0.0662)	1.00 (0.0881)	-0.00 (0.2663)
		5	0.70 (0.0450)	0.49 (0.0611)	5.02 (0.4284)	-0.11 (1.3148)

Table 7.3. $n = 250$, α-stable estimation, 0.2 – 0.7

α	β	γ	$\hat{\alpha}$	$\hat{\beta}$	$\hat{\gamma}$	$\hat{\mu}$
0.2	-0.5	1	0.20 (0.0100)	-0.49 (0.0458)	1.08 (0.3176)	0.00 (0.0012)
		5	0.20 (0.0107)	-0.49 (0.0451)	5.45 (1.5223)	0.00 (0.0059)
	0.0	1	0.20 (0.0104)	-0.00 (0.0494)	1.09 (0.4644)	0.00 (0.0015)
		5	0.20 (0.0102)	-0.00 (0.0502)	5.44 (1.5519)	0.00 (0.0067)
	0.5	1	0.20 (0.0104)	0.48 (0.0472)	1.08 (0.3033)	0.00 (0.0017)
		5	0.20 (0.0103)	0.48 (0.0444)	5.50 (1.5389)	0.00 (0.0064)
0.5	-0.5	1	0.50 (0.0360)	-0.50 (0.0547)	1.01 (0.1246)	0.01 (0.0949)
		5	0.50 (0.0270)	-0.49 (0.0516)	5.07 (0.6108)	0.00 (0.2897)
	0.0	1	0.50 (0.0272)	-0.00 (0.0569)	1.01 (0.1185)	0.00 (0.0505)
		5	0.50 (0.0270)	-0.00 (0.0547)	5.02 (0.5678)	0.02 (0.2421)
	0.5	1	0.50 (0.0306)	0.48 (0.0575)	1.01 (0.1175)	0.00 (0.0812)
		5	0.50 (0.0266)	0.49 (0.0519)	5.11 (0.6745)	0.00 (0.2922)
0.7	-0.5	1	0.70 (0.0546)	-0.50 (0.0625)	1.00 (0.0898)	0.02 (0.2943)
		5	0.70 (0.0478)	-0.50 (0.0609)	5.01 (0.4433)	0.09 (1.2013)
	0.0	1	0.70 (0.0449)	-0.00 (0.0662)	1.00 (0.0846)	0.02 (0.4887)
		5	0.70 (0.0415)	-0.00 (0.0631)	5.03 (0.4520)	0.05 (0.6811)
	0.5	1	0.70 (0.0474)	0.49 (0.0662)	1.00 (0.0881)	-0.00 (0.2663)
		5	0.70 (0.0450)	0.49 (0.0611)	5.02 (0.4284)	-0.11 (1.3148)

Table 7.4. *n = 500, α-stable estimation, 0.2 – 0.7*

Tables 7.11, 7.12, 7.13 and 7.14 show the results of our estimator for different sets of α, β, γ, and μ parameters as well as different sample sizes n for values of $\alpha > 1$ whilst Tables 7.15, 7.16, 7.17 and 7.18 show the same results obtained using the McCulloch estimator.

It can be observed that the results are slightly worse compared to the results given in Tables 7.3–7.6 and 7.7–7.10, particularly in standard deviations. In fact, the standard deviations of the two methods given in Tables 7.11–7.14 and 7.15–7.18 (when $\alpha > 1$), even for different values of n, are larger than those given in Tables 7.3–7.10 (when $\alpha < 1$).

Nonetheless, it can be noted that our algorithm gives a better estimate of the symmetry parameter β, in particular for large-sized samples.

α	β	γ	$\hat{\alpha}$	$\hat{\beta}$	$\hat{\gamma}$	$\hat{\mu}$
0.2	-0.5	1	0.20 (0.0036)	-0.49 (0.0159)	1.02 (0.0946)	0.00 (0.0002)
		5	0.20 (0.0039)	-0.49 (0.0156)	5.17 (0.5255)	0.00 (0.0013)
	0.0	1	0.20 (0.0036)	-0.00 (0.0168)	1.01 (0.0985)	0.00 (0.0002)
		5	0.20 (0.0038)	-0.00 (0.0167)	5.13 (0.5897)	0.00 (0.0012)
	0.5	1	0.20 (0.0035)	0.49 (0.0159)	1.01 (0.0943)	0.00 (0.0002)
		5	0.20 (0.0040)	0.49 (0.0160)	5.15 (0.5576)	0.00 (0.0013)
0.5	-0.5	1	0.50 (0.0111)	-0.49 (0.0201)	1.00 (0.0411)	0.00 (0.0234)
		5	0.50 (0.0101)	-0.49 (0.0180)	5.02 (0.2021)	0.00 (0.0974)
	0.0	1	0.50 (0.0101)	0.00 (0.0195)	1.00 (0.0409)	0.00 (0.0171)
		5	0.50 (0.0103)	0.00 (0.0199)	5.02 (0.2037)	0.00 (0.0848)
	0.5	1	0.50 (0.0116)	0.49 (0.0196)	1.00 (0.0425)	0.00 (0.0234)
		5	0.49 (0.0102)	0.49 (0.0187)	5.01 (0.1986)	0.00 (0.1003)
0.7	-0.5	1	0.70 (0.0220)	-0.49 (0.0259)	1.00 (0.0350)	0.01 (0.1270)
		5	0.70 (0.0178)	-0.50 (0.0238)	5.01 (0.1673)	0.06 (0.4675)
	0.0	1	0.70 (0.0179)	0.00 (0.0242)	1.00 (0.0344)	0.00 (0.0513)
		5	0.70 (0.0163)	0.00 (0.0225)	5.01 (0.1648)	0.00 (0.2378)
	0.5	1	0.70 (0.0204)	0.49 (0.0271)	1.00 (0.0341)	0.00 (0.1138)
		5	0.70 (0.0183)	0.49 (0.0245)	5.01 (0.1640)	0.01 (0.5005)

α	β	γ	$\hat{\alpha}$	$\hat{\beta}$	$\hat{\gamma}$	$\hat{\mu}$
0.2	-0.5	1	0.20 (0.0030)	-0.50 (0.0118)	1.01 (0.0828)	0.00 (0.0002)
		5	0.20 (0.0030)	-0.49 (0.0124)	5.12 (0.4233)	0.00 (0.0010)
	0.0	1	0.20 (0.0027)	0.00 (0.0120)	1.02 (0.0777)	0.00 (0.0002)
		5	0.20 (0.0031)	0.00 (0.0129)	5.07 (0.3784)	0.00 (0.0009)
	0.5	1	0.20 (0.0025)	0.49 (0.0154)	1.02 (0.0839)	0.00 (0.0002)
		5	0.20 (0.0030)	0.49 (0.0126)	5.11 (0.4289)	0.00 (0.0012)
0.5	-0.5	1	0.50 (0.0087)	-0.49 (0.0161)	1.00 (0.0339)	0.00 (0.0177)
		5	0.49 (0.0081)	-0.49 (0.0149)	5.01 (0.1651)	0.00 (0.0759)
	0.0	1	0.50 (0.0084)	0.00 (0.0156)	1.00 (0.0316)	0.00 (0.0140)
		5	0.50 (0.0080)	0.00 (0.0151)	5.01 (0.1545)	0.00 (0.0637)
	0.5	1	0.50 (0.0086)	0.49 (0.0147)	1.00 (0.0317)	0.00 (0.0170)
		5	0.50 (0.0083)	0.49 (0.0152)	5.01 (0.1571)	0.00 (0.0836)
0.7	-0.5	1	0.69 (0.0164)	-0.49 (0.0215)	1.00 (0.0289)	0.00 (0.0883)
		5	0.70 (0.0157)	-0.49 (0.0205)	5.01 (0.1360)	0.02 (0.4150)
	0.0	1	0.70 (0.0156)	0.00 (0.0201)	1.00 (0.0277)	0.00 (0.0435)
		5	0.70 (0.0132)	0.00 (0.0196)	5.01 (0.1327)	0.00 (0.2044)
	0.5	1	0.69 (0.0173)	0.49 (0.0213)	1.00 (0.0285)	0.00 (0.0930)
		5	0.70 (0.0160)	0.49 (0.0208)	5.01 (0.1363)	0.04 (0.4201)

Table 7.5. $n = 5,000$, α-stable estimation, $0.2 - 0.7$

α	β	γ	$\hat{\alpha}$	$\hat{\beta}$	$\hat{\gamma}$	$\hat{\mu}$
0.2	-0.5	1	0.20 (0.0030)	-0.50 (0.0118)	1.01 (0.0828)	0.00 (0.0002)
		5	0.20 (0.0030)	-0.49 (0.0124)	5.12 (0.4233)	0.00 (0.0010)
	0.0	1	0.20 (0.0027)	0.00 (0.0120)	1.02 (0.0777)	0.00 (0.0002)
		5	0.20 (0.0031)	0.00 (0.0129)	5.07 (0.3784)	0.00 (0.0009)
	0.5	1	0.20 (0.0025)	0.49 (0.0154)	1.02 (0.0839)	0.00 (0.0002)
		5	0.20 (0.0030)	0.49 (0.0126)	5.11 (0.4289)	0.00 (0.0012)
0.5	-0.5	1	0.50 (0.0087)	-0.49 (0.0161)	1.00 (0.0339)	0.00 (0.0177)
		5	0.49 (0.0081)	-0.49 (0.0149)	5.01 (0.1651)	0.00 (0.0759)
	0.0	1	0.50 (0.0084)	0.00 (0.0156)	1.00 (0.0316)	0.00 (0.0140)
		5	0.50 (0.0080)	0.00 (0.0151)	5.01 (0.1545)	0.00 (0.0637)
	0.5	1	0.50 (0.0086)	0.49 (0.0147)	1.00 (0.0317)	0.00 (0.0170)
		5	0.50 (0.0083)	0.49 (0.0152)	5.01 (0.1571)	0.00 (0.0836)
0.7	-0.5	1	0.69 (0.0164)	-0.49 (0.0215)	1.00 (0.0289)	0.00 (0.0883)
		5	0.70 (0.0157)	-0.49 (0.0205)	5.01 (0.1360)	0.02 (0.4150)
	0.0	1	0.70 (0.0156)	0.00 (0.0201)	1.00 (0.0277)	0.00 (0.0435)
		5	0.70 (0.0132)	0.00 (0.0196)	5.01 (0.1327)	0.00 (0.2044)
	0.5	1	0.69 (0.0173)	0.49 (0.0213)	1.00 (0.0285)	0.00 (0.0930)
		5	0.70 (0.0160)	0.49 (0.0208)	5.01 (0.1363)	0.04 (0.4201)

Table 7.6. $n = 10,000$, α-stable estimation, $0.2 - 0.7$

α	β	γ	$\hat{\alpha}$	$\hat{\beta}$	$\hat{\gamma}$	$\hat{\mu}$
0.2	-0.5	1	0.5188 (0.0131)	-0.9638 (0.1403)	8.4629 (6.7437)	19.2340 (16.6239)
		5	0.5187 (0.0136)	-0.9605 (0.1492)	44.0291 (34.3708)	100.0039 (85.5797)
	0.0	1	0.5633 (0.0259)	0.0143 (0.5768)	2.7807 (2.0169)	-0.0567 (2.3619)
		5	0.5623 (0.0258)	-0.0154 (0.5872)	12.5885 (8.9279)	0.7862 (11.2772)
	0.5	1	0.5172 (0.0101)	0.9777 (0.1033)	9.0573 (8.7198)	-20.3268 (16.7490)
		5	0.5188 (0.0135)	0.9608 (0.1621)	41.3637 (29.2884)	-93.7654 (72.1596)
0.5	-0.5	1	0.5590 (0.0382)	-0.7325 (0.2653)	0.8934 (0.3917)	0.4439 (0.4138)
		5	0.5603 (0.0454)	-0.7445 (0.2563)	4.3736 (1.8325)	2.2674 (2.0338)
	0.0	1	0.5844 (0.0135)	0.0135 (0.2391)	1.0127 (0.2387)	-0.0118 (0.3383)
		5	0.5836 (0.0135)	-0.0025 (0.2517)	4.9671 (1.1959)	0.0529 (1.6594)
	0.5	1	0.5592 (0.0429)	0.7408 (0.2561)	0.8856 (0.3613)	-0.4672 (0.4178)
		5	0.5597 (0.0388)	0.7427 (0.2692)	4.4746 (2.0433)	-2.1848 (1.9647)
0.7	-0.5	1	0.7134 (0.0849)	-0.5906 (0.2133)	0.9320 (0.2504)	0.3136 (0.9265)
		5	0.7146 (0.0884)	-0.5899 (0.2149)	4.6527 (1.3515)	1.6574 (4.9961)
	0.0	1	0.7033 (0.0711)	-0.0181 (0.1743)	0.9602 (0.1616)	0.0297 (0.3709)
		5	0.7014 (0.0699)	0.0107 (0.1828)	4.7900 (0.8228)	-0.1375 (1.9261)
	0.5	1	0.7185 (0.0886)	0.5955 (0.2199)	0.9418 (0.2583)	-0.3414 (0.9045)
		5	0.7173 (0.0855)	0.5996 (0.2120)	4.6265 (1.3248)	-1.7295 (5.1308)

Table 7.7. $n = 250$, McCulloch estimation, $0.2 - 0.7$

α	β	γ	$\hat{\alpha}$	$\hat{\beta}$	$\hat{\gamma}$	$\hat{\mu}$
0.2	-0.5	1	0.5158 (0.0068)	-0.9913 (0.0671)	7.8370 (4.6916)	18.6715 (11.5353)
		5	0.5152 (0.0052)	-0.9959 (0.0504)	39.2014 (18.2783)	94.2303 (45.4315)
	0.0	1	0.5725 (0.0191)	-0.0552 (0.4278)	2.7573 (1.3159)	0.1761 (1.5591)
		5	0.5715 (0.0196)	0.0020 (0.4452)	13.3655 (6.4244)	-0.1315 (8.1083)
	0.5	1	0.5154 (0.0045)	0.9965 (0.0360)	7.1520 (3.7307)	-17.1249 (9.0901)
		5	0.5157 (0.0057)	0.9928 (0.0515)	36.6105 (16.6436)	-87.2594 (41.3631)
0.5	-0.5	1	0.5482 (0.0237)	-0.7755 (0.2139)	0.8055 (0.2613)	0.4177 (0.2894)
		5	0.5473 (0.0217)	-0.7714 (0.2120)	4.0051 (1.4385)	1.9838 (1.2949)
	0.0	1	0.5873 (0.0062)	0.0048 (0.1543)	1.0432 (0.1599)	-0.0101 (0.2307)
		5	0.5872 (0.0054)	0.0061 (0.1517)	5.1905 (0.8011)	-0.0364 (1.1531)
	0.5	1	0.5492 (0.0260)	0.7660 (0.2116)	0.8102 (0.2884)	-0.3983 (0.2432)
		5	0.5506 (0.0248)	0.7442 (0.2159)	4.2016 (1.4839)	-1.9526 (1.3542)
0.7	-0.5	1	0.7107 (0.0659)	-0.5828 (0.1663)	0.9355 (0.2190)	0.2369 (0.6952)
		5	0.7123 (0.0608)	-0.5814 (0.1667)	4.6907 (1.0349)	1.0797 (2.1052)
	0.0	1	0.7015 (0.0494)	-0.0042 (0.1242)	0.9575 (0.1043)	0.0154 (0.2638)
		5	0.7031 (0.0442)	0.0088 (0.1289)	4.8416 (0.5662)	-0.1055 (1.3533)
	0.5	1	0.7084 (0.0640)	0.5816 (0.1663)	0.9245 (0.2077)	-0.2059 (0.5451)
		5	0.7097 (0.0644)	0.5718 (0.1719)	4.7197 (1.0425)	-0.8797 (2.4869)

Table 7.8. $n = 500$, McCulloch estimation, 0.2 – 0.7

α	β	γ	$\hat{\alpha}$	$\hat{\beta}$	$\hat{\gamma}$	$\hat{\mu}$
0.2	-0.5	1	0.5140 (0.0005)	-1.0000 (0.0000)	6.5419 (0.9776)	15.8336 (2.4174)
		5	0.5140 (0.0005)	-1.0000 (0.0000)	32.9854 (4.8350)	79.8604 (11.9497)
	0.0	1	0.5881 (0.0037)	0.0028 (0.1293)	2.9384 (0.3374)	-0.0110 (0.5853)
		5	0.5880 (0.0039)	-0.0067 (0.1325)	14.6809 (1.6854)	0.1586 (2.9691)
	0.5	1	0.5140 (0.0005)	1.0000 (0.0000)	6.5588 (0.9535)	-15.8757 (2.3565)
		5	0.5140 (0.0005)	1.0000 (0.0000)	33.0529 (5.0163)	-80.0152 (12.4111)
0.5	-0.5	1	0.5404 (0.0049)	-0.8106 (0.0822)	0.7068 (0.0818)	0.3868 (0.0680)
		5	0.5404 (0.0052)	-0.8104 (0.0878)	3.5579 (0.4408)	1.9576 (0.3552)
	0.0	1	0.5910 (0.0014)	-0.0004 (0.0502)	1.0704 (0.0512)	0.0009 (0.0828)
		5	0.5909 (0.0014)	0.0002 (0.0525)	5.3279 (0.2381)	-0.0030 (0.4327)
	0.5	1	0.5406 (0.0051)	0.8071 (0.0863)	0.7121 (0.0877)	-0.3892 (0.0694)
		5	0.5407 (0.0048)	0.8065 (0.0800)	3.5644 (0.3993)	-1.9436 (0.3348)
0.7	-0.5	1	0.7129 (0.0211)	-0.5407 (0.0596)	0.9687 (0.0768)	0.1283 (0.1268)
		5	0.7126 (0.0204)	-0.5447 (0.0614)	4.8306 (0.3694)	0.6745 (0.5940)
	0.0	1	0.7023 (0.0156)	0.0008 (0.0412)	0.9841 (0.0316)	-0.0023 (0.0901)
		5	0.7022 (0.0167)	-0.0011 (0.0434)	4.9298 (0.1756)	0.0129 (0.4728)
	0.5	1	0.7146 (0.0211)	0.5407 (0.0573)	0.9721 (0.0734)	-0.1409 (0.1311)
		5	0.7118 (0.0202)	0.5405 (0.0587)	4.8239 (0.3624)	-0.6021 (0.6217)

Table 7.9. $n = 5,000$, McCulloch estimation, 0.2 – 0.7

α	β	γ	α̂	β̂	γ̂	μ̂
0.2	-0.5	1	0.5140 (0.0003)	-1.0000 (0.0000)	6.5563 (0.6998)	15.8735 (1.7273)
		5	0.5139 (0.0003)	-1.0000 (0.0000)	32.6053 (3.3260)	78.9393 (8.2150)
	0.0	1	0.5896 (0.0024)	0.0020 (0.0905)	2.9725 (0.2247)	-0.0089 (0.4212)
		5	0.5897 (0.0022)	-0.0032 (0.0883)	14.8871 (1.1739)	0.0797 (2.0654)
	0.5	1	0.5139 (0.0003)	1.0000 (0.0000)	6.5194 (0.6750)	-15.7836 (1.6648)
		5	0.5140 (0.0003)	1.0000 (0.0000)	32.9284 (3.4183)	-79.7449 (8.4429)
0.5	-0.5	1	0.5402 (0.0033)	-0.8139 (0.0554)	0.7037 (0.0550)	0.3941 (0.0457)
		5	0.5403 (0.0032)	-0.8120 (0.0545)	3.5346 (0.2760)	1.9765 (0.2272)
	0.0	1	0.5914 (0.0011)	-0.0006 (0.0375)	1.0734 (0.0351)	0.0009 (0.0626)
		5	0.5914 (0.0011)	-0.0011 (0.0375)	5.3650 (0.1805)	0.0094 (0.3155)
	0.5	1	0.5402 (0.0034)	0.8136 (0.0573)	0.7030 (0.0566)	-0.3928 (0.0453)
		5	0.5402 (0.0032)	0.8136 (0.0539)	3.5191 (0.2765)	-1.9692 (0.2245)
0.7	-0.5	1	0.7136 (0.0145)	-0.5339 (0.0423)	0.9766 (0.0523)	0.1223 (0.0901)
		5	0.7133 (0.0145)	-0.5377 (0.0437)	4.8614 (0.2689)	0.6266 (0.4311)
	0.0	1	0.7016 (0.0119)	-0.0001 (0.0312)	0.9877 (0.0250)	0.0001 (0.0682)
		5	0.7022 (0.0114)	-0.0000 (0.0294)	4.9409 (0.1200)	-0.0028 (0.3203)
	0.5	1	0.7135 (0.0147)	0.5343 (0.0396)	0.9762 (0.0520)	-0.1234 (0.0909)
		5	0.7128 (0.0145)	0.5363 (0.0433)	4.8658 (0.2725)	-0.6057 (0.4599)

Table 7.10. $n = 10,000$, McCulloch estimation, $0.2 - 0.7$

α	β	γ	α̂	β̂	γ̂	μ̂
1.3	-0.5	1	1.3951 (0.1509)	-0.5575 (0.2588)	1.0173 (0.0797)	0.0812 (0.4347)
		5	1.3605 (0.1291)	-0.5721 (0.2059)	5.0374 (0.4143)	0.1051 (2.2526)
	0.0	1	1.3736 (0.1713)	-0.0133 (0.2298)	1.0081 (0.0849)	-0.0125 (0.2772)
		5	1.3458 (0.1336)	-0.0115 (0.1956)	4.9922 (0.4086)	-0.1323 (1.5510)
	0.5	1	1.3873 (0.1389)	0.5420 (0.2326)	1.0127 (0.0841)	-0.1353 (0.3726)
		5	1.3591 (0.1252)	0.5380 (0.2111)	5.0426 (0.3895)	-0.3908 (2.0331)
1.5	-0.5	1	1.5439 (0.1485)	-0.5718 (0.2720)	1.0039 (0.0746)	-0.0237 (0.2412)
		5	1.5305 (0.1412)	-0.5673 (0.2742)	4.9707 (0.3739)	-0.1621 (1.3031)
	0.0	1	1.5579 (0.1688)	0.0003 (0.3252)	1.0031 (0.0776)	-0.0161 (0.1974)
		5	1.5431 (0.1661)	-0.0214 (0.3222)	4.9926 (0.3901)	-0.1066 (1.0187)
	0.5	1	1.5454 (0.1430)	0.5146 (0.2903)	1.0010 (0.0789)	-0.0362 (0.2240)
		5	1.5273 (0.1370)	0.5204 (0.2854)	5.0099 (0.3758)	-0.0821 (1.1384)
1.8	-0.5	1	1.8013 (0.1397)	-0.3451 (0.5432)	0.9938 (0.0643)	-0.0115 (0.1518)
		5	1.7923 (0.1388)	-0.3942 (0.5248)	4.9609 (0.3351)	-0.0589 (0.7634)
	0.0	1	1.8073 (0.1363)	-0.0288 (0.5562)	0.9935 (0.0680)	-0.0214 (0.1428)
		5	1.8117 (0.1378)	-0.0724 (0.5929)	4.9551 (0.3407)	-0.1412 (0.7420)
	0.5	1	1.7972 (0.1350)	0.2471 (0.5336)	0.9972 (0.0658)	-0.0427 (0.1389)
		5	1.7977 (0.1330)	0.2895 (0.5302)	4.9690 (0.3360)	-0.2010 (0.6933)

Table 7.11. $n = 250$, α-stable estimation, $1.3 - 1.8$

α	β	γ	$\hat{\alpha}$	$\hat{\beta}$	$\hat{\gamma}$	$\hat{\mu}$
1.3	-0.5	1	1.3739 (0.1198)	-0.5394 (0.1928)	1.0139 (0.0627)	0.0862 (0.3036)
		5	1.3454 (0.0901)	-0.5431 (0.1434)	5.0386 (0.2902)	0.1366 (1.6287)
	0.0	1	1.3536 (0.1384)	-0.0109 (0.1745)	1.0081 (0.0645)	-0.0181 (0.1911)
		5	1.3216 (0.0890)	-0.0130 (0.1225)	5.0030 (0.2925)	-0.1130 (1.0061)
	0.5	1	1.3661 (0.1168)	0.5298 (0.1939)	1.0122 (0.0638)	-0.0972 (0.2994)
		5	1.3477 (0.0924)	0.5263 (0.1493)	5.0453 (0.2893)	-0.3433 (1.4487)
1.5	-0.5	1	1.5402 (0.1134)	-0.5534 (0.2283)	1.0026 (0.0557)	-0.0018 (0.1666)
		5	1.5340 (0.1120)	-0.5597 (0.1968)	5.0115 (0.2824)	-0.0310 (0.8027)
	0.0	1	1.5469 (0.1303)	-0.0144 (0.2080)	1.0054 (0.0596)	-0.0128 (0.1330)
		5	1.5266 (0.1143)	-0.0120 (0.1823)	4.9944 (0.2682)	-0.0584 (0.6505)
	0.5	1	1.5342 (0.1158)	0.5259 (0.2354)	1.0019 (0.0556)	-0.0229 (0.1577)
		5	1.5254 (0.1062)	0.5242 (0.2013)	4.9984 (0.2775)	-0.1245 (0.7442)
1.8	-0.5	1	1.8007 (0.1173)	-0.4212 (0.4453)	0.9950 (0.0512)	-0.0039 (0.1030)
		5	1.8114 (0.1162)	-0.4683 (0.4117)	4.9866 (0.2439)	-0.0024 (0.5173)
	0.0	1	1.8394 (0.1182)	0.0013 (0.5093)	1.0015 (0.0516)	-0.0102 (0.0925)
		5	1.8329 (0.1144)	-0.0475 (0.4960)	5.0089 (0.2352)	-0.0438 (0.4690)
	0.5	1	1.8081 (0.1124)	0.3597 (0.4740)	0.9993 (0.0500)	-0.0259 (0.0976)
		5	1.8037 (0.1093)	0.3958 (0.4451)	4.9914 (0.2464)	-0.1032 (0.5062)

Table 7.12. $n = 500$, α-stable estimation, 1.3 – 1.8

α	β	γ	$\hat{\alpha}$	$\hat{\beta}$	$\hat{\gamma}$	$\hat{\mu}$
1.3	-0.5	1	1.3332 (0.0471)	-0.5171 (0.0584)	1.0083 (0.0232)	0.0643 (0.1292)
		5	1.3262 (0.0393)	-0.5159 (0.0516)	5.0338 (0.1083)	0.2340 (0.5904)
	0.0	1	1.3117 (0.0394)	0.0011 (0.0441)	1.0040 (0.0228)	-0.0004 (0.0728)
		5	1.3082 (0.0355)	0.0001 (0.0424)	5.0139 (0.1057)	-0.0082 (0.3670)
	0.5	1	1.3311 (0.0462)	0.5177 (0.0574)	1.0068 (0.0234)	-0.0595 (0.1269)
		5	1.3240 (0.0412)	0.5146 (0.0556)	5.0290 (0.1122)	-0.2159 (0.6159)
1.5	-0.5	1	1.5200 (0.0488)	-0.5236 (0.0770)	1.0040 (0.0201)	0.0072 (0.0581)
		5	1.5173 (0.0419)	-0.5212 (0.0708)	5.0173 (0.0999)	0.0326 (0.2701)
	0.0	1	1.5130 (0.0449)	-0.0001 (0.0621)	1.0033 (0.0204)	-0.0005 (0.0474)
		5	1.5107 (0.0411)	0.0020 (0.0585)	5.0135 (0.0982)	0.0014 (0.2296)
	0.5	1	1.5180 (0.0475)	0.5148 (0.0806)	1.0044 (0.0200)	-0.0096 (0.0590)
		5	1.5155 (0.0446)	0.5161 (0.0736)	5.0151 (0.0966)	-0.0373 (0.2742)
1.8	-0.5	1	1.8187 (0.0554)	-0.5323 (0.2453)	1.0024 (0.0185)	0.0050 (0.0344)
		5	1.8156 (0.0504)	-0.5633 (0.1971)	5.0108 (0.0895)	0.0146 (0.1673)
	0.0	1	1.8403 (0.0674)	-0.0017 (0.2554)	1.0064 (0.0189)	0.0006 (0.0297)
		5	1.8336 (0.0612)	0.0088 (0.2028)	5.0299 (0.0962)	0.0036 (0.1537)
	0.5	1	1.8186 (0.0567)	0.5455 (0.2692)	1.0038 (0.0197)	-0.0050 (0.0336)
		5	1.8134 (0.0504)	0.5561 (0.2004)	5.0124 (0.0877)	-0.0130 (0.1644)

Table 7.13. $n = 5,000$, α-stable estimation, 1.3 – 1.8

208 Metaheuristics for Intelligent Electrical Networks

α	β	γ	$\hat{\alpha}$	$\hat{\beta}$	$\hat{\gamma}$	$\hat{\mu}$
1.3	-0.5	1	1.3287 (0.0385)	-0.5113 (0.0473)	1.0075 (0.0187)	0.0631 (0.1055)
		5	1.3207 (0.0349)	-0.5103 (0.0446)	5.0236 (0.0945)	0.2154 (0.5007)
	0.0	1	1.3108 (0.0326)	0.0004 (0.0362)	1.0038 (0.0180)	0.0007 (0.0601)
		5	1.3066 (0.0307)	0.0011 (0.0356)	5.0121 (0.0861)	0.0102 (0.2987)
	0.5	1	1.3289 (0.0406)	0.5138 (0.0492)	1.0082 (0.0198)	-0.0578 (0.1151)
		5	1.3200 (0.0342)	0.5096 (0.0445)	5.0234 (0.0905)	-0.2143 (0.5044)
1.5	-0.5	1	1.5162 (0.0406)	-0.5127 (0.0611)	1.0034 (0.0163)	0.0118 (0.0475)
		5	1.5136 (0.0363)	-0.5150 (0.0574)	5.0147 (0.0786)	0.0268 (0.2285)
	0.0	1	1.5097 (0.0347)	-0.0023 (0.0503)	1.0029 (0.0165)	-0.0020 (0.0375)
		5	1.5084 (0.0331)	-0.0012 (0.0492)	5.0092 (0.0780)	-0.0044 (0.1930)
	0.5	1	1.5161 (0.0412)	0.5145 (0.0607)	1.0048 (0.0169)	-0.0088 (0.0485)
		5	1.5142 (0.0357)	0.5131 (0.0566)	5.0142 (0.0764)	-0.0439 (0.2343)
1.8	-0.5	1	1.8134 (0.0462)	-0.5420 (0.1949)	1.0024 (0.0149)	0.0042 (0.0275)
		5	1.8166 (0.0415)	-0.5636 (0.1672)	5.0127 (0.0714)	0.0107 (0.1319)
	0.0	1	1.8362 (0.0569)	0.0031 (0.1988)	1.0063 (0.0164)	-0.0010 (0.0264)
		5	1.8249 (0.0483)	-0.0000 (0.1384)	5.0255 (0.0745)	-0.0004 (0.1250)
	0.5	1	1.8135 (0.0461)	0.5353 (0.1902)	1.0017 (0.0144)	-0.0055 (0.0263)
		5	1.8158 (0.0414)	0.5606 (0.1710)	5.0153 (0.0705)	-0.0152 (0.1306)

Table 7.14. $n = 10{,}000$, α-stable estimation, $1.3 - 1.8$

α	β	γ	$\hat{\alpha}$	$\hat{\beta}$	$\hat{\gamma}$	$\hat{\mu}$
1.3	-0.5	1	1.3173 (0.1339)	-0.5458 (0.1906)	0.9916 (0.0904)	-0.1354 (0.8843)
		5	1.3146 (0.1424)	-0.5510 (0.1826)	4.9687 (0.5083)	-1.0200 (3.7072)
	0.0	1	1.3046 (0.1135)	-0.0070 (0.1984)	0.9938 (0.0901)	-0.0141 (0.4547)
		5	1.3142 (0.1162)	0.0150 (0.1886)	4.9634 (0.4098)	0.1167 (2.2671)
	0.5	1	1.3087 (0.1305)	0.5450 (0.1707)	0.9832 (0.0941)	0.1712 (0.8818)
		5	1.3066 (0.1357)	0.5198 (0.1818)	4.9418 (0.4687)	0.7455 (4.3048)
1.5	-0.5	1	1.5258 (0.1452)	-0.5797 (0.2481)	0.9929 (0.0866)	-0.0424 (0.2473)
		5	1.5026 (0.1582)	-0.5549 (0.2526)	4.9277 (0.4251)	-0.2451 (1.3573)
	0.0	1	1.5085 (0.1386)	0.0158 (0.2768)	0.9994 (0.0786)	0.0010 (0.2290)
		5	1.5151 (0.1465)	-0.0070 (0.2891)	4.9844 (0.4197)	-0.0570 (1.0431)
	0.5	1	1.5122 (0.1456)	0.5640 (0.2479)	0.9938 (0.0838)	0.0472 (0.2459)
		5	1.5238 (0.1516)	0.5833 (0.2418)	4.9772 (0.4348)	0.2962 (1.3701)
1.8	-0.5	1	1.8144 (0.1524)	-0.5185 (0.4560)	1.0037 (0.0824)	0.0107 (0.1350)
		5	1.8104 (0.1595)	-0.4582 (0.4969)	5.0100 (0.3936)	0.0439 (0.7217)
	0.0	1	1.8146 (0.1488)	0.0396 (0.5932)	1.0051 (0.0782)	-0.0047 (0.1307)
		5	1.8220 (0.1591)	-0.0103 (0.5706)	5.0366 (0.4100)	0.0499 (0.6431)
	0.5	1	1.8132 (0.1546)	0.4446 (0.5020)	0.9968 (0.0807)	-0.0167 (0.1366)
		5	1.8145 (0.1490)	0.4676 (0.5021)	5.0190 (0.3878)	-0.0457 (0.7065)

Table 7.15. $n = 250$, McCulloch estimation, $1.3 - 1.8$

α	β	γ	$\hat{\alpha}$	$\hat{\beta}$	$\hat{\gamma}$	$\hat{\mu}$
1.3	-0.5	1	1.3056 (0.0891)	-0.5245 (0.1262)	0.9887 (0.0698)	-0.1128 (0.4938)
		5	1.3069 (0.0917)	-0.5414 (0.1403)	4.9617 (0.3475)	-0.6365 (2.6845)
	0.0	1	1.3037 (0.0797)	-0.0067 (0.1259)	0.9986 (0.0624)	-0.0067 (0.2808)
		5	1.3028 (0.0738)	-0.0064 (0.1349)	4.9661 (0.2943)	-0.0479 (1.4243)
	0.5	1	1.3104 (0.0947)	0.5349 (0.1262)	0.9903 (0.0644)	0.0992 (0.4584)
		5	1.3049 (0.0920)	0.5268 (0.1287)	4.9708 (0.3406)	0.5697 (2.5334)
1.5	-0.5	1	1.5059 (0.1005)	-0.5458 (0.1781)	0.9938 (0.0579)	-0.0270 (0.1696)
		5	1.5121 (0.1093)	-0.5758 (0.1879)	4.9833 (0.2943)	-0.2150 (0.8817)
	0.0	1	1.5026 (0.0923)	-0.0060 (0.1710)	0.9925 (0.0579)	-0.0008 (0.1446)
		5	1.5061 (0.0898)	-0.0064 (0.1677)	4.9983 (0.2882)	-0.0492 (0.7007)
	0.5	1	1.5146 (0.1081)	0.5669 (0.1949)	0.9990 (0.0617)	0.0319 (0.1769)
		5	1.5130 (0.1000)	0.5493 (0.1814)	5.0007 (0.2843)	0.1423 (0.7790)
1.8	-0.5	1	1.8151 (0.1191)	-0.5591 (0.3724)	0.9985 (0.0566)	0.0039 (0.1011)
		5	1.8231 (0.1280)	-0.6012 (0.3530)	5.0087 (0.2700)	0.0186 (0.5138)
	0.0	1	1.8095 (0.1255)	0.0361 (0.4558)	0.9952 (0.0593)	-0.0003 (0.0884)
		5	1.8093 (0.1225)	0.0336 (0.4797)	5.0088 (0.2850)	0.0052 (0.4810)
	0.5	1	1.8020 (0.1184)	0.5371 (0.3828)	0.9952 (0.0551)	-0.0028 (0.0987)
		5	1.8203 (0.1223)	0.5758 (0.3795)	5.0109 (0.2600)	0.0266 (0.5314)

Table 7.16. $n = 500$, McCulloch estimation, $1.3 - 1.8$

α	β	γ	$\hat{\alpha}$	$\hat{\beta}$	$\hat{\gamma}$	$\hat{\mu}$
1.3	-0.5	1	1.3033 (0.0300)	-0.5334 (0.0402)	0.9914 (0.0217)	-0.0419 (0.1207)
		5	1.3063 (0.0305)	-0.5331 (0.0406)	4.9588 (0.1058)	-0.1490 (0.5967)
	0.0	1	1.3039 (0.0239)	0.0005 (0.0427)	0.9978 (0.0188)	0.0012 (0.0768)
		5	1.3035 (0.0242)	0.0021 (0.0427)	4.9837 (0.0958)	0.0159 (0.3818)
	0.5	1	1.3057 (0.0292)	0.5332 (0.0394)	0.9925 (0.0199)	0.0328 (0.1184)
		5	1.3050 (0.0302)	0.5325 (0.0399)	4.9655 (0.1122)	0.1790 (0.6173)
1.5	-0.5	1	1.5034 (0.0339)	-0.5257 (0.0548)	0.9955 (0.0186)	-0.0130 (0.0517)
		5	1.5031 (0.0329)	-0.5294 (0.0542)	4.9784 (0.0905)	-0.0815 (0.2584)
	0.0	1	1.5011 (0.0290)	-0.0013 (0.0502)	0.9976 (0.0183)	-0.0041 (0.0426)
		5	1.5049 (0.0289)	-0.0005 (0.0513)	4.9925 (0.0903)	0.0020 (0.2182)
	0.5	1	1.5045 (0.0321)	0.5294 (0.0557)	0.9964 (0.0180)	0.0140 (0.0490)
		5	1.5037 (0.0317)	0.5302 (0.0531)	4.9843 (0.0910)	0.0817 (0.2376)
1.8	-0.5	1	1.8062 (0.0443)	-0.6025 (0.1879)	0.9980 (0.0168)	-0.0108 (0.0278)
		5	1.8078 (0.0475)	-0.6103 (0.1955)	4.9953 (0.0935)	-0.0554 (0.1402)
	0.0	1	1.8045 (0.0431)	0.0030 (0.1335)	1.0005 (0.0186)	0.0001 (0.0288)
		5	1.8026 (0.0433)	-0.0022 (0.1352)	4.9948 (0.0866)	-0.0062 (0.1462)
	0.5	1	1.8059 (0.0455)	0.5973 (0.1905)	0.9989 (0.0176)	0.0077 (0.0296)
		5	1.8035 (0.0438)	0.5898 (0.1857)	4.9919 (0.0854)	0.0547 (0.1539)

Table 7.17. $n = 5,000$, McCulloch estimation, $1.3 - 1.8$

α	β	γ	$\hat{\alpha}$	$\hat{\beta}$	$\hat{\gamma}$	$\hat{\mu}$
1.3	-0.5	1	1.3060 (0.0217)	-0.5332 (0.0290)	0.9921 (0.0150)	-0.0272 (0.0861)
		5	1.3059 (0.0208)	-0.5337 (0.0294)	4.9599 (0.0722)	-0.1427 (0.4197)
	0.0	1	1.3036 (0.0173)	-0.0001 (0.0309)	0.9980 (0.0133)	-0.0010 (0.0553)
		5	1.3033 (0.0181)	0.0007 (0.0303)	4.9905 (0.0692)	0.0027 (0.2693)
	0.5	1	1.3050 (0.0211)	0.5319 (0.0277)	0.9917 (0.0152)	0.0285 (0.0859)
		5	1.3055 (0.0216)	0.5335 (0.0287)	4.9593 (0.0747)	0.1503 (0.4249)
1.5	-0.5	1	1.5034 (0.0239)	-0.5265 (0.0385)	0.9963 (0.0133)	-0.0135 (0.0357)
		5	1.5038 (0.0232)	-0.5292 (0.0391)	4.9824 (0.0645)	-0.0717 (0.1787)
	0.0	1	1.5041 (0.0210)	0.0006 (0.0351)	0.9993 (0.0131)	-0.0006 (0.0316)
		5	1.5024 (0.0201)	-0.0009 (0.0359)	4.9912 (0.0647)	-0.0043 (0.1573)
	0.5	1	1.5023 (0.0233)	0.5257 (0.0372)	0.9956 (0.0125)	0.0142 (0.0363)
		5	1.5024 (0.0242)	0.5275 (0.0403)	4.9798 (0.0642)	0.0742 (0.1822)
1.8	-0.5	1	1.8050 (0.0311)	-0.5915 (0.1371)	0.9982 (0.0120)	-0.0117 (0.0203)
		5	1.8033 (0.0317)	-0.5829 (0.1422)	4.9911 (0.0605)	-0.0569 (0.1010)
	0.0	1	1.8013 (0.0305)	-0.0000 (0.0908)	0.9987 (0.0127)	0.0007 (0.0207)
		5	1.8030 (0.0314)	0.0027 (0.0984)	4.9964 (0.0640)	0.0029 (0.1054)
	0.5	1	1.8047 (0.0312)	0.5874 (0.1434)	0.9982 (0.0119)	0.0115 (0.0205)
		5	1.8036 (0.0317)	0.5794 (0.1350)	4.9908 (0.0615)	0.0538 (0.0991)

Table 7.18. *n = 10,000, McCulloch estimation, 1.3 – 1.8*

In general, solving the optimization problem described in section 7.3.2 and, specifically, the minimization of the Kolmogorov–Smirnov statistic (equation [7.25]) by our algorithm is in any case better than that of the McCulloch algorithm. In effect, Figure 7.4 shows that the box-plots of the optimized objective are largely below the acceptance threshold and this is true for any value of α, β, γ and μ and for any sample size n. On the contrary, Figure 7.5 shows that the box-plots of the Kolmogorov–Smirnov statistic calculated for McCulloch estimates are close to rejection boundaries, sometimes even exceeding that threshold.

Another important point to note in the light of these results is the asymptotic convergence of the two estimators (Tables 7.6, 7.10, 7.14 and 7.18). The difficulty in estimating the four parameters of the α-stable distributions when $\alpha > 1$ for small sample sizes n lies in the fact that the tail of the distribution does not remain consistent (that is to say it exhibits few variations), knowing that the slope of the probability distribution in loglog characterizes the stability index α of α-stable distributions.

7.4.2. *Parallelization of the process on a GP/GPU card*

The algorithm that we have developed is inherently parallelizable. We wanted to implement it in order to estimate the gains in computation times. In this section, we directly present the procedure used to perform the implementation of our α-stable estimator on a GP/GPU card.

The "kstest2.m" function in Matlab achieves a Kolmogorov–Smirnov statistical hypothesis test with two independent sample sets X_1 and X_2. The result of the test determines if X_1 and X_2 come from the same distribution law (Boolean H). The series X_1 is the reference series whose α-stable distribution parameters are to be determined (this can be, for instance, the distribution of faults in an electrical network). It is assumed that the latter follows an α-stable distribution. The series X_2 is generated by the parameters of the α-stable distribution of the OEP particles. This function is the objective function of the OEP developed in section 7.3.

The initial idea is to calculate in parallel, in a synchronous manner and for all particles, the function *kstest2:*

$$[H, P, KSSTAT] = kstest2(X_1, X_2, ALPHA, TYPE)$$

with, as input:

- X_1 sample series;

- X_2 sample series;

- $Alpha$: level of confidence;

- $Type$: "unequal", "larger" and "smaller";

and as output:

- $KSSTAT$: test statistics;

- P: asymptotic value;

- H: a binary number for the acceptance or rejection of the hypothesis.

The Matlab code analysis $kstest2.m$ shows that this function can be broken down sequentially into parallelizable tasks:

– sort;

– histograms;

– cumulative sums;

– determination of the maximal value of a series.

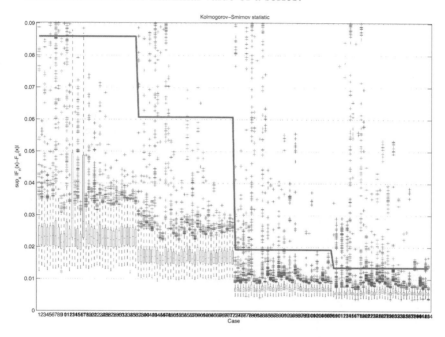

Figure 7.4. *Application of the algorithm to the benchmark with:*
$\alpha = 0.2$, $\beta = [-0, 5, 0, 0, 5]$, $\gamma = [1, 5]$, $\mu = 0$. *For a color version of this figure, see www.iste.co.uk/heliodore/metaheuristics.zip*

These are encoded in a language similar to the C language in the form of kernels that will be able to be compiled and then downloaded onto the target (GPU) from the Python program running on the host (CPU). This is not, from an algorithmic perspective, a simple translation of the existing sequential algorithms for these operations. It is necessary to find or develop algorithms that are as inherently parallel as possible. This is the first level of parallelism.

The second level of parallelism concerns the data according to the *single instruction multiple data* computing paradigm, which is the paradigm used by the GPU. In fact, the same instruction $kstest2$ can be applied to the data of the OEP particles. In order to use this level of parallelism, the series generated by the parameters (α-stable distribution) of the particles are concatenated in the same table. The processing of the latter is then achieved in a synchronous manner. An underlying low-level mechanism makes it possible to distribute these tasks on the *streaming multiprocessor* (SM) of the GPU according to a queue mechanism ("*queueing*").

These low-level operations (compiled during runtime and downloaded onto the target) are carried out by the advanced commands of the pyOpenCL Python module and take place at the beginning of the program. The pyOpenCL module achieves the interface between Python and OpenCL (open standard with specifications concerning programming and parallel computing on heterogeneous platforms). The Python code is executed by the CPU (host), the kernels compiled and transferred are executed by the GPU (target).

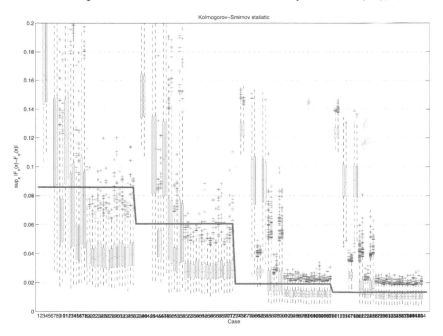

Figure 7.5. *Application of the algorithm to the benchmark with:*
$\alpha = 0.2$, $\beta = [-0.5, 0, 0.5]$, $\gamma = [1, 5]$, $\mu = 0$. *For a color version of this figure, see www.iste.co.uk/heliodore/metaheuristics.zip*

It is imperative to minimize data transfers between the host and the target. For this purpose, it is important to *a priori* allocate memory resources on the GPU during the initialization of the program. In the case of the $kstest2$ function, the variables to which memory space has to be allocated on the GPU are:

– the series X_1 and X_2;

– the parameters α_i, β_i, γ_i and μ_i determining the distribution parameters of the series X_2 for particles i;

– storage and intermediate processing tables necessary for the sorting, cumulative sum and histogram algorithms.

Table 7.19 gives the description of the OpenCL files utilized for the previous operations.

Files	Descriptions
copy.cl	Formatting of memory allocations in the GPU (copy)
copy.cl	Formatting of memory allocations in the GPU (filling)
stab_rnd1.cl	Random number generator following an α-stable distribution
stab_rnd2.cl	Random number generator following an α-stable distribution
pyopencl-ranluxcl.cl	Random number generator following a uniform distribution
radix.cl	Modified "radix" sorting algorithm (origin Nvidia)
histogram.cl	Parallelized algorithm for the computation of histograms
cumsum_large.cl	Cumulative sum parallelized algorithm (origin Nvidia)
KSstatistic.cl	Determination of maxima and deltaCDF. Results formatting

Table 7.19. *List of OpenCL files*

7.4.2.1. *Distribution generator according to an α-stable distribution*

Distribution is achieved based on the stabrnd.m Matlab function (algorithm 7.1). The basic generator is a random number generator following a uniform distribution law coded in C in the form of kernels and directly executed on the GPU. It is based on the RANLUX algorithm (*RANdom LUXury*) [JAM 94, LUS 94]. There is no massive data transfer between the host and the target. The memory spaces of series X2 corresponding to the particles of the OEP algorithm are directly filled by the OpenCL kernels (libraries pyopencl-ranluxcl.cl, stab_rnd.cl, fill.cl and copy.cl). The only variables that are subject to a transfer between the host and the target and vice versa are the parameters α_i, β_i, γ_i and μ_i determining the parameters of the α-stable distribution of series X_2 for particles i.

7.4.2.2. *Sorting*

This function is based on a "Radix" sorting algorithm or base sorting. The basic principle is understandable through the following example:

Sort the list: 170, 45, 75, 90, 2, 24, 802, 66.

1) sorting by least significant digit (units): 170, 90, 2, 802, 24, 45, 75, 66;

2) sorting by the following digit (tens): 2, 802, 24, 45, 66, 170, 75, 90;

3) sorting by most significant digit (hundreds): 2, 24, 45, 66, 75, 90, 170, 802.

These operations are based on binary masking operations (using AND, OR and XOR operators) and not on comparison operators.

This algorithm initially intended for sorting positive integers has been adapted to real ones (FLOAT32 mantissa + exponent + sign type coded in 32-bit) with minor modifications. The reference [FEL 10] describes in detail the Radix algorithm. The OpenCL implementation is largely based on an example taken from the OpenCL SDK (*Sample Development Kit*) from Nvidia [CUD 17]. It is coded in C++ (instead of Python). It took extensive reverse engineering work to achieve the interface with pyOpenCL (identification of the various kernels and their parameters, variables and used tables).

7.4.2.3. *Histogram*

At the GPU level, histograms are massively used in image processing [FRE 11] because they can provide evaluations of the contrast of an image (overexposure or underexposure for example). They utilize direct indexing methods. The classes of these histograms have a fixed width (grayscale coding in 8 bits, for example) and employ a direct indexing method.

This is an original algorithm based on the use of dichotomy and functions known as "atomic" in the OpenCL standard [GRO]. For each value in the series to sort, a dichotomy algorithm is applied. The value is first compared to the bounds of the classes of the histogram and to the median value. The result of these comparisons allows the restriction of the interval to which the class of the value of the series under consideration belongs. Gradually, when the interval is small enough (the number of interval classes is divided by 2 at each iteration), the class is determined. The histogram index corresponding to the previously determined class is then incremented by one. Multiple instances of this process can be launched in parallel. In fact, the determination of the class to which a value of the series belongs does not depend on that of the other values. Using a so-called "atomic" function to perform the increment operations makes it possible to ensure that all increments will be taken into account and that there will be no masking (no taking into account), for example in the event that two instances of the algorithm increment the same index at the same time (same memory address).

7.4.2.4. *Cumulative sum*

The studies [HIL 86] and [BLE 90] describe in detail the parallelized cumulative sum algorithms.

Let a sequence of numbers x_0, x_1, x_2 ... x_n be the cumulative parallel sum algorithm described by the pseudo-code 7.3, where N is the number of elements in the sequence whose cumulative sum is to be calculated.

Figure 7.6 graphically shows the evolution of the cumulative sum computation process for a series of 16 samples.

The OpenCL implementation is largely based on an example taken from the OpenCL SDK (*Sample Development Kit*) of Nvidia [CUD 17]. The latter is coded in C++ (instead of Python). Due to optimizations in terms of memory access (global/local) and intermediate storage variables, the code is visibly more complex than the pseudo-code previously presented. An extensive work of reverse engineering has been necessary in order to achieve the interface with pyOpenCL (identification of the different kernels, variables and tables used).

7.4.2.5. *Maximum*

The maximum value of a series is determined by means of a parallel "reduction" algorithm. The series is divided into subsections. An instance of the kernel compiled and downloaded is assigned to each subsection in order to determine the maximum value following a sequential process. The local maximum values thus determined are collected in a new smaller table (hence the term "reduction"). Next, the maximum value in the table is determined or a process of decomposition into subsections is resumed. The number of subsections and the number of reduction steps can be optimized according to the GPU. Multiple instances of this algorithm can be initiated based on the number of particles.

Algorithm 7.3: Cumulative sum

```
/* We want to compute the cumulative sum of N vector
   elements.                                            */
```
1 **For** d *ranging from* 1 *to* $\log_2(N)$ **Do**
2   **For** k *in parallel* **Do**
3   **If** $k > 2^d$ **Then**
4       $x[out][k] \leftarrow x[in][k - 2^{(d-1)}] + x[in][k]$
5   **Else**
6       $x[out][k] := x[in][k]$
7   **End**
8   **End**
9   **Swap** (in,out)
10 **End**

7.4.2.6. *Results*

Table 7.20 shows the comparison of GPU Python + OpenCL/CPU Matlab execution times of the function $kstest2$ for different sizes of series X_1 and X_2. The number of simulated particles is 32. Eight workstations are equipped with the GP/GPU card. The GTX 570 card is more powerful (twice the number of SMs and higher kernel and memory frequency). Its results are given as an indication. The analysis of the results shows that in all cases, the GPU is significantly faster than the CPU (from 4 to 16 times), all the more when series are long.

Case	1	2	3	4	5
Series X1 (Nb samples N1)	1,023	2,047	4,095	8,191	16,383
Series X2(Nb samples N2)	7,167	14,335	28,671	57,343	114,686
N1+N2	8,190	16,382	32,766	65,534	131,070
GPU Quadro 4000 Python/OpenCL (Execution time in ms)	30,2	27.0	37.4	100	144
GPU GTX 570 Python/OpenCL (Execution time in ms)	28.5	22.1	26,.0	45.5	60.0
CPU X5690 Matlab (Execution time in ms)	53.9	106	195	419	959
GPU acceleration Quadro 4000	1.78	3.93	**5.21**	**4.19**	**6.66**
GPU acceleration GTX 570	1.89	4.79	**7.5**	**9.2**	**15.98**

Table 7.20. *Execution time of kstest2. Comparison GPU Python+pyopencl/CPU Matlab*

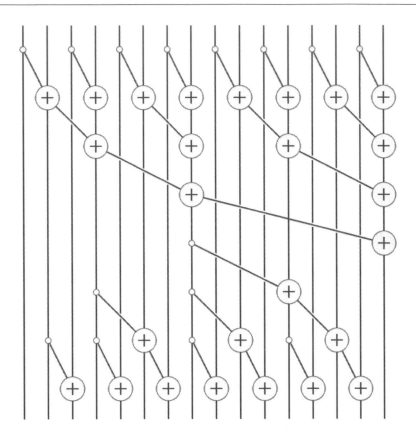

Figure 7.6. *Representation of a 16-element circuit*

The implementation of the algorithm in Python GPU/OpenCL is compared to its sequential version on Matlab and its parallel CPU version of MATLAB (*parfor*). The *cores pool* mechanism of Matlab is similar to that of OpenCL. In the parallel version of Matlab, at each iteration of the algorithm the objective function [7.24] is calculated in a single pass for the 32 particles (replacing the loop *for* by *parfor*). The processor used is a 3.46 GHz 6-core INTEL XEON X5690. Figure 7.7(a) shows the execution time of an iteration of algorithm 7.2 with its different versions. In all cases, the implementation of the algorithm in Python GPU/OpenCL is better than the other two and this is all the more so when the lengths of the two series X_1 and X_2 are large. In addition, for smaller sized series, the parallel version of Matlab is slower than its corresponding sequential version. This figure also shows that the sensitivity of the algorithm implemented in Python GPU/OpenCL compared to the length of the series X_1 ($N1$) is low.

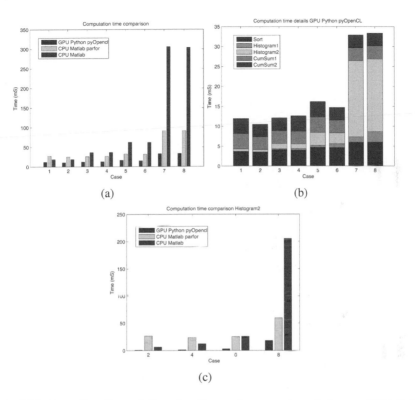

(a)   (b)

(c)

Figure 7.7. *Execution time of the algorithm: a) comparison between GPU Python OpenCL, CPU Matlab in sequential and CPU Matlab in parallel, b) details of the GPU Python OpenCL algorithm and c) details of Histogram2. The tests are performed on different sizes of series X_1 and X_2 described in Table 7.21. For a color version of this figure, see www.iste.co.uk/heliodore/metaheuristics.zip*

Case	1	2	3	4	5	6	7	8
N1	256	512	{1,024}	2,048	2,048	{4,096}	4,096	{8,192}
N2	3,840	{3,584}	7,168	6,144	14,336	12,288	61,440	57,344
N1+N2	4,096	4,096	8,192	8,192	16,384	16,384	65,536	65,536

Table 7.21. *Description of studied cases: N_1 and N_2 correspond to the size of the series X_1 and X_2 respectively*

Figure 7.7(b) gives details of the execution time of the algorithm implemented on GPU/OpenCL. Except for the histogram, the computational time of the algorithm is hardly dependent on the length of the series X_1. This low dependence can be explained by the fact that the boundaries of the GPU/OpenCL queue process are not reached. Figure 7.7(c) gives details about the computation time of the "Histogram2" algorithm. This figure shows that the GPU/OpenCL histogram parallel algorithm largely outperforms both the sequential and the parallel version of the Matlab "histc" function with accelerations of 11.3 and 3.3 respectively for case 8.

7.5. Conclusion

A new non-parametric estimator of α-stable distributions has been proposed. This estimator presents two particularities:

– its originality regarding the use of metaheuristics in this field of statistics;

– it makes no restrictions on the parameters to be estimated.

The algorithm presented in this chapter obtains very good results, particularly for values of the stability index $\alpha < 1$, thus exceeding one of the most efficient and most widely used estimators, namely the McCulloch estimator.

Another advantage of our estimator is that it is inherently parallelizable. In effect, in the second part of the results, we have proposed parallelized functions (sort, histogram, cumulative sum and maximum value of a series) performing the computations on GPU cards. These developed or adapted parallelized functions are more than just granular and reusable because these are extremely common basic functions in the fields of probability and statistics among others.

8

SmartGrid and *MicroGrid* Perspectives

This last chapter is intended to be the application framework of the tools that we have developed throughout the book. Whether referring to optimization techniques or focusing on the statistical contribution of data, the implementation of real solutions remains the only tangible expression of the development and the promotion of innovative ideas. The reflection conducted about the new concepts of production, management, trade and electrical energy consumption provides consistency to a whole thought process where only action is entitled to be mentioned.

8.1. New *SmartGrid* concepts

SmartGrid technologies appear as the solution to the transformation of electrical networks taken in their entirety to respond and adapt to ever increasing demand, to the integration of the intermittent and distributed production of renewable energy and more generally to address issues of decarbonization of the energy system.

By 2020, about 50 billion diverse and varied devices will likely be connected to each other by means of a new "Internet of Things". As such, electricity networks gradually acquire a new integrative role of "systems of systems", composed of, to put it metaphorically, "constellations of micro-networks" performing energy transactions between themselves and making use of the new possibilities of information and communication technologies (ICTs) to enable transactional controls at different levels of energy subsystems.

All of these systems interacting with each other, regardless of the scale being considered, constitute the global *SmartGrid* system which allows for the management and distribution of energy in an optimal manner through the coordination of the operations of these *MicroGrids*. This new era cannot be conceived without reconsidering the way in which the principles of control are designed in order to integrate a real potential for communication and for managing bidirectional energy flows. These principles should also integrate all of the production sources (conventional and renewable), after the customers' demand has been made flexible and after considering how transactions are organized along the wholesale energy markets' chain of value of energy. The result is to allow for the management of the interaction between "production, consumption and storage aggregators" toward the management of retail portfolios incorporating the flexibility of end-users and the distributed means of production.

Electricity companies have gradually progressed toward these new *SmartGrid* concepts by means of a series of pilot projects and demonstrations with the aim of defining an optimal transition path while maintaining the same reliability standards on their critical infrastructures.

As a matter of fact, networks have historically been operated by means of one-way real-time communication, requiring connections of small numbers of "dispatchable" production points and by considering IT architectures in which "dispatch" optimization was managed by a limited number of centralized computational platforms.

Similarly, data manipulation has always been done with the aim of reconciliation. The prediction of most data related to consumption was intended to minimize errors at the scale of large network areas, with the purpose of minimizing forecasting errors and in order to financially reconcile, by way of a few meter readings a few months later, the profiles based on theoretical load profiles. Distribution operators have always had very limited access to real-time data originating from their demand.

With *SmartGrids*, communication becomes multidimensional, with information flowing between several layers in energy systems, involving real-time transactions between the players of the market from generation to demand. The ultimate goal is to allow the whole of the system to work in a much more flexible manner, to enable a wider penetration of intermittent renewable energy production through interactive network infrastructures, by integrating interaction with consumers by means of various processes for demand management (*Demand Response* or load management), the management, of distributed storage and the recharging of electric vehicles.

In the long term, *SmartGrid* technology will make it possible to coordinate the needs and flexibility capabilities of all the centralized or distributed stakeholders of transport and distribution network infrastructures up to end users and aggregator participants of the electricity market. This will result in optimally managing all of the parts constituting this complex system in a given regulatory context. The ultimate goal of this optimization is to minimize the cost of operating the energy system as a whole, taking into account the costs of operating the various constituent components, the costs of environmental impacts and associated penalties, while maintaining the reliability of the system as a whole, its resilience and its dynamic stability.

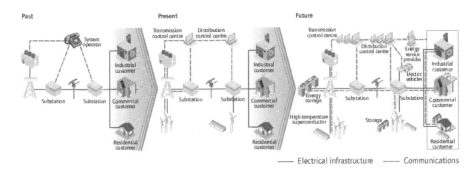

Figure 8.1. *Smart electric systems [IEA 11]. For a color version of this figure, see www.iste.co.uk/heliodore/metaheuristics.zip*

SmartGrids also allow for the implementation of new regulatory options by offering new services and incentives for now active consumers. By exposing them to new offers of electricity prices, reflecting in real time not only the supply–demand balance of the energy system but also the costs associated with the technical constraints related to energy transit in networks. The objective of these new offers is to propose new incentives to consumers ready to change their behavior and make them responsible for their individual carbon footprint.

8.2. Key elements for *SmartGrid* deployment

Between 2010 and 2030, economic growth should more than double the global energy demand. During this period, world global emissions of CO_2 should grow even faster. The effort required to reduce these CO_2 emissions has reached a critical stage and the introduction of new renewable energy sources has become a priority. According to the International Energy Agency (IEA), renewable energy and biofuels will lead to a reduction of 23% of greenhouse gases by 2030. This will result in an increase in the share of renewable energy in electrical networks to more than 30% of the total demand by 2030, which means that the renewable energy share will reach, in real-time scales, proportions largely exceeding 50% of the consumption of energy systems. This strong growth has had the effect of considerably reducing the production costs of renewable energy, which has reached network parity in many parts of the world.

Furthermore, electrical network operators are the most directly and largely exposed economic players to the consequences of environmental disasters, which force them to review their technology options in order to increase the resilience of their infrastructures against extreme weather conditions. These technologies are designed to achieve greater reliability in networks and to minimize the impact of large power outages (*blackouts*) by implementing new strategies for self-healing so as to allow for the division of networks into *MicroGrids* which will result in the impact of major network incidents at the end customers' level to be minimized.

Finally, electric operators continue their efforts to improve the effectiveness of the network, seeking to reduce losses, to minimize network balancing and congestion costs induced by the integration of renewable energy and to optimize their network-building strategies.

Throughout the world, electrical systems are, in this context, facing many challenges, namely aging infrastructures, the development of new interconnections integrating distributed renewable energy, the increasing integration of renewable energy sources and electric vehicles, the need to improve supply safety and the obligation to reduce carbon dioxide emissions.

8.2.1. *Improvement of network resilience in the face of catastrophic climate events*

The recent failures of electrical systems during extreme weather conditions have recently drawn the attention of the public to the critical role of network operators in modern society. Network reliability is the ability of the system to meet customers' requirements in terms of power and energy, taking into consideration forced outages (following interruption) as well as the planned maintenance of equipment outages in the system. The *North American Electric Reliability Corporation* defines the reliability of an interconnected electrical network by two basic and functional aspects: "adequacy and security".

8.2.1.1. *System adequacy*

Production/consumption adequacy is the capacity of the energy system to satisfy the energy and power needs of all its customers at any time, taking into account the constraints of planned maintenance and faults evaluated under a reasonable risk of occurrence.

SmartGrid technologies indirectly contribute to improving this system adequacy by means of an optimized redistribution of power flows in every node of the network. In addition, ever more abundant data gathered at the consumer level allows for a finer analysis of market scenarios through estimates closer to real-time consumption and renewable energy production at different temporal and geographic levels.

The term adequacy includes, in particular, new concerns regarding flexibility related to the deployment of means for the production of renewable energy having an intermittent nature, which require the implementation of new management flexibility mechanisms, such as the deployment of mechanisms for managing real-time adjustments as well as the reserve of the system at the level of transport operators and the deployment of management mechanisms of technical constraints at the distribution operator level.

8.2.1.2. *System operating safety*

The operating safety is the capacity of the system to remain in service during disturbances such as short circuits, the loss of operating equipment, extreme meteorological events or acts of terrorism.

When these interruptions remain circumscribed in a localized area, they are considered as faults or unintended disruptions. When they are spread over large areas, this is then referred to as a phenomenon of "cascading outages", resulting from successive and uncontrolled failures of the system elements, triggered by an incident that could have occurred anywhere.

SmartGrid technologies are capable of containing and improving the security of the system by means of innovative defense planning systems. By deploying sensors throughout the electrical network, they can monitor and anticipate any system failure before it occurs and prepare targeted actions aimed at minimizing operating losses in the system. When faults occur, these technologies constitute a means to reduce their propagation and interface with new tools for the management of the mobility of maintenance crews spread on the ground in order to automate and accelerate restoration strategies.

Resistance to computer attacks (cyber security) also represents a critical dimension of the security of the energy system as a whole. The penetration of digital technology at the heart of the operating system of *SmartGrids* introduces new vulnerabilities by offering new access to computer hackers. Cyber security is becoming a key parameter in design criteria for smart electrical networks and, regarded as a new constraint, it must be considered in a global approach both at the level of contingency analysis scenarios and at the level of strategic defense planning.

8.2.1.3. *Energy quality*

Energy quality is another fundamental indicator of energy systems, with the objective of identifying distortions in voltage and current waveforms, as well as phase shifts caused by transient disturbances. These distortions or phase shifts are likely to generate serious failures, to the extent of disabling equipment at the interface of the electric network. The most important aspect refers to the quality of the voltage provided to customers, which requires diversions and disruptions to be followed with respect to steady-state operating conditions.

8.2.1.4. *Integration of energy production sources following a distributed nature*

The radial distribution of medium and low voltage energy is one of the key features of networks, as opposed to high-voltage transport networks which are very largely meshed. The redundancy capacity of the distribution system is very limited, at the expense of the quality of service guaranteed to consumers.

On the other hand, defects caused to high-voltage (HV) transport networks rarely translate into a loss of energy supply.

One of the advantages inherent to distributed energy sources (generation or energy storage) connected to medium and/or low voltage networks is their intrinsic ability to offer an alternative supply in case of failure of the main distribution network.

This led to a significant development in network architectures, which involved redesigning conventional centralized control architectures into new distributed multi-level control architectures allowing for flow optimization between *MicroGrids* located at different levels of the main network.

8.2.2. *Increasing electrical network efficiency*

8.2.2.1. *Increasing electric energy consumption*

Electricity is and remains one of the growing components of global energy demand, particularly in developing economics where the structures of electrical networks have not yet reached their maturity.

In OECD countries, with more modest energy consumption growth rates, *SmartGrid* solutions offer new advantages by facilitating the connection of production sources of intermittent renewable energy, allowing the structural reinforcement needed for growing network areas (typically urban centers) and facing environmental requirements (in particular the distribution of transportation means without CO_2 emissions whether they be public transport or electric vehicles). These new connections are the focus of new cost benefit analyses to minimize the enhancement needs of existing infrastructures, and to maximize the use of *SmartGrid* technologies such as the active management of demand or storage.

In developing regions with high energy consumption growth rates, *SmartGrid* technologies are considered to be directly incorporated into new infrastructures in order to maximize the use of these infrastructures.

Everywhere, *SmartGrid* technologies allow for a better understanding of the needs of innovative planning by anticipating induced efficiency gains, by reducing the criticality of power demand at peak state and, in a general manner, by smoothing the solicitations to which the network is exposed.

8.2.2.2. *Peak consumption*

Electricity demand varies throughout the day and according to seasons (Figure 8.2). Electricity system infrastructures are designed to face extreme solicitations, and *a contrario*, outside of rush hour, the system is generally underutilized. However, building a system to address occasional peak demand translates into financial surcharges, whereas smoothing the curve of energy demand would enable them to be reduced.

SmartGrids make it possible in particular to reduce this peak demand by offering new pricing and incentive information to consumers to allow them to shift their flexible consumption outside of peak periods. This real-time management of demand (load management) – the mechanism by which users at the end of the chain (at the industrial, service or residential sector levels) adapt their consumption according to tariff conditions or other indicators–enables the peak demand to be smoothed and thus better amortization of network infrastructures. This can also contribute to bringing flexibility to the operation of the system in order to integrate larger variable production capacities. Peak demand management (load or demand-side management (DSM)) is usually the first priority in the deployment of smart networks, because it is the most cost-effective way to provide the system with new sources of flexibility.

8.2.2.3. *Aging infrastructure planning*

The electrification of developed countries has taken place over the last hundred years; it is important to constantly invest in order to continue to guarantee the reliability and the quality of the supply. While consumption requirements do develop, in quantity and quality, as well as distributed energy production tends to spread out, the aging of energy transport and distribution infrastructures has to be dealt with.

SmartGrid technologies offer the opportunity to maximize the usage of existing infrastructures through better real-time monitoring of the operating conditions of the network equipment so as to allow for an estimation of the reserve capacities of infrastructures in real-time. They also make it possible to better define replacement strategies for electrical network equipment by anticipating the replacement of the most sought after equipment and by considering the extension of their use beyond the lifetime assigned for other equipment that would have been underutilized.

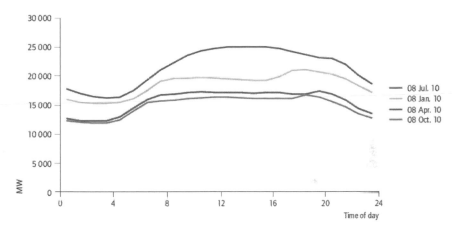

Figure 8.2. *Example of a demand curve of the electricity system over 24 hours, corresponding to several dates of the year (source: data from the independent operator of the electricity network, Ontario, Canada [IEA 11]). For a color version of this figure, see www.iste.co.uk/heliodore/metaheuristics.zip*

8.2.3. *Integration of the variability of renewable energy sources*

Efforts aiming to reduce CO_2 emissions related to electricity production have led to a significant penetration of intermittent renewable production technologies. This continuous increase is gradually extending to all regions (Figure 8.3).

Unlike traditional production methods, the production of energy sources known as "variable" is very closely correlated with weather conditions in different parts of the network. This leads to new constraints for balancing the electricity system, associated with the prediction, the monitoring and the control of the adequacy between supply and demand, and with reserve management. When the contribution of variable energy sources, with respect to the global production base, exceeds 15–20%, it becomes necessary to implement new management strategies to provide network operators with new flexibility in order to ensure system balancing (Figure 8.4).

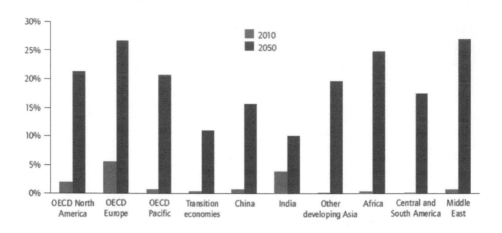

Figure 8.3. *Proportion of variable character energy production, by region (IEA Blue Map Scenario [IEA 11]). For a color version of this figure, see www.iste.co.uk/heliodore/metaheuristics.zip*

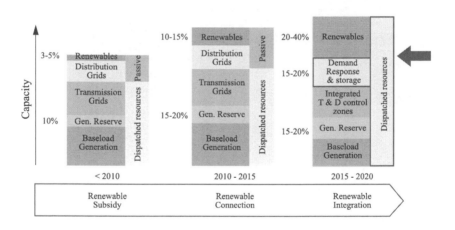

Figure 8.4. *Development of Grid flexibility versus Variable Renewable Resources [FEN 09]. For a color version of this figure, see www.iste.co.uk/heliodore/metaheuristics.zip*

SmartGrid technologies enable the deployment of larger amounts of intermittent resources by means of integrating new artificial intelligence and *machine learning* technologies in order to best predict production and demand and to improve the economic "dispatch" of the system in its entirety.

8.3. *SmartGrids* and components technology architecture

8.3.1. *Global SmartGrid architecture*

As has been previously developed, *SmartGrid* technologies have the ability to coordinate the production and consumption related to the available network capacities in line with energy market managements. They consist of an integrated architecture of the value chain from start to finish according to specific principles.

– *System design.* The system can no longer be considered as a system operated by a single entity, but as a "system of systems" wich allow several subsystems to interact. These are interconnected to each other through real-time transactional control systems.

Deployment. In the value chain, the system must realize the interconnection of a very large number of geographically dispersed components based on different IP communication formats by integrating communication standards clearly identified at each connection node (the communication infrastructure can, *in fine*, be the property of network managers or be partially externalized depending on the case).

– *The synchronized processing of very large Big Data volumes of time data series.* Since these technologies must provide means to understand the constraints for operating the system in real-time, the IT infrastructure must be able to synchronize and process chronological series in real time, with different sampling capabilities varying from the fraction of a millisecond (for stability problems in electrical networks) to the second (for system balancing and congestion management), or even several minutes (for optimization algorithms of energy flows and pricing on energy markets).

The new IT infrastructures of *SmartGrid* technologies open the way for a better optimization of the electrical system as a whole, through a better real-time estimation of network assets and of means of production, through sensors distributed at the interfaces of the system, the *GridEdge*, by way of automata and computers distributed in substations and control centers, up to every power feeder, or even in consumers' homes in order to enable a flexible dynamic control of expenses.

These new architectures combine centralized computerized processing in control centers, and even the *Cloud* depending on the nature of the data and their criticality, with concepts of distributed intelligence deployed at different levels of the network, from control centers in thermal plants up to control systems in renewable energy parks and load management in consumers' homes.

These systems are based on hybrid unified architectures (Figure 8.5) combining *On-Premise, Cloud Substation* and *GridEdge* multilevel automated systems, incorporating the latest communication standards developed in the industry, and especially the IEC61850 *Common Information Model* (unified data model) and the *SmartGrid* SGAM architecture model.

They comprise expert user interfaces, derived from advanced technologies for real-time decision support of the nearby environment (*situational awareness*), as well as *middleware* software integration layers to enable significant scalability in terms of application, interfaces, processing mechanisms and data storage. These tools integrate with physical network infrastructures, superposing an information technology layer.

These systems provide operators with real-time information about every asset in the network (quality, measures, oscillations, counters, etc.) to enable the real-time management of transactions between means of production, storage and flexible demand while ensuring an optimal balancing of the system as a whole.

8.3.2. *Basic technological elements for SmartGrids*

The previous "systems of systems" *SmartGrid* architecture is composed of several key technological building blocks interacting with one another at different levels of the electric network. Some of these components already exist in the network, others considered as mature are being deployed while some still require development and demonstration stages.

For this purpose, close collaborations between electric operators and market participants are essential to update associated technologies and deployment strategies.

When examining the various technology layers of systems, multiple blocks can be distinguished:

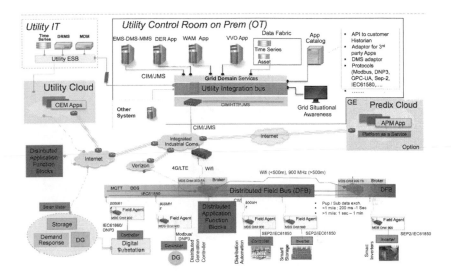

Figure 8.5. *New generation of computerized platforms for Smart Grid deployment (source: GE Grid Solution 2016). For a color version of this figure, see www.iste.co.uk/heliodore/metaheuristics.zip*

– at the lowest levels, new *Smart Inverter* technologies which integrate power electronics technology associated with high-speed controllers deployed for the management of power conversion and of the quality of AC-DC power. These include in particular:

- AC/DC conversion substations for interconnections between networks or renewable farms' remote connections. Originally intended for connection purposes, their use is evolving towards a more complex function for network support,

- FACTS and "smart" STATCOM to provide compensation for reactive power to the system. Initially deployed in very high voltage, the technology is developing for low voltage (at the *GridEdge's* level) where the massive integration of photovoltaic resources generates new voltage constraints,

- inverters associated with photovoltaics and storage incorporating DC/AC conversion functions and providing auxiliary services – frequency and voltage control – to manage network stability and its inertial reserve,

- fast electric vehicle chargers;

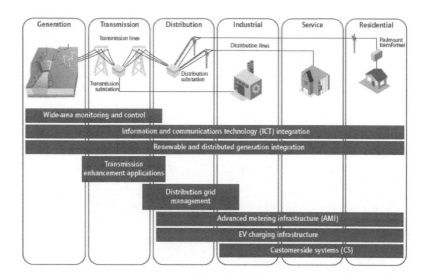

Figure 8.6. *Smart Grid Technology areas (source: IEA Smart Grid Roadmap). For a color version of this figure, see www.iste.co.uk/heliodore/metaheuristics.zip*

– at a higher level, computerized substation technologies, for *MicroGrid* control and operating electric feeders. They include all fast protection and control equipment to protect assets or to self-heal the system during emergency situations. These solutions are usually composed of the following technology components:

- digital and analog current and voltage sensors for detecting electrical waveforms,

- devices for the surveillance of the good health of substations and primary equipment,

- controllers associated with substations and electric feeders,

- controllers associated with *MicroGrids* and regional defense plans (*Wide Area Measurement System*);

– at a third level, control technologies of distributed energy resources. These technologies are usually deployed on the consumer side, that is, close to flexible distributed energy resources (located downstream of *GridEdge* interfaces). They usually include:

- smart meter management systems (AMI, MDM and others),

- decentralized production controllers,

- energy management and control systems in buildings,

- energy management and control systems in residences, in particular the recharge infrastructure for electric vehicles;

– at the last level, the management tools of the energy system as a whole. Although historically they were very centralized in a few control centers, associated architectures tend to evolve into new hybrid distributed architectures. They thus allow for a distribution of application catalogues at different levels of the subsystems located within the IT infrastructures of *Utility Premise* network operators, in the *Cloud* or even at the *GridEdge* interfaces level depending on the criticality of associated data and computational constraints. These tools comprise all ICTs required for monitoring, controlling and the optimization of the energy system, in particular, tools for:

- congestion management and contingency analysis,

- stability management,

- dynamic management of asset conditions,

- renewable energy forecasts and real-time estimation of the system state,

- dynamic management of incidents and reconfiguration-reconnection strategies,

- management of distributed energy resources (integrating decentralized production, storage and demand management),

- energy market management,

- geographical data management.

8.3.3. *Integration of new MicroGrid layers: definition*

A *MicroGrid* is a section contiguous to the electrical network. The commercial incorporation of its distributed energy resources (namely, its means of production, expenses, storage means and the electric vehicles allocated thereto) all contribute to its operation in a coordinated manner in response to its consumption requirements and to the specific constraints of the network, generally related to its congestion and its quality problems.

MicroGrids can operate in a completely autonomous fashion (small disconnected electrical networks) in scenarios where the main network requires it. They are generally attached to an "aggregator" unit operating a virtual power plant (VPP) composed of the aggregation of distributed energy resources of *MicroGrids*.

The growing demand in distributed renewable energy, the development of information system architectures towards distributed architectures and the active participation of customers in the market through services such as demand-side management are points of convergence towards decentralized *MicroGrid* architectures, thus offering new business models to network operators. The main advantages of *MicroGrids* can be outlined as follows:

– they naturally encourage the self-consumption of private renewable energy by end-users produced within the boundaries of *MicroGrids*, thus minimizing operating losses and the impact on congestions in the main network;

– it offers new opportunities of service continuity on the critical loads of *MicroGrids* during a network incident at "*GridEdge*" interfaces;

– it allows the optimization of distributed energy production with regard to the requirements of the energy market, even the balancing and reserve requirements of the network;

– it offers new options for reprofiling capital investments necessary to the consolidation of the network;

– it allows for the emergence of new business models among *MicroGrid* users.

The qualitative and quantitative evaluations of the advantages largely depend on the *MicroGrid* business model and on the services offered to the main network. *MicroGrids* can be defined according to the following usage contexts:

– *MicroGrids* attached to private industrial and commercial infrastructures:

- they are private property, operated by private infrastructure managers and integrate limited interaction with networks,

- the main objective is to offer a reliable and economic supply to infrastructure owners,

- more recently, new developments have been observed around university campuses focusing on innovation that can be deployed in connection with these campuses;

– *MicroGrids* attached to government agencies:

- military *MicroGrid* particularly focusing on the reliability of energy and infrastructure resilience,

- these organisms take interest in the economic impact of the approach by utilizing their *MicroGrid* in addition to the energy supplied through the main network,

- some cities have begun to consider *MicroGrids* as a key factor for the development of their *SmartCity* vision of energy;

– *MicroGrids* attached to electrical network operators:

- electric network operators are considering the deployment of *MicroGrids* to supply customers with specific and localized requirements, in areas exposed to strong network constraints (Figure 8.7, example of Enedis in France as part of the *NiceGrid* project, around Carros),

- deregulated public services work together with the aggregators of energy resources in order to improve service quality through distribution networks and *MicroGrid* operators,

- the deployment of these solutions requires coordination with the aggregators of production and consumption means in order to stay in line with market rules.

MicroGrid management functionalities are mainly derived from management and portfolio optimization applications of distributed energy resources (DER). These applications derive largely from applications initially deployed in control rooms of public distribution operators which, in the case of private *MicroGrids*, are operated by other commercial entities.

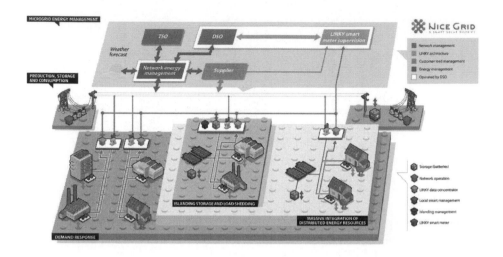

Figure 8.7. *Smart Grid Technology areas [SOL 16]. For a color version of this figure, see www.iste.co.uk/heliodore/metaheuristics.zip*

These systems generally cover the following technological building blocks:

– supervision, control and communication data acquisition:

- industrial communications equipment employing wireless technology or power-line communication (PLC).

- automation equipment for substations and electrical feeders,

- control algorithms for the *dispatch* of distributed energy resources;

– *MicroGrids* real-time management applications:

- islanding detection, resynchronization and economic *dispatch* in interconnected mode,

- power balancing and frequency control,

- voltage control,

- *MicroGrid* topology evaluation,

- alarm management and event logging;

– forecasting and planning:

- renewable resources forecasting, namely including photovoltaics, wind energy and electricity-steam combined cycles.

- load, load management and storage availability forecasting,

- energy price forecasting,

- distributed energy *dispatching* optimization;

– transactional control with network operators and markets:

- retail aggregators with contracts, compliance and performance,

- real-time *trading* of flexibility and available reserves,

- billing and regulations follow-up.

In the future, the operation of electric networks will evolve into a multi-level coordinated network control interfacing with *MicroGrid* constellations operated through flexibility aggregators (*Virtual Power Plant*) which interface with network and market operators. Even if the real-time control of each of these *MicroGrids* will still be managed by local control facilities, a new aggregation layer is emerging in order to ensure the coordination of these *MicroGrids* regarding the whole of the energy system.

Figure 8.8 illustrates these new integration approaches in which the electrical network plays a new unifying optimization role between different *MicroGrid* infrastructures deployed at the *GridEdge* interfaces of the electrical network.

MicroGrids appear as a new cornerstone of interconnections between consumers/users – transformed into "prosumers" likely to offer a new level of flexibility to the system – and the infrastructures of the electric network whose control layers are evolving. This leads to the implementation of new information and communication infrastructures facilitating a global integration of these systems between them, while allowing for distributed control and optimization strategies at all levels of the electricity system, depending on the technical and business model constraints under consideration.

In cities in particular, where energy systems are particularly constrained, these architectures should also enable an extension beyond the limit of the power system, by means of interconnecting with other gas, heat or even electric vehicle recharging networks through open interfaces allowing the exchange of flexibility between these systems.

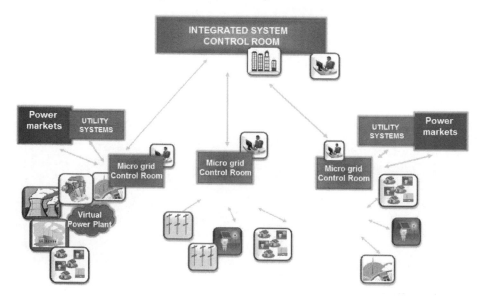

Figure 8.8. *Diagram of MicroGrid integration in the energy system. For a color version of this figure, see www.iste.co.uk/heliodore/metaheuristics.zip*

A major challenge for the deployment of these new architectures is their potential to open up sufficient new avenues to be able to interrelate historically isolated information while responding to new rules of confidentiality and minimizing risks in terms of cyber-security. These new systems will aim to establish optimal control strategies between energy infrastructures.

Over the past years, architecture specifications and the standardization of interfaces have remained confined to "single infrastructure silos" relying on highly personalized platforms and specific to each field. Recent developments in ICTs nevertheless enable the consideration of new "Industrial Internet" platforms, focusing on re-using *Big Data* and *Machine Learning* applications capable of considering new avenues for "System of systems" deployment, thus making a decompartmentalization of the energy system by data possible.

A1.1. Test functions

In this section, we will present the benchmarks functions utilized in the experimentation of the algorithms. The main test functions are the following:

– Sphere function:

$$f_1(x) = \sum_{i=1}^{n} x_i^2 \qquad\qquad [A1.1]$$

– Rosenbrock function:

$$f_2(x) = \sum_{i=1}^{n} (100(x_i^2 - x_{i+1})^2 + (x_i - 1)^2) \qquad\qquad [A1.2]$$

– Akley function:

$$f_3(x) = -20exp\left(-0.2\sqrt{\frac{1}{n}\sum_{i=1}^{n} x_i^2}\right)$$

$$-exp\left(\frac{1}{n}\sum_{i=1}^{n} cos(2\pi x_i)\right) + 20 + e \qquad\qquad [A1.3]$$

– Rastringin function:

$$f_4(x) = \sum_{i=1}^{n}(x_i^2 - 10cos(2\pi x_i) + 10)$$ [A1.4]

– Weierstrass function:

$$f_5(x) = \sum_{i=1}^{n}\left(\sum_{k=0}^{k_{max}}\left[a^k cos(2\pi b^k(x_i + 0.5))\right]\right)$$

$$-D\sum_{k=0}^{k_{max}}\left[a^k cos(2\pi b^k.0.5)\right]$$ [A1.5]

$$a = 0.5, \quad b = 3, \quad k_{max} = 20$$

– Griewank function:

$$f_6(x) = \sum_{i=1}^{n}\frac{x_i^2}{4000} - \prod_{i=1}^{n}cos\left(\frac{x_i}{\sqrt{i}}\right) + 1$$ [A1.6]

Figure A1.1 represents the form of test functions.

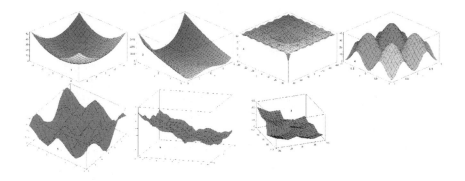

Figure A1.1. *Benchmark functions*

Table A1.1 represents the parameters of the benchmark functions.

f	Name	Global optimum x^*	$f(x^*)$	Research space
f_1	Sphere function	(0, 0, ..., 0)	0	$[-100, 100]^N$
f_2	Quadratic function	(0, 0, ..., 0)	0	$[-100, 100]^N$
f_3	Rosenbrock's function	(1, 1, ..., 1)	0	$[-2.048, 2.048]^N$
f_4	Ackley's function	(0, 0, ..., 0)	0	$[-32.768, 32.768]^N$
f_5	Rastrigin's function	(0, 0, ..., 0)	0	$[-5.12, 5.12]^N$
f_6	Weierstrass's function	(0, 0, ..., 0)	0	$[-0.5, 0.5]^N$
f_8	Griewank's function	(0, 0, ..., 0)	0	$[-600, 600]$

Table A1.1. *Benchmark functions*

A2.1. Application to the multi-objective case

The introduction of an economic criterion on the cost of installed reactive power requires an estimate of that cost. This will be based on relations [A2.1]. Figure A2.1 presents the evolution of this cost according to the installed power, S, $\tilde{S}$ and $\hat{S}$, for different FACTS types.

$$Price_{SVC} = Price_{STATCOM} = (0.0003\ S^2 - 0.3051\ S + 127.38) \times S\ 10^3$$

$$price_{TCSC} = (0.0015\ \tilde{S}^2 - 0.7130\ \tilde{S} + 153.75) \times \tilde{S}\ 10^3 \qquad [A2.1]$$

$$price_{UPFC} = (0.0003\ \hat{S}^2 - 0.2691\ \hat{S} + 188.22) \times \hat{S}\ 10^3$$

with, respectively, S_i, $\hat{S}_i$ and $\tilde{S}_i$ the installed powers of the STATCOM i or SVC i, of the TCSC i and of the UPFC i.

The costs incurred by the placement and dimensioning of each type of FACTS will thus be (by interpolation of Figure A2.1)

$$P_1 = \sum_{i=1}^{N_1}(0.0003.S_i^2 - 0.3051.S_i + 127.38) \times S_i.10^3$$

$$P_2 = \sum_{i=1}^{N_2}(0.0015.\tilde{S}_i^2 - 0.7130.\tilde{S}_i + 153.75) \times \tilde{S}_i.10^3 \qquad [A2.2]$$

$$P_3 = \sum_{i=1}^{N_3}(0.0003.\hat{S}_i^{\,2} - 0.2691.\hat{S}_i + 188.22) \times \hat{S}_i.10^3$$

with, respectively, N_i, N_2 and N_3 the total number of STATCOMs and SVCs, TCSCs and UPFCs installed in the network.

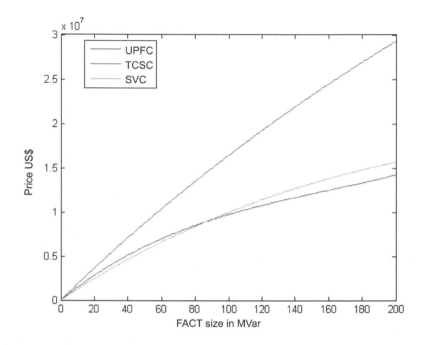

Figure A2.1. *Cost of FACTS depending on their size and their types.*

Finally, the cost criterion to be optimized will be:

$$J_6 = P_1 + P_2 + P_3 \hspace{4cm} \text{[A2.3]}$$

For testing and comparison purposes with a number of multi-objective particle swarm optimization methods (in particular, the ϵ-Constraint approach, the H-GA-PSO and H-PSO algorithms defined in Chapter 1), two criteria are chosen to be optimized, namely:

– the minimization of nodal voltage differences (J_3, equation [4.10]).

– the minimization of the total cost of FACTS installed in the network (J_6, equation [A2.3]).

Unless otherwise stated, the initial adjustment parameters common to the three methods are fixed as follows:

– the validated algorithm: α-SLPSO (same parameters as in the single-objective case).

– swarm size: $Nb_{particle} = 50$.

– number of iterations: $1,000$;

– choice of network: IEEE 57-node.

A2.1.1. *Results obtained by the ϵ-Constraint approach*

Here, the dimension of $\overrightarrow{\epsilon}$ is 2 (that is: two objectives). Figure A2.2(a) shows the Pareto front (in blue) found when varying c_2 (corresponding to the cost objective) from $2 * 10^5$ to $500 * 10^5$.

The α–SLPSO algorithm is executed several times, here 400 times, (variation of c_2) to recover the Pareto region, but in terms of searching for the latter, this corresponds to a single execution.

The algorithm has found 72 solutions on the Pareto front, with $1,000$ iterations, that is a solution every fourteen iterations, which is not satisfactory given the necessary time for each of them. On the other hand, we notice a good variety of solutions, which are expected results given that the α–SLPSO algorithm has already been validated in the single-objective case.

A2.1.2. *Results obtained by the Pareto approach*

The H-GA-PSO algorithm (*Hybrid Genetic Algorithm PSO*): Figure A2.2(b) shows the Pareto front obtained corresponding to a simulation where the size of the archive (neighbors) is fixed to 3.

The algorithm proposes 161 solutions for the Pareto front, corresponding to six iterations/solution which is significantly better than the ϵ-Constraint approach for a computation time nearly 140 times lower. In addition, the proposed solutions are, in most cases better, what shown in Figure A2.2(d). On the other hand, a variety of solutions worse than with the algorithm based on the ϵ-Constraint approach.

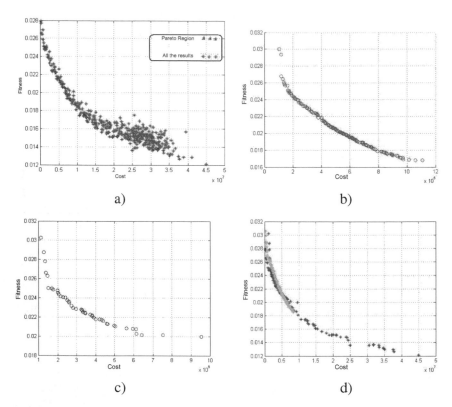

Figure A2.2. *Illustration of the results obtained with the multi-objective case: a) Pareto front, ε-Constraint approach, 35 particles and 500 iterations; b) Pareto front, H-GA-PSO approach, 50 particles and 1,000 iterations; c) Pareto front, H-PSO approach 50 particles and 1,000 iterations. d) Pareto front, H-PSO approach (50 particles and 1,000 iterations), H-GA-PSO approach (50 particles and 1,000 iterations) and ε-Constraint approach (35 particles and 500 iterations). For a color version of this figure, see www.iste.co.uk/heliodore/metaheuristics.zip*

The *H-PSO* algorithm (*Homogeneous PSO*): Figure A2.2(c) shows the Pareto front obtained by executing: H- PSO where also the size of the archive (neighbours) is fixed to 3.

The algorithm yields 45 solutions for the Pareto front, corresponding to a solution every 22 iterations; which is better compared to the ϵ-Constraint approach (when the computational time factor is taken into account). On the other hand, it can be noted that this method presents a weakness in the diversification (that is, it only suggests part of the Pareto region).

It should be noted that according to Figure A2.2(d), the quality of the solutions of the two H-PSO and H-GA-PSO methods is virtually identical.

According to Figures A2.2(b) and A2.2(d) and to the results presented, the H-GA-PSO algorithm seems to be the best approach for our optimization problem, taking into account the required computation time and the number q of proposed solutions. Nonetheless, its difficulty in proposing new solutions (namely to ensure the diversity of solutions) remains a weakness. By allowing the algorithm to execute for longer, it proposes increasingly more new solutions, which illustrates Figure A2.2(a). The algorithm proposes $1,590$ solutions for the Pareto front, yielding 0.0159 solutions/iteration which proves that the algorithm exhibits the ergodicity property (capacity to propose the whole Pareto region).

Figure A2.2(b) displays on the same graph the solution obtained by FACTS placement and dimensioning in addition to the Pareto front obtained in the case of the placement and dimensioning of several FACTS of different types. The examination of this figure highlights the interest of a multi-objective approach. As a matter of fact, for an identical "physical" performance (identical criterion J_3) the cost proposed by the multi-objective approach is significantly less (3 million dollars compared with eight million dollars for two FACTS).

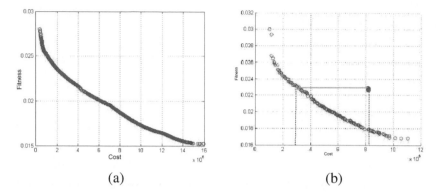

(a)   (b)

Figure A2.3. *Illustration of the Pareto fronts obtained: a) Pareto region, H-GA-PSO approach (50 particles, 90,000 iterations). b) Comparison of solutions with 2 FACTS and solutions with several FACTS*

Bibliography

[AGE 11] AGENCY I.E., "International energy Agency, Technology Roadmap Smart Grids", *IEA 2011*, AIP Publishing, 2011.

[ALB 02] ALBERT R., BARABÁSI A.-L., "Statistical mechanics of complex networks", *Rev. Mod. Phys.*, vol. 74, pp. 47–97, American Physical Society, January 2002.

[ALB 04] ALBERT R., ALBERT I., NAKARADO G., "Structural vulnerability of the North American power grid", *Phys. Rev. E*, vol. 69, p. 025103, American Physical Society, February 2004.

[BAC 00] BÄCK T., FOGEL D., MICHALEWICZ Z., *Evolutionary Computation 1: Basic Algorithms and Operators*, vol. 1, CRC Press, 2000.

[BAR 87] BARNARD S., "Stereo matching by hierarchical, microcanonical annealing", *Joint Conference on Artificial Intelligence*, Milan, Italy, pp. 832–835, 1987.

[BAT 94] BATTITI R., TECCHIOLLI G., "The Reactive Tabu Search", *INFORMS Journal on Computing*, vol. 6, no. 2, pp. 126–140, 1994.

[BEN 78] BENDER E., CANFIELD E., "The asymptotic number of labeled graphs with given degree sequences", *Journal of Combinatorial Theory, Series A*, vol. 24, no. 3, pp. 296–307, Elsevier, May 1978.

[BEN 05] BÉNICHOU O., COPPEY M., MOREAU M. *et al.*, "Optimal search strategies for hidden targets", *Physical review letters*, vol. 94, no. 19, p. 198101, APS, May 2005.

[BER 73] BERGE C., *Graphes et hypergraphes*, Dunod, Paris, 1973.

[BLE 90] BLELLOCH G., Prefix Sums and Their Applications, Report no. CMU-CS-90-190, School of Computer Science, Carnegie Mellon University, November 1990.

[BLU 04] BLUM C., DORIGO M., "The hyper-cube framework for ant colony optimization", *IEEE Transactions on Systems, Man, and Cybernetics, Part B: Cybernetics*, vol. 34, no. 2, pp. 1161–1172, April 2004.

[BOC 06] BOCCALETTI S., LATORA V., MORENO Y. *et al.*, "Complex Networks: Structure and Dynamics", *Phys. Rep.*, vol. 424, pp. 175–308, Elsevier, February 2006.

[BRA 85] BRANS J.-P., VINCKE P., "Note-A Preference Ranking Organisation Method: (The PROMETHEE Method for Multiple Criteria Decision-Making)", *Management science*, vol. 31, no. 6, pp. 647–656, INFORMS, 1985.

[BRA 03] BRAUNSTEIN L., BULDYREV S., COHEN R. *et al.*, "Optimal paths in disordered complex networks", *Physical review letters*, vol. 91, no. 16, p. 168701, APS, August 2003.

[BRO 83] BROTHERS K., DuMOUCHEL W., PAULSON A., Fractiles of the stable laws, Report, Rensselaer Polytechnic Institute, Troy, NY, 1983.

[CAR 99] CARLSON J., DOYLE J., "Highly optimized tolerance: A mechanism for power laws in designed systems", *Physical Review E*, vol. 60, no. 2, pp. 1412–1427, APS, August 1999.

[CAR 01] CARRERAS B., LYNCH V., SACHTJEN M. *et al.*, "Modeling blackout dynamics in power transmission networks with simple structure", *HICSS*, vol. 1, p. 2018, 2001.

[CAR 02] CARRERAS B., LYNCH V., DOBSON I. *et al.*, "Critical points and transitions in an electric power transmission model for cascading failure blackouts | Browse - Chaos", *Chaos*, vol. 12, pp. 985–994, American Institute of Physics, December 2002.

[CAR 09] CARVALHO R., BUZNA L., BONO F. *et al.*, "Robustness of trans-European gas networks", *Phys. Rev. E*, vol. 80, p. 016106, American Physical Society, July 2009.

[CHA 76] CHAMBERS J., MALLOWS C., STUCK B., "A method for simulating stable random variables", *Journal of the American Statistical Association*, vol. 71, no. 354, pp. 340–344, Taylor & Francis Group, June 1976.

[CHA 93] CHARON I., HUDRY O., "The noising method: a new method for combinatorial optimization", *Operations Research Letters*, vol. 14, no. 3, pp. 133–137, 1993.

[CHA 06] CHARON I., HUDRY O., "Noising methods for a clique partitioning problem", *Discrete Applied Mathematics*, vol. 154, no. 5, pp. 754–769, Elsevier, 2006.

[CLE 02] CLERC M., KENNEDY J., "The particle swarm - explosion, stability, and convergence in a multidimensional complex space", *IEEE Transactions on Evolutionary Computation*, vol. 6, no. 1, pp. 58–73, 2002.

[CLE 06] CLERC M., Confinements and Biases in Particle Swarm Optimization, available at: http://clerc.maurice.free.fr/pso/Confinements_and_bias.pdf, 2006.

[CLE 07] CLERC M., Binary Particle Swarm Optimisers: toolbox, derivations, and mathematical insights, available at: https://hal.archives-ouvertes.fr/hal-00122809/document, January 2007.

[COH 00] COHEN R., EREZ K., BEN AVRAHAM D. *et al.*, "Resilience of the Internet to Random Breakdowns", *Phys. Rev. Lett.*, vol. 85, pp. 4626–4628, American Physical Society, November 2000.

[COH 01] COHEN R., EREZ K., AVRAHAM D. *et al.*, "Breakdown of the Internet under Intentional Attack", *Physical Review Letters*, vol. 86, pp. 3682–3685, American Physical Society, April 2001.

[COH 02] COHEN R., BEN AVRAHAM D., HAVLIN S., "Percolation critical exponents in scale-free networks", *Phys. Rev. E*, vol. 66, p. 036113, American Physical Society, September 2002.

[COH 03] COHEN R., HAVLIN S., "Scale-Free Networks Are Ultrasmall", *Phys. Rev. Lett.*, vol. 90, p. 058701, American Physical Society, February 2003.

[COR 06] CORREA E., FREITAS A., JOHNSON C., "A New Discrete Particle Swarm Algorithm Applied to Attribute Selection in a Bioinformatics Data Set", *Proceedings of the 8th Annual Conference on Genetic and Evolutionary Computation*, GECCO'06, New York, NY, USA, ACM, pp. 35–42, 2006.

[COS 07] COSTA L., RODRIGUES F., TRAVIESO G. *et al.*, "Characterization of Complex Networks: A Survey of Measurements", *Advances in Physics*, vol. 56, no. 1, pp. 167–242, Taylor & Francis, February 2007.

[CRE 83] CREUTZ M., "Microcanonical monte carlo simulation", *Physical Review Letters*, vol. 50, no. 19, pp. 1411–1414, APS, 1983.

[CRU 04] CRUCITTI P., LATORA V., MARCHIORI M., "Model for cascading failures in complex networks", *Phys. Rev. E*, vol. 69, p. 045104, American Physical Society, April 2004.

[CRU 05] CRUCITTI P., LATORA V., MARCHIORI M., "Locating critical lines in high-voltage electrical power grids", *Fluctuation and Noise Letters*, vol. 5, no. 02, pp. L201–L208, World Scientific, 2005.

[CUD 17] CUDA, NVIDIA OpenCL SDK Code Samples, https://developer.nvidia.com/opencl, 2017.

[DAS 08] DAS S., ABRAHAM A., KONAR A., "Particle Swarm Optimization and Differential Evolution Algorithms: Technical Analysis, Applications and Hybridization Perspectives", in LIU Y., SUN A., LOH H. *et al.* (eds.), *Advances of Computational Intelligence in Industrial Systems*, Springer, Berlin-Heidelberg, 2008.

[DEN 90] DENEUBOURG J., ARON S., GOSS S. *et al.*, "The self-organizing exploratory pattern of the argentine ant", *Journal of Insect Behavior*, vol. 3, no. 2, pp. 159–168, 1990.

[DEV 86] DEVROYE L., *Non-uniform Random Variate Generation*, Springer-Verlag, 1986.

[DOB 01] DOBSON I., CARRERAS B., LYNCH V. *et al.*, "An initial model fo complex dynamics in electric power system blackouts", *Proceedings of the 34th Annual Hawaii International Conference on System Sciences*, pp. 710–718, January 2001.

[DOR 91] DORIGO M., MANIEZZO V., COLORNI A., Positive feedback as a search strategy, Technical report 91–016, June 1991.

[DOR 96] DORIGO M., MANIEZZO V., COLORNI A., "The ant systems: optimization by a colony of cooperative agents", *IEEE Transactions on Man, Machine and Cybernetics-Part B*, vol. 26, no. 1, 1996.

[DOR 97] DORIGO M., GAMBARDELLA L., "Ant colony system: a cooperative learning approach to the traveling salesman problem", *IEEE Transactions on Evolutionary Computation*, vol. 1, no. 1, pp. 53–66, 1997.

[DOR 99a] DORIGO M., DI CARO G., "The Ant Colony Optimization Meta-heuristic", in *New Ideas in Optimization*, McGraw-Hill, Maidenhead, 1999.

[DOR 99b] DORIGO M., DI CARO G., GAMBARDELLA L., "Ant Algorithms for Discrete Optimization", *Artif. Life*, vol. 5, no. 2, pp. 137–172, MIT Press, April 1999.

[DOR 03] DOROGOVTSEV S., MENDES J., *Evolution of Networks: From Biological Nets to the Internet and WWW (Physics)*, Oxford University Press, New York, 2003.

[DOR 05] DORIGO M., BLUM C., "Ant colony optimization theory: A survey", *Theoretical Computer Science*, vol. 344, nos. 2 3, pp. 243–278, 2005.

[DOR 08] DOROGOVTSEV S., GOLTSEV A., MENDES J., "Critical phenomena in complex networks", *Rev. Mod. Phys.*, vol. 80, pp. 1275–1335, American Physical Society, October 2008.

[DOY 00] DOYLE J., CARLSON J., "Power laws, highly optimized tolerance, and generalized source coding", *Physical Review Letters*, vol. 84, no. 24, pp. 5656–9, APS, June 2000.

[DRE 03] DREO J., PETROWSKI A., TAILLARD E. *et al.*, *Métaheuristiques pour l'optimisation difficile*, Eyrolles, 2003.

[DUV 71] DUVANENKO V., Parallel In-Place N-bit-Radix Sort, PhD Thesis, New Haven, 1971.

[EBE 95] EBERHART R., KENNEDY J., "A new optimizer using particle swarm theory", *MHS'95, Proceedings of the Sixth International Symposium on Micro Machine and Human Science*, pp. 39–43, 1995.

[EBE 96] EBERHART R., SIMPSON P., DOBBINS R., *Computational Intelligence PC Tools*, Academic Press Professional, 1996.

[EBE 01] EBERHART R., SHI Y., KENNEDY J., *Swarm Intelligence*, 1st edition, Morgan Kaufmann, 2001.

[EFT 04] EFTEKHARI A., "Fractal dimension of electrochemical reactions", *Journal of the Electrochemical Society*, vol. 151, no. 9, pp. E291–E296, The Electrochemical Society, August 2004.

[ELA 09] EL-ABD M., "Preventing premature convergence in a PSO and EDA hybrid", *IEEE Congress on Evolutionary Computation, CEC'09*, pp. 3060–3066, May 2009.

[ELD 12a] EL DOR A., CLERC M., SIARRY P., "Hybridization of Differential Evolution and Particle Swarm Optimization in a New Algorithm: DEPSO-2S", *Proceedings of the 2012 International Conference on Swarm and Evolutionary Computation*, SIDE'12, Berlin, Heidelberg, Springer-Verlag, pp. 57–65, 2012.

[ELD 12b] EL DOR A., CLERC M., SIARRY P., "A Multi-swarm PSO Using Charged Particles in a Partitioned Search Space for Continuous Optimization", *Comput. Optim. Appl.*, vol. 53, no. 1, pp. 271–295, Kluwer Academic Publishers, September 2012.

[ERD 59] ERDŐS P., RÉNYI A., "On random graphs I.", *Publ. Math. Debrecen*, vol. 6, pp. 290–297, 1959.

[FAM 65] FAMA E., "The Behavior of Stock-Market Prices", *The Journal of Business*, vol. 38, no. 1, pp. 34–105, The University of Chicago Press, January 1965.

[FAM 68] FAMA E., ROLL R., "Some properties of symmetric stable distributions", *J. Am. Stat. Assoc.*, vol. 63, no. 323, pp. 817–836, American Statistical Association, September 1968.

[FAM 71] FAMA E., ROLL R., "Parameter estimates for symmetric stable distributions", *Journal of the American Statistical Association*, vol. 66, no. 334, pp. 331–338, Taylor & Francis, June 1971.

[FEL 66] FELLER W., *An Introduction to Probability Theory and its Applications, Vol. II.*, John Wiley and Sons, New York, 1966.

[FEL 10] FELLER W., "An introduction to probability theory and its applications. Vol. II.", *Dr. Dobb's Journal*, August 2010.

[FEN 09] FENIX PROJECT, http//www.fenix-project.org/, 2009.

[FEO 95] FEO T., RESENDE M., "Greedy Randomized Adaptive Search Procedures", *Journal of Global Optimization*, vol. 6, no. 2, pp. 109–133, 1995.

[FER 03] FERRER I CANCHO, SOLÉ R., "Optimization in complex networks", *Statistical mechanics of complex networks*, pp. 114–126, Springer, 2003.

[FEU 81] FEUERVERGER A., MCDONNOUGH P., "On efficient inference in symmetric stable laws and processes", *Canadian Journal of Statistics*, vol. 18, no. 2, pp. 109–122, Statistics and Related topics, 1981.

[FIE 72] FIELITZ B., SMITH E., "Asymmetric stable distributions of stock price changes", *Journal of the American Statistical Association*, vol. 67, no. 340, pp. 813–814, Taylor & Francis, January 1972.

[FIG 05] FIGUEIRA J., MOUSSEAU V., ROY B., "ELECTRE methods", *Multiple criteria decision analysis. State of the art surveys*, pp. 133–153, Springer, 2005.

[FRE 81] FREUND R., LITTELL R., *SAS for linear models: a guide to the ANOVA and GLM procedures*, vol. 1, Sas Institute, 1981.

[FRE 11] FREEMAN M., *Digital Slr Handbook*, Ilex, 3rd edition, 2011.

[GAL 05] GALLOS L., COHEN R., ARGYRAKIS P. *et al.*, "Stability and topology of scale-free networks under attack and defense strategies", *Physical review letters*, vol. 94, no. 18, p. 188701, APS, May 2005.

[GEH 65a] GEHAN E., "A generalized two-sample Wilcoxon test for doubly censored data", *Biometrika*, pp. 650–653, JSTOR, 1965.

[GEH 65b] GEHAN E., "A generalized Wilcoxon test for comparing arbitrarily singly-censored samples", *Biometrika*, vol. 52, nos. 1–2, pp. 203–223, Biometrika Trust, 1965.

[GEN 16] GENERAL ELECTRIC GRID SOLUTIONS, Internal resources, 2016.

[GEO 74] GEOFFRION A., "Lagrangean relaxation for integer programming", dans BALINSKI M. (eds.), *Approaches to Integer Programming*, vol. 2, *Mathematical Programming Studies*, pp. 82–114, Springer, Berlin-Heidelberg, 1974.

[GLO 86a] GLOVER F., "Future paths for integer programming and links to artificial intelligence", *Computers & Operations Research*, vol. 13, no. 5, pp. 533–549, 1986.

[GLO 86b] GLOVER F., MCMILLAN C., "The general employee scheduling problem. An integration of MS and AI", *Computers & Operations Research*, vol. 13, no. 5, pp. 563–573, Elsevier, 1986.

[GOL 89] GOLDBERG D., *Genetic Algorithms in Search, Optimization and Machine Learning*, Addison-Wesley Longman Publishing Co., 1st edition, 1989.

[GOL 91] GOLDBERG D., DEB K., "A comparative analysis of selection schemes used in genetic algorithms", *Foundations of Genetic Algorithms*, vol. 1, pp. 69–93, 1991.

[GOT 82] GOTOH O., "An improved algorithm for matching biological sequences", *Journal of Molecular Biology*, vol. 162, no. 3, pp. 705–708, 1982.

[GRO] GROUP T.K., "OpenCL API 1.1 Quick Reference Card", http://www.khronos.org.

[HAN 95] HANSEN N., OSTERMEIER A., GAWELCZYK A., "On the adaptation of arbitrary normal mutation distributions in evolution strategies: The generating set adaptation", *Proceedings of the Sixth International Conference on Genetic Algorithms*, pp. 57–64, 1995.

[HAN 00] HANSEN P., JAUMARD B., MLADENOVIĆ N. *et al.*, "Variable neighborhood search for weight satisfiability problem", *Les Cahiers du GERARD*, G-2000-62, 2000.

[HAN 01a] HANSEN P., MLADENOVI N., "Variable neighborhood search: Principles and applications", *European Journal Of Operational Research*, vol. 130, no. 3, pp. 449–467, 2001.

[HAN 01b] HANSEN P., MLADENOVIĆ N., PEREZ-BRITOS D., "Variable neighborhood decomposition search", *Journal of Heuristics*, vol. 7, no. 4, pp. 335–350, 2001.

[HAN 09] HANSEN N., FINCK S., ROS R. *et al.*, Real-Parameter Black-Box Optimization Benchmarking 2009: Noiseless Functions Definitions, Research Report no. RR–6829, INRIA, 2009.

[HAU 04] HAUPT R., HAUPT S., *Practical Genetic Algorithms*, John Wiley & Sons, 2004.

[HEP 90] HEPPNER F, GRENANDER U., "A stochastic nonlinear model for coordinated bird flocks", *American Association for the Advancement of Science*, 1990.

[HER 93] HERAULT L., HORAUD R., "Figure-ground discrimination: A combinatorial optimization approach", *IEEE Transactions on Pattern Analysis and Machine Intelligence*, vol. 15, no. 9, pp. 899–914, 1993.

[HIL 86] HILLIS W., STEELE JR. G., "Data Parallel Algorithms", *Commun. ACM*, vol. 29, no. 12, pp. 1170–1183, ACM, December 1986.

[HIL 90] HILLIS W., "Simulated Evolution", *Optimization*, vol. 42, pp. 228–234, 1990.

[HOL 73] HOLD D., CROW E., "Tables and graphs of the stable probability functions", *Journal of Rechearch of the National Bureau of Standards*, vols. 3–4, no. 77b, pp. 143–198, B. Mathematical Sciences, July 1973.

[HOL 92] HOLLAND J., *Adaptation in Natural and Artificial Systems*, 1992.

[HSI 09] HSIEH S.-T., SUN T.-Y., LIU C.-C. *et al.*, "Efficient population utilization strategy for particle swarm optimizer", *IEEE Transactions on Systems, Man, and Cybernetics, Part B: Cybernetics*, vol. 39, no. 2, pp. 444–456, April 2009.

[HSU 08] HSU H., LACHENBRUCH P., "Paired t test", *Wiley Encyclopedia of Clinical Trials*, Wiley Online Library, 2008.

[IEA 11] IEA, Technology Roadmap Smart Grids, International Energy Agency, 2011.

[JAM 94] JAMES F., "RANLUX: A Fortran implementation of the high-quality pseudorandom number generator of Lüscher", *Computer Physics Communications*, vol. 79, no. 1, pp. 111–114, Elsevier, September 1994.

[JUN 94] JUN G., HUANG X., "Efficient local search with search space smoothing: a case study of the traveling salesman problem (TSP)", *IEEE Transactions on Systems, Man and Cybernetics*, vol. 24, no. 5, pp. 728–735, May 1994.

[KAN 75] KANTER M., "Stable densities under change of scale and total variation inequalities", *The Annals of Probability*, vol. 3, no. 4, pp. 697–707, Institute of Mathematical Statistics, August 1975.

[KAR 72] KARP R., "Reducibility among combinatorial problems", in *Complexity of Computer Computations*, Yorktown Heights, 1972.

[KAR 98] KARYPIS G., KUMAR V., METIS: A Software Package for Partitioning Unstructured Graphs, Partitioning Meshes, and Computing Fill-Reducing Orderings of Sparse Matrices, September 1998.

[KEN 95] KENNEDY J., EBERHART R., "Particle swarm optimization", *IEEE International Conference on Neural Networks*, Perth, Australia, pp. 1942–1948, 1995.

[KEN 02] KENNEDY J., MENDES R., "Population structure and particle swarm performance", *Proceedings of the 2002 Congress on Evolutionary Computation, CEC 2002*, vol. 2, pp. 1671–1676, 2002.

[KIM 00] KIM H.-J., KIM H.-J., FAY M.P., FEUER E.J., MIDTHUNE D.N., "Permutation tests for joinpoint regression with applications to cancer rates", *Statistics in Medicine*, vol. 19, pp. 335–351, 2000.

[KIN 05] KINNEY R., CRUCITTI P., ALBERT R. *et al.*, "Modeling cascading failures in the North American power grid", *The European Physical Journal B - Condensed Matter and Complex Systems*, vol. 46, no. 1, pp. 101–107, EDP Sciences, July 2005.

[KIR 83] KIRKPATRICK S., GELATT C. D. JR., VECCHI M. P., "Optimization by Simulated Annealing", *Science*, vol. 220, pp. 671–680, 1983.

[KIR 84] KIRKPATRICK S., "Optimization by simulated annealing: Quantitative studies", *Journal of Statistical Physics*, vol. 34, pp. 975–986, 1984.

[KOG 98] KOGON S., WILLIAMS D., *A Practical Guide to Heavy Tails*, Birkhauser Boston Inc., 1998.

[KOU 80] KOUTROUVELIS I., "Regression-type estimation of the parameters of stable laws", *Journal of the American Statistical Association*, vol. 75, no. 372, pp. 918–928, Taylor & Francis, December 1980.

[LEI 75] LEITCH R., PAULSON A., "Estimation of stable law parameters: stock price behavior application", *Journal of the American Statistical Association*, vol. 70, no. 351a, pp. 690–697, Taylor & Francis, September 1975.

[LEV 02] LÉVY VÉHEL J., WALTER C., *Les Marchés fractals*, PUF, Paris, 2002.

[LIA 13] LIANG J., QU B., SUGANTHAN P. *et al.*, Problem definitions and evaluation criteria for the CEC 2013 special session on real-parameter optimization, Computational Intelligence Laboratory, Zhengzhou University, Zhengzhou, China and Nanyang Technological University, Singapore, Technical Report, 2013.

[LIN 96] LINDGREN F., HANSEN B., KARCHER W. *et al.*, "Model validation by permutation tests: Applications to variable selection", *Journal of Chemometrics*, vol. 10, nos. 5–6, pp. 521–532, Wiley Online Library, 1996.

[LIU 05] LIU J., LAMPINEN J., "A Fuzzy Adaptive Differential Evolution Algorithm", *Soft Computing*, vol. 9, no. 6, pp. 448–462, Springer-Verlag, 2005.

[LOU 01] LOURENCÓ H., MARTIN O., STÜTZLE T., "A beginner's introduction to Iterated Local Search", *Proceeding of the 4th Metaheuristics International Conference*, pp. 1–11, 2001.

[LOU 03] LOURENCÓ H., MARTIN O., STÜTZLE T., "Iterated Local Search", in GLOVER F., KOCHENBERGER G. (eds.), *Handbook of Metaheuristics*, Springer US, 2003.

[LUK 09] ŁUKASIK S., ŻAK S., "Firefly Algorithm for Continuous Constrained Optimization Tasks", in NGUYEN N., KOWALCZYK R., CHEN S.-M. (eds.), *Computational Collective Intelligence. Semantic Web, Social Networks and Multiagent Systems*, Springer, Berlin-Heidelberg, 2009.

[LUS 94] LÜSCHER M., "A portable high-quality random number generator for lattice field theory simulations", *Computer Physics Communications*, vol. 79, no. 1, pp. 100–110, Elsevier, February 1994.

[MA 10] MA H., "An analysis of the equilibrium of migration models for biogeography-based optimization", *Information Sciences*, vol. 180, no. 18, pp. 3444–3464, Elsevier, 2010.

[MAC 67] MACARTHUR R., WILSON E., *The Theory of Island Biogeography*, vol. 1, Princeton University Press, 1967.

[MAN 63] MANDELBROT B., "The Variation of Certain Speculative Prices", *The Journal of Business*, vol. 36, pp. 394–419, The University of Chicago Press, 1963.

[MAN 94] MANTEGNA R., "Fast, accurate algorithm for numerical simulation of Lévy stable stochastic processes", *Phys. Rev. E*, vol. 49, pp. 4677–4683, American Physical Society, May 1994.

[MAN 05] MANNING M., CARLSON J., DOYLE J., "Highly optimized tolerance and power laws in dense and sparse resource regimes", *Physical Review E*, vol. 72, no. 1, p. 016108, APS, July 2005.

[MAR 04] MARSHALL L.F., "The Lagrangian Relaxation Method for Solving Integer Programming Problems", *Management Science*, vol. 50, no. 12, supplément, pp. 1861–1871, 2004.

[MAS 51] MASSEY JR F., "The Kolmogorov-Smirnov test for goodness of fit", *Journal of the American Statistical Association*, vol. 46, no. 253, pp. 68–78, Taylor & Francis Group, March 1951.

[MCC 86] McCulloch J., "Simple consistent estimators of stable distribution parameters", *Communications in Statistics-Simulation and Computation*, vol. 15, no. 4, pp. 1109–1136, Taylor & Francis, 1986.

[MET 53] Metropolis N., Rosenbluth A., Rosenbluth M. *et al.*, "Equation of state calculations by fast computing machines", *The Journal of Chemical Physics*, vol. 21, no. 6, pp. 1087–1092, AIP Publishing, 1953.

[MIL 56] Miller L., "Table of percentage points of Kolmogorov statistics", *Journal of the American Statistical Association*, vol. 51, no. 273, pp. 111–121, Taylor & Francis, March 1956.

[MIT 01] Mittnik S., *Stable Non-Gaussian Models in Finance and Econometrics*, vol. 34, Pergamon Press, New York, 2001.

[MLA 97] Mladenović N., Hansen P., "Variable neighborhood search", *Computers & Operations Research*, vol. 24, no. 11, pp. 1097–1100, 1997.

[MON 84] Montgomery D., *Design and Analysis of Experiments*, Wiley, 1984.

[MOT 02] Motter A., Lai Y.-C., "Cascade-based attacks on complex networks", *Phys. Rev. E*, vol. 66, p. 065102, American Physical Society, December 2002.

[NAK 13] Nakib A., Siarry P., "Performance Analysis of Dynamic Optimization Algorithms", in Alba E., Nakib A., Siarry P. (eds.), *Metaheuristics for Dynamic Optimization*, Springer, Berlin Heidelberg, 2013.

[NAK 15] Nakib A., Thibault B., Siarry P., "Bayesian based metaheuristic for large scale continuous optimization", *IEEE/ACM International Parallel and Distributed Processing*, Hyderabad, India, May 2015.

[NEL 65] Nelder J., Mead R., "A Simplex Method for Function Minimization", *The Computer Journal*, vol. 7, no. 4, pp. 308–313, 1965.

[NEW 02] Newman M., "Assortative Mixing in Networks", *Phys. Rev. Lett.*, vol. 89, p. 208701, American Physical Society, October 2002.

[NEW 03] Newman M., "The Structure and Function of Complex Networks", *SIAM Review*, vol. 45, pp. 167–256, SIAM, August 2003.

[NIK 95] Nikias C., Shao M., *Signal Processing with Alpha-stable Distributions and Applications*, Wiley-Interscience, New York, 1995.

[NOL 98] Nolfi S., Floreano D., "Coevolving predator and prey robots: do "arms races" arise in artificial evolution", *Artificial life*, vol. 4, no. 4, pp. 311–335, 1998.

[NOT 11] Nottale L., *Scale Relativity and Fractal Space-Time: A New Approach to Unifying Relativity and Quantum Mechanics*, Imperial College Press, 2011.

[PAN 92] Panton D., "Cumulative distribution function values for symmetric standardized stable distributions", *Communications in Statistics-Simulation and Computation*, vol. 21, no. 2, pp. 485–492, Taylor & Francis, 1992.

[PAS 01] Pastor-Satorras R., Vázquez A., Vespignani A., "Dynamical and Correlation Properties of the Internet", *Phys. Rev. Lett.*, vol. 87, p. 258701, American Physical Society, November 2001.

[PAU 75] PAULSON A., HOLCOMB E., LEITCH R., "The estimation of the parameters of the stable laws", *Biometrika*, vol. 62, no. 1, pp. 163–170, Biometrika Trust, April 1975.

[PAU 07] PAUL G., COHEN R., SREENIVASAN S. *et al.*, "Graph Partitioning Induced Phase Transitions", *Phys. Rev. Lett.*, vol. 99, p. 115701, American Physical Society, September 2007.

[POO 95] POON P., CARTER J., "Genetic algorithm crossover operators for ordering applications", *Computers & Operations Research*, vol. 22, no. 1, pp. 135–147, 1995.

[POT 94] POTTER M., DE JONG K., "A cooperative coevolutionary approach to function optimization", *Parallel Problem Solving from Nature*, pp. 249–257, 1994.

[PRE 72] PRESS S., "Estimation in univariate and multivariate stable distributions", *Journal of the American Statistical Association*, vol. 67, no. 340, pp. 842–846, Taylor & Francis Group, December 1972.

[PRE 92] PRESS W., *Numerical Recipes in C: The Art of Scientific Computing*, no. 4, William H. Press, Cambridge University Press, 1992.

[QIN 05] QIN A., SUGANTHAN P., "Self-adaptive differential evolution algorithm for numerical optimization", *2005 IEEE Congress on Evolutionary Computation*, vol. 2, pp. 1785–1791, September 2005.

[QIN 09a] QIN A., HUANG V., SUGANTHAN P., "Differential evolution algorithm with strategy adaptation for global numerical optimization", *IEEE Transactions on Evolutionary Computation*, vol. 13, no. 2, pp. 398–417, April 2009.

[QIN 09b] QING A., *Benchmarking a Single-Objective Optimization Test Bed for Parametric Study on Differential Evolution*, John Wiley & Sons, 2009.

[RAD 91] RADCLIFFE N., "Equivalence class analysis of genetic algorithms", *Complex Systems*, vol. 5, no. 2, pp. 183–205, 1991.

[REC 73] RECHENBERG I., "Evolution Strategy: optimization of technical systems by means of biological evolution", *Fromman-Holzboog*, vol. 104, 1973.

[REY 87] REYNOLDS C., "Flocks, herds and schools: a distributed behavioral model", *SIGGRAPH Comput. Graph.*, vol. 21, no. 4, pp. 25–34, ACM, July 1987.

[REY 94] REYNOLDS R., ZANNONI E., POSNER R., "Learning to understand software using cultural algorithms", *Conference On Evolutionary Programming*, San Diego, CA, pp. 150–157, 1994.

[REY 05] REYNOLDS R., PENG B., "Cultural Algorithms: Computational Modeling of How Cultures Learn To Solve Problems: an Engineering Example", *Cybernetics & Systems*, vol. 36, no. 8, pp. 753–771, 2005.

[RON 97] RONALD S., "Robust encodings in genetic algorithms: a survey of encoding issues", *Proceedings of 1997 IEEE International Conference on Evolutionary Computation (ICEC '97)*, 1997.

[ROS 97] ROSIN C., BELEW R., "New methods for competitive coevolution", *Evolutionary Computation*, vol. 5, no. 1, pp. 1–29, 1997.

[ROS 12] ROSAS CASALS M., COROMINAS MURTRA B. *et al.*, Assessing European power grid reliability by means of topological measures, Report, 2012.

[ROW 04] ROWE J., WHITLEY D., BARBULESCU L. *et al.*, "Properties of gray and binary representations.", *Evolutionary Computation*, vol. 12, no. 1, pp. 47–76, 2004.

[ROY 68] ROY B., "Classement et choix en présence de points de vue multiples", *Revue française d'automatique, d'informatique et de recherche opérationnelle. Recherche opérationnelle*, vol. 2, no. 1, pp. 57–75, 1968.

[ROZ 09] ROZEL B., La sécurisation des infrastructures critiques: recherche d'une méthodologie d'identification des vulnérabilités et modélisation des interdépendances, PhD Thesis, Paris, France, 2009.

[RUX 06] RUXTON G., "The unequal variance t-test is an underused alternative to Student's t-test and the Mann–Whitney U test", *Behavioral Ecology*, vol. 17, no. 4, pp. 688–690, ISBE, 2006.

[SAM 69] SAMUELSON P., "Lifetime portfolio selection by dynamic stochastic programming", *The Review of Economics and Statistics*, vol. 51, no. 3, pp. 239–246, 1969.

[SCH 81] SCHWEFEL H.-P., *Numerical Optimization of Computer Models*, John Wiley & Sons, 1981.

[SCH 02] SCHWARTZ N., COHEN R., BEN AVRAHAM D. *et al.*, "Percolation in directed scale-free networks", *Physical Review E*, vol. 66, no. 1, p. 015104, APS, August 2002.

[SHA 03] SHARGEL B., SAYAMA H., EPSTEIN I. *et al.*, "Optimization of Robustness and Connectivity in Complex Networks", *Phys. Rev. Lett.*, vol. 90, p. 068701, American Physical Society, February 2003.

[SHI 98] SHI Y., EBERHART R., "A modified particle swarm optimizer", *IEEE International Conference on Evolutionary Computation Proceedings. IEEE World Congress on Computational Intelligence (Cat. No.98TH8360)*, pp. 69–73, 1998.

[SHI 99] SHI Y., EBERHART R., "Empirical study of particle swarm optimization", *Proceedings of the 1999 Congress on Evolutionary Computation-CEC99*, pp. 1945–1950, 1999.

[SIM 08] SIMON D., "Biogeography-Based Optimization", *IEEE Transactions on Evolutionary Computation*, vol. 12, no. 6, pp. 702–713, December 2008.

[SOI 96] SOILLE P., RIVEST J., "On the Validity of Fractal Dimension Measurements in Image Analysis", *Journal of Visual Communication and Image Representation*, vol. 7, no. 3, pp. 217–229, Elsevier, September 1996.

[SOL 08] SOLÉ R., ROSAS-CASALS M., COROMINAS-MURTRA B. *et al.*, "Robustness of the European power grids under intentional attack", *Phys. Rev. E*, vol. 77, p. 026102, American Physical Society, February 2008.

[SOL 16] SOLUTIONS G.E.G., Internal report on Smart Grids, Report, 2016.

[SON 07] SONG C., GALLOS L.K., HAVLIN S. *et al.*, "How to calculate the fractal dimension of a complex network: the box covering algorithm", *Journal of Statistical Mechanics: Theory and Experiment*, vol. 2007, no. 03, p. P03006, IOPscience, January 2007.

[SPE 62] SPENDLEY W., HEXT G., HIMSWORTH F., "Sequential application of simplex designs in optimisation and evolutionary operation", *Technometrics*, vol. 4, no. 4, pp. 441–461, Taylor & Francis Group, 1962.

[STE 70] STEPHENS M., "Use of the Kolmogorov-Smirnov, Cramér-Von Mises and related statistics without extensive tables", *Journal of the Royal Statistical Society. Series B (Methodological)*, vol. 32, no. 1, pp. 115–122, JSTOR, 1970.

[STE 03] STÉPHANE G., Métaheuristiques appliquées au placement optimal de dispositifs FACTS dans un réseau électrique, PhD Thesis, Lausanne, Suisse, 2003.

[STO 95] STORN R., PRICE K., *Differential Evolution: A Simple and Efficient Adaptive Scheme for Global Optimization Over Continuous Spaces*, vol. 3, ICSI Berkeley, 1995.

[STU 00] STÜTZLE T., HOOS H., "Ant System", *Future Generation Computer Systems*, vol. 16, no. 8, pp. 889–914, 2000.

[TAI 91] TAILLARD E., "Robust tabu search for the quadratic assignment problem", *Parallel computing*, vol. 17, pp. 443–455, 1991.

[TAL 09] TALBI E.-G., *Metaheuristics: From Design to Implementation*, John Wiley & Sons, 2009.

[TAN 05] TANIZAWA T., PAUL G., COHEN R. *et al.*, "Optimization of network robustness to waves of targeted and random attacks", *Phys. Rev. E*, vol. 71, p. 047101, American Physical Society, April 2005.

[TAN 10] TAN Y., ZHU Y., "Fireworks algorithm for optimization", *Lecture Notes in Computer Science (including subseries Lecture Notes in Artificial Intelligence and Lecture Notes in Bioinformatics)*, vol. 6145 LNCS, no. PART 1, pp. 355–364, 2010.

[TAN 15] TAN Y., *Fireworks Algorithm: A Novel Swarm Intelligence Optimization Method*, Springer, 2015.

[TEA 06] TEAM B., Areva, Internal Report, 2006.

[THE 90] THEILER J., "Estimating fractal dimension", *JOSA A*, vol. 7, no. 6, pp. 1055–1073, Optical Society of America, June 1990.

[TOL 03] TOLLE C., MCJUNKIN T., GORISCH D., "Suboptimal minimum cluster volume cover-based method for measuring fractal dimension", *IEEE Transactions on Pattern Analysis and Machine Intelligence*, vol. 25, no. 1, pp. 32–41, January 2003.

[VOU 99] VOUDOURIS C., TSANG E., "Guided local search and its application to the traveling salesman problem", *European Journal of Operational Research*, vol. 113, no. 2, pp. 469–499, 1999.

[WAN 06] WANG B., TANG H., GUO C. *et al.*, "Entropy optimization of scalefree networksrobustness to random failures", *Physica A: Statistical Mechanics and its Applications*, vol. 363, no. 2, pp. 591–596, Elsevier, May 2006.

[WAN 08a] WANG B., KAZUYUKI A., LUONAN C., "Traffic jamming in disordred flow distribution networks", *Operations Research and Its Applications: The 7th International Symposium, ISORA '08*, Lecture notes in operations research, Lijiang, Chine, World Publishing Corporation, pp. 465–469, 2008.

[WAN 08b] WANG Y., XIAO S., XIAO G. *et al.*, "Robustness of Complex Communication Networks Under Link Attacks", *Proceedings of the 2008 International Conference on Advanced Infocomm Technology (ICAIT '08)* , New York, pp. 61:1–61:7, 2008.

[WAS 94] WASSERMAN S., FAUST K., *Social Network Analysis: Methods and Applications*, vol. 8, *Structural Analysis in the Social Sciences*, Cambridge University Press, Cambridge, 1994.

[WAT 98] WATTS D., STROGATZ S., "Collective dynamics of 'small-world'networks", *Nature*, vol. 393, no. 6684, pp. 440–442, Nature Publishing Group, April 1998.

[WAT 02] WATTS D., "A simple model of global cascades on random networks", *Proceedings of the National Academy of Sciences of the United States of America*, vol. 99, no. 9, p. 5766, National Academy of Sciences, May 2002.

[WER 95] WERON R., Performance of the estimators of stable law parameters, HSC Research Reports no. HSC/95/01, Hugo Steinhaus Center, Wroclaw University of Technology, 1995.

[WHI 01] WHITLEY E., BALL J., "Statistics review 1: Presenting and summarising data", *Critical Care*, vol. 6, no. 1, p. 66, BioMed Central Ltd, 2001.

[WOR 75] WORSDALE G., "Tables of cumulative distribution functions for symmetric stable distributions", *Applied Statistics*, vol. 24, no. 1, pp. 123–131, JSTOR, November 1975.

[WU 06] WU Z., BRAUNSTEIN L., COLIZZA V. *et al.*, "Optimal paths in complex networks with correlated weights: The worldwide airport network", *Phys. Rev. E*, vol. 74, p. 056104, American Physical Society, November 2006.

[WU 08] WU Z., PENG G., WANG W.-X. *et al.*, "Cascading failure spreading on weighted heterogeneous networks", *Journal of Statistical Mechanics: Theory and Experiment*, vol. 2008, p. P05013, IOPscience, March 2008.

[XU 14] XU J., ZHANG J., "Exploration-exploitation tradeoffs in metaheuristics: Survey and analysis", *33rd Chinese Control Conference (CCC)*, Nanjing, China, pp. 8633–8638, July 2014.

[YAN 08] YANG X.-S., *Nature-Inspired Metaheuristic Algorithms*, Luniver Press, 2008.

[YAN 09a] YANG X.-S., *Firefly Algorithms for Multimodal Optimization*, Springer, Berlin, 2009.

[YAN 09b] YANG X.-S., DEB S., "Cuckoo Search via Lévy flights", *Nature Biologically Inspired Computing, NaBIC 2009*, Coimbatore, India, pp. 210–214, December 2009.

[YAN 10] YANG X.-S., "Firefly algorithm, stochastic test functions and design optimisation", *International Journal of Bio-Inspired Computation*, vol. 2, no. 2, pp. 78–84, 2010.

[YOS 00] YOSHIDA H., KAWATA K., FUKUYAMA Y. *et al.*, "A particle swarm optimization for reactive power and voltage control considering voltage security assessment", *IEEE Transactions on Power Systems*, vol. 15, no. 4, pp. 1232–1239, 2000.

[ZEM 81] ZEMEL E., "Measuring the Quality of Approximate Solutions to Zero-One Programming Problems", *Mathematics of Operations Research*, vol. 6, no. 3, pp. 319–332, 1981.

[ZHA 10] ZHANG Z., GAO S., CHEN L. *et al.*, "Mapping Koch curves into scale-free small-world networks", *Journal of Physics A: Mathematical and Theoretical*, vol. 43, no. 39, p. 395101, IOP Publishing, 2010.

[ZLO 02] ZLOCHIN M., DORIGO M., "Model-based search for combinatorial optimization: A comparative study", *Parallel Problem Solving from Nature-PPSN VII*, pp. 651–661, Springer, 2002.

[ZOL 66] ZOLOTAREV V., "On representation of stable laws by integrals", *Selected Translations in Mathematical Statistics and Probability*, vol. 6, no. 1, pp. 84–88, American Mathematical Society Providence, 1966.

Index

Other titles from

in

Computer Engineering

2017

MA Haiping, SIMON Dan
Evolutionary Computation with Biogeography-based Optimization
(Metaheuristics Set – Volume 8)

PÉTROWSKI Alain, BEN-HAMIDA Sana
Evolutionary Algorithms
(Metaheuristics Set – Volume 9)

2016

BLUM Christian, FESTA Paola
Metaheuristics for String Problems in Bio-informatics
(Metaheuristics Set – Volume 6)

DEROUSSI Laurent
Metaheuristics for Logistics
(Metaheuristics Set – Volume 4)

DHAENENS Clarisse and JOURDAN Laetitia
Metaheuristics for Big Data
(Metaheuristics Set – Volume 5)

LABADIE Nacima, PRINS Christian, PRODHON Caroline
Metaheuristics for Vehicle Routing Problems
(Metaheuristics Set – Volume 3)

LEROY Laure
Eyestrain Reduction in Stereoscopy

LUTTON Evelyne, PERROT Nathalie, TONDA Albert
Evolutionary Algorithms for Food Science and Technology
(Metaheuristics Set – Volume 7)

MAGOULÈS Frédéric, ZHAO Hai-Xiang
Data Mining and Machine Learning in Building Energy Analysis

RIGO Michel
Advanced Graph Theory and Combinatorics

2015

BARBIER Franck, RECOUSSINE Jean-Luc
*COBOL Software Modernization: From Principles to Implementation with
the BLU AGE® Method*

CHEN Ken
*Performance Evaluation by Simulation and Analysis with Applications to
Computer Networks*

CLERC Maurice
Guided Randomness in Optimization
(Metaheuristics Set – Volume 1)

DURAND Nicolas, GIANAZZA David, GOTTELAND Jean-Baptiste,
ALLIOT Jean-Marc
Metaheuristics for Air Traffic Management
(Metaheuristics Set – Volume 2)

MAGOULÈS Frédéric, ROUX François-Xavier, HOUZEAUX Guillaume
Parallel Scientific Computing

MUNEESAWANG Paisarn, YAMMEN Suchart
Visual Inspection Technology in the Hard Disk Drive Industry

2014

BOULANGER Jean-Louis
Formal Methods Applied to Industrial Complex Systems

BOULANGER Jean-Louis
Formal Methods Applied to Complex Systems:
Implementation of the B Method

GARDI Frédéric, BENOIST Thierry, DARLAY Julien, ESTELLON Bertrand,
MEGEL Romain
Mathematical Programming Solver based on Local Search

KRICHEN Saoussen, CHAOUACHI Jouhaina
Graph-related Optimization and Decision Support Systems

LARRIEU Nicolas, VARET Antoine
Rapid Prototyping of Software for Avionics Systems: Model-oriented
Approaches for Complex Systems Certification

OUSSALAH Mourad Chabane
Software Architecture 1
Software Architecture 2

PASCHOS Vangelis Th
Combinatorial Optimization – 3-volume series, 2nd Edition
Concepts of Combinatorial Optimization – Volume 1, 2nd Edition
Problems and New Approaches – Volume 2, 2nd Edition
Applications of Combinatorial Optimization – Volume 3, 2nd Edition

QUESNEL Flavien
Scheduling of Large-scale Virtualized Infrastructures: Toward Cooperative
Management

RIGO Michel
Formal Languages, Automata and Numeration Systems 1:
Introduction to Combinatorics on Words
Formal Languages, Automata and Numeration Systems 2:
Applications to Recognizability and Decidability

SAINT-DIZIER Patrick
Musical Rhetoric: Foundations and Annotation Schemes

TOUATI Sid, DE DINECHIN Benoit
Advanced Backend Optimization

2013

ANDRÉ Etienne, SOULAT Romain
The Inverse Method: Parametric Verification of Real-time Embedded Systems

BOULANGER Jean-Louis
Safety Management for Software-based Equipment

DELAHAYE Daniel, PUECHMOREL Stéphane
Modeling and Optimization of Air Traffic

FRANCOPOULO Gil
LMF — Lexical Markup Framework

GHÉDIRA Khaled
Constraint Satisfaction Problems

ROCHANGE Christine, UHRIG Sascha, SAINRAT Pascal
Time-Predictable Architectures

WAHBI Mohamed
Algorithms and Ordering Heuristics for Distributed Constraint Satisfaction Problems

ZELM Martin *et al.*
Enterprise Interoperability

2012

ARBOLEDA Hugo, ROYER Jean-Claude
Model-Driven and Software Product Line Engineering

BLANCHET Gérard, DUPOUY Bertrand
Computer Architecture

BOULANGER Jean-Louis
Industrial Use of Formal Methods: Formal Verification

BOULANGER Jean-Louis
Formal Method: Industrial Use from Model to the Code

CALVARY Gaëlle, DELOT Thierry, SÈDES Florence, TIGLI Jean-Yves
Computer Science and Ambient Intelligence

MAHOUT Vincent
*Assembly Language Programming: ARM Cortex-M3 2.0: Organization,
Innovation and Territory*

MARLET Renaud
Program Specialization

SOTO Maria, SEVAUX Marc, ROSSI André, LAURENT Johann
Memory Allocation Problems in Embedded Systems: Optimization Methods

2011

BICHOT Charles-Edmond, SIARRY Patrick
Graph Partitioning

BOULANGER Jean-Louis
Static Analysis of Software: The Abstract Interpretation

CAFERRA Ricardo
Logic for Computer Science and Artificial Intelligence

HOMES Bernard
Fundamentals of Software Testing

KORDON Fabrice, HADDAD Serge, PAUTET Laurent, PETRUCCI Laure
Distributed Systems: Design and Algorithms

KORDON Fabrice, HADDAD Serge, PAUTET Laurent, PETRUCCI Laure
Models and Analysis in Distributed Systems

LORCA Xavier
Tree-based Graph Partitioning Constraint

TRUCHET Charlotte, ASSAYAG Gerard
Constraint Programming in Music

VICAT-BLANC PRIMET Pascale *et al.*
Computing Networks: From Cluster to Cloud Computing

2010

AUDIBERT Pierre
Mathematics for Informatics and Computer Science

BABAU Jean-Philippe *et al.*
Model Driven Engineering for Distributed Real-Time Embedded Systems 2009

BOULANGER Jean-Louis
Safety of Computer Architectures

MONMARCHE Nicolas *et al.*
Artificial Ants

PANETTO Hervé, BOUDJLIDA Nacer
Interoperability for Enterprise Software and Applications 2010

SIGAUD Olivier *et al.*
Markov Decision Processes in Artificial Intelligence

SOLNON Christine
Ant Colony Optimization and Constraint Programming

AUBRUN Christophe, SIMON Daniel, SONG Ye-Qiong *et al.*
Co-design Approaches for Dependable Networked Control Systems

2009

FOURNIER Jean-Claude
Graph Theory and Applications

GUEDON Jeanpierre
The Mojette Transform / Theory and Applications

JARD Claude, ROUX Olivier
Communicating Embedded Systems / Software and Design

LECOUTRE Christophe
Constraint Networks / Targeting Simplicity for Techniques and Algorithms

2008

BANÂTRE Michel, MARRÓN Pedro José, OLLERO Hannibal, WOLITZ Adam
Cooperating Embedded Systems and Wireless Sensor Networks

MERZ Stephan, NAVET Nicolas
Modeling and Verification of Real-time Systems

PASCHOS Vangelis Th
Combinatorial Optimization and Theoretical Computer Science: Interfaces and Perspectives

WALDNER Jean-Baptiste
Nanocomputers and Swarm Intelligence

2007

BENHAMOU Frédéric, JUSSIEN Narendra, O'SULLIVAN Barry
Trends in Constraint Programming

JUSSIEN Narendra
A to Z of Sudoku

2006

BABAU Jean-Philippe *et al.*
From MDD Concepts to Experiments and Illustrations – DRES 2006

HABRIAS Henri, FRAPPIER Marc
Software Specification Methods

MURAT Cecile, PASCHOS Vangelis Th
Probabilistic Combinatorial Optimization on Graphs

PANETTO Hervé, BOUDJLIDA Nacer
Interoperability for Enterprise Software and Applications 2006 / IFAC-IFIP I-ESA'2006

2005

GÉRARD Sébastien *et al.*
Model Driven Engineering for Distributed Real Time Embedded Systems

PANETTO Hervé
Interoperability of Enterprise Software and Applications 2005

Printed and bound by CPI Group (UK) Ltd, Croydon, CR0 4YY